NEW ARABIAN STUDIES

6

مَجَلَّة
ٱلدِّرَاسَاتِ ٱلعَرَبِيَّةِ ٱلجَدِيدَةِ

NEW ARABIAN STUDIES 6

EDITED BY
G. REX SMITH
J.R. SMART
AND
B.R. PRIDHAM

UNIVERSITY
of
EXETER
PRESS

First published 2004 by
University of Exeter Press
Reed Hall, Streatham Drive
Exeter, Devon EX4 4QR
UK

www.exeterpress.co.uk

British Library Cataloguing in Publication Data
A catalogue record of this book
is available from the British Library

ISSN 1351–4709
ISBN 0 85989 706 0

Typeset in Times New Roman
by Colin Bakké Typesetting, Exmouth

Printed and bound in Great Britain
by Short Run Press Limited, Exeter

Contents

Editorial Foreword

Again the editors would like to express their extreme gratitude to H.H. Dr Shaikh Sultan bin Muhammad al-Qasimi, Ruler of Sharjah, whose generous financial support has made the publication of this volume possible.

Readers are reminded that *NAS* is designed to cater for all academic fields in the humanities, in so far as they relate to the Arabian Peninsula, and that we continue to seek articles and reviews for future issues. Potential contributors are reminded that, with Volume 3 published in 1996, the transliteration and house rules changed radically and they are asked to follow to the letter the guidlines published in Volumes 3, 4, 5 and in this volume immediately after this foreword. Failure to do so in future will by necessity result in the return of the articles to the author without assessment. Contributors should send *two* copies of their articles *with double line spacing* and, if possible, computer disks, stating exactly which word processing programme was used, to the following address:

New Arabian Studies
University of Exeter Press
Reed Hall
Streatham Drive
Exeter
EX4 4QR, U.K.

Originals of photographs, diagrams and other art work should *not* be sent to the editors. Please ensure that you retain these and send a copy, as *NAS* cannot be held responsible. Photographs, slides, etc. should also be *clearly labelled*, and precise indication given of where they should be included in the text. Brief biographical details should also be supplied for the 'Notes on Contributors' section.

GUIDELINES AND TRANSLITERATION SCHEME FOR CONTRIBUTORS

Transliteration

ا When used as a ‘seat’ for *hamzah* transliterate with the original vowel of the *hamzah*, even if this is technically elided, e.g. *wa-ismuhu*. The definite article should always be *al-*, even with sun letters, e.g. *wa-al-salām*.

Vowels: a, ā, i, ī, u, ū
Dipthongs: aw, ay

ء Transliterate as ’ when medial or final; do not transliterate inital *hamzah*, e.g. *su’āl*, *nisā’*, but *islām*.

ة Normallly h (*raḥmah*), but t in *iḍāfah* constructions (*raḥmat allāh*).

Case and mood endings: Except in quotations from the Qur’ān, and classical poetry those case endings which consist only of short vowels should generally be omitted unless they are essential to the meaning, or some special point is to be made, e.g. *fī al-qarn al-sādis*.

One-letter words: These should be separated by a hyphen from the word to which they are joined in Arabic, e.g. *wa-al-natīǧah*, *bi-al-raḡm*.

Other letters:

ب	b	ز	z	ف	f
ت	t	س	s	ق	q
ث	ṯ	ش	š	ك	k
ج	ǧ	ص	ṣ	ل	l
ح	ḥ	ض	ḍ	م	m
خ	ẖ	ط	ṭ	ن	n
د	d	ظ	ẓ	ه	h
ذ	ḏ	ع	‘	و	w
ر	r	غ	ḡ	ي	y

Alif maqṣūrah should be transliterated by *-ā*. If there is a sound linguistic need to distinguish between final *alif* and *alif maqṣūrah*, then *-à* may be used for the latter.

Personal and place names: Where these are well known and have accepted English spellings, they should not be transliterated (Riyadh, Muscat, Khartoum, Mecca, Medina, Dhofar, Nasser, Saladin). There are grey areas here and, where in doubt, the name should be fully transliterated. Contributors using primarily European archive sources may employ the spelling of names as they find them in the original. However, an *early* footnote should explain precisely the method followed.

Vernacular Arabic: Contributors dealing with dialect pronunciation (e.g. proverbs, folklore) may deviate from the above system, but should list in an *early* footnote the symbols they intend to use and their phonetic descriptions.

Bibliography

The bibliography should follow the Harvard system using the author-date form. References should be listed at the end of the article in alphabetical order of author. Works by the same author should be listed chronologically, with those published the same year labelled 1990a, 1990b, etc. Works by a single author should precede those written by the same author with collaborators. If there are three or more authors, the first name should be followed by '*et al.*'. Please follow the following examples exactly:

1) Article in a journal:

Beeston, A.F.L. 1975a. Epigraphic South Arabian auxiliaries. *JSS* 20: 191–2.
Beeston, A.F.L. 1975b. The Realm of King Uusuf (Dhu Nuwas). *BSOAS* 38: 124–6.
Gingrich, A. and Heiss, J. 1986. A Note on traditional agricultural tools in Ṣa'da province. *PSAS* 16: 51–63.

NB: Common journals may be abbreviated as above. Other titles should be given in full. NB also where capital letters should be used in titles and where not. No inverted commas are needed.

2) Book:

Serjeant, R.B. 1974. *The South Arabian Hunt*. London.

NB: Capitals on all words in the title with the exception of prepositions and articles with the exception of an initial article.

3) Contribution:

Müller, W.W. 1988. Outline of the history of ancient Southern Arabia. In Daum, W. (ed.), *Yemen: 3000 Years of Art and Civilization in Arabia Felix*. Innsbruck and Frankfurt/Main, 49–54.

4) Book published in series:

Potts, D. 1991. *The Pre-Islamic Coinage of Eastern Arabia*. Copenhagen: Carsten Niebuhr Institute Publications no. 14.

5) Multi-volume books:

Löfgren, Oscar. 1936–50. *Arabische Texte zur Kenntnis der Stadt Aden im Mittelalter*. Uppsala. 2 vols.

6) Unpublished dissertation:

Hakeim, Abd al-Aziz. 1977. A Critical and comparative study of early Arabian coins on the basis of Arabic textual evidence and actual finds. PhD thesis. University of Leeds.

Citations

Where possible and appropriate, simple citations should be given in the text in brackets and should give the author, year of publication and page reference as follows:

(Beeston 1975a: 192)
(Potts 1991: 33)

Apart from these, all notes should be given as end notes. It is appreciated that short citations in brackets in the text are not always appropriate and contributors working for example from manuscript sources, or from medieval edited texts, or from archives may certainly use end notes rather than the simple citation method outlined above. If the author's name forms part of the text, it should not be repeated in the brackets.

E.g. The domestic architecture had significantly changed since the beginning of the occupation (Jones 1992: 137–9).

Several researchers have addressed this issue, most notably Assaf (1937) and Strauss (1951: 255–7).

In multi-volume works, the volume number should be given as in the work (1, i, I), if it is possible to decide. If this is not clear, please use lower case Roman as follows: Löfgren 1936–50 i: 48.

Dates

Contributors mentioning Islamic dates should ALWAYS provide the corresponding Christian date or century and vice versa. The former should stand first followed by an oblique stroke followed by the Christian date/century. AD and AH are not necessary. E.g. 386/996; 7th/13th century (always using Arabic numerals, not, in these circumstances, writing out the numerals in full.

Addenda & Corrigenda

The editors apologize for the fact that some inconsistencies occurred in two articles in the last volume. While regretting this, it should be pointed out that, in some cases, the texts received on disk varied from those in the hard copy.

Since we generally process articles directly from the disks supplied, it is incumbent on contributors to make sure that the disk/hard copy texts are consistent with each other. We also note that, in some cases, certain improvements have been made in the revised versions supplied.

Since this is a subsidized publication subject to a limited budget, it is not always practical to send out proofs to contributors, but we shall try to do this in future whenever possible.

The articles concerned are as follows:

1. ElMahi, 'The Ibex Hunt in the Rock Art of Oman':

p. 33, second paragraph, line 2. Insert between 'Oman,' and '(Harrison)':

which are believed to portray ibex hunt activities. It aims at understanding the ibex hunting methods and techniques used in the past and delineated by the ancient Dhofari artist. Traditional ibex hunting methods in southern Arabia, namely in Ḥaḍramawt and in other regions will be examined to attain a reasonable understanding of these rock scenes. In doing so, the paper views rock scenes as a series of snapshots. A rock scene presenting certain figures can be one single snapshot of a series of snapshots, which actually form the main theme of a particular activity that the artist had in mind when he depicted the scene. In other words, the ancient artist had chosen to depict a certain moment of activity from a wider temporally extended activity. On that account, the paper focusses on the essential quality (the moment of activity depicted by the artist) of rock scenes that convenes beyond the mere graphic delineation and aesthetic property. Yet before proceeding with this attempt, it would be more useful to have a closer look at the ibex (*capra ibex*) which constitutes our main theme. There are several subspecies of *capra ibex* distributed over a wide geographical range. Among these is the Nubian ibex (*capra ibex nubiana*) which inhabits the desert mountain ranges of the Arabian Peninsula including Oman (Map2). Today, in Oman, the Nubian ibex is known from southern Oman

Page 38, immediately after the quotation from Serjeant:

Furthermore, it is worthy of mention that Winnet and Reed (1973:80) in their archaeological-epigraphical survey report of the Ha'il area in northern Saudi Arabia have recorded a rock drawing of a group of ibex, a dog, and a hunter armed with a bow.

2. *Freitag and Schönig, 'Wise Men Control Wasteful Woman …'*

The following list, supplied by the authors, has been modified in some places as the suggested amendments did not conform to *NAS* house style.

page/line		*read*
67/3 and *pasim*	Kathīrī	Kaṯīrī
68/22	āfasādū	[fasād]
73/23	fatwā	*fatwā*
74/6	sayyid	*sayyid*
75/28	Rushayd	Rušayd
76/8	Ja'far	Ǧa'far
	Ghālib	Ḡālib
76/12	[was decided]	was decided
77/2	khaṭrah	*ḫaṭrah*
77/33	Ja'far	Ǧa'far
77/36	Dhū	Ḏū
80/3	Shibām	Šibām
80/30	gusl	*ḡusl*
81/16+18	*haṭrah*	*ḫaṭrah*
81/36	*'ishrīn*	*'išrīn*
83/plate	Say'un	Say'ūn
84/6	*ḥūbs*	*ḥbūs*
84/f.n.	Ḥāḍsan (twice)	Ḥasan
	Ḥāḍšwān	Ḥašwān
86/21	Khudhab123	Khudhab[123]
	popular.124	popular.[124]
87/2	*huṭum*	*ḥuṭum*
87/18	*al-aṣīd*	*al-'aṣīd*
87/21	sayyid	*sayyid*

88/32	*buhr*	*buḥūr*
89/2	al-Šihr.164	al-Šihr.[164]
	darī	*darī*
89/3	ğīm = yīm	*ğīm = yīm*

page/note

89/1	in 1996.	in 1996 (U.F.) resp. 1997 (H.Sch.).
	Kr,ger	Krüger
	Katīrī	Kaṯīrī
	(in print)	251–259
89/2	Katīrī	Kaṯīrī
89/3	*alKatīriyyah*	*al-Kaṯīriyyah*
89/4	*alAḥqāf*	*al-Aḥqāf*
89/5	āthār	āṯār
89/6	Makallā	Mukallā
	al-Siḥr	al-Šiḥr
90/16	*al-ākhirah*	*al-āḫirah*
90/22	*Uurban*	*Urban*
91/30	*nasr*	*našr*
	al-Gunaydiyyah	*al-Ğunaydiyyah*
91/36	*al-Ikhā'*	*al-Iḫā'*
91/37	*al-Irshād*	*al-Iršād*
91/42	sayyids	*sayyid*s
	qabīlīṣ	*qabīlīs*
	masāḳīn	*masākīn*
91/43	*al-Katiriyyah*	*al-Katīriyyah*
	'Āḍāṭ	*'Āḍāt*
92/47	sayyids	*sayyid*s
92/55	mûriyya	*mûriyya*
92/58	*gamasa*	*ğamasa*
	al-dhahab	*al-ḏahab*
	gmz	*ğmz*
92/62	form_as	form—as
92/65	*gussah*	*ğussah*
92/67	*Daṭînois*	*Daṯînois*
92/69	(forthcoming)	22–23
93/73	Schönig.	Schönig,
93/77	Survey	*Survey*
93/78	'Āḍāṭ	*'Āḍāt*
	ẓallah	*ẓallah*
	wufā'	*wufā'*

93/79	*sagīrah*	*ṣaġīrah*
93/89	*means*	means
94/96	*al-sa'biyyah*	*al-ša'biyyah*
94/99	Start	Stark
94/111	*Āḍāṭ*	*'Āḍāṭ*
94/113	(ṣmṭ)	(*ṣmṭ*)
94/123	*ẖudab* (*ẖidāb*)	*ẖuḍāb* (*ẖiḍāb*)
95/126	M,ller	Müller
	Introduction	*introduction*
95/131	*khidāb*	*khidāb'*
95/146	Ibid.	ibid.
96/150	al-Ṣabbān	al-Ṣabbān
96/157	al-Ṣān	al-Ṣabbān
96/162	al-Ṣābbān	al-Ṣabbān
96/165	g	ǧ

Review Notices

Historic Mosques and Shrines of Oman

by Paolo M. Costa (with a contribution by E. Baldissera),
BAR S 938, Archaeopress: Oxford
2001, figs 239, colour plates 43, xiv, 270 pp. £36.

The book under review is the fruit of many years research on the part of the author, working on the mosques and shrines of Oman both during his period as archaeological adviser to the Government of the Sultanate and also more recently during several return visits to the country. A cursory glance reveals a plethora of black and white plates and more than forty colour plates, as well as maps and drawings; some illustration on each page in fact.

Sundry miscellaneous items begin the work, before the Introduction (pp. 1–7). Chapter 1 is entitled 'The natural and built environment of Oman' (pp. 7–34). Chapter 2, dealing more precisely with the subject in hand by geographical area, covers the subject of the mosque in the Ibāḍī interior (pp. 34–121). In Chapter 3, the author deals with the mosques and shrines of the Omani coastal areas (pp. 121–212) and the book is brought to a close with Chapter 4, 'Main aspects of the religious architecture of Oman' (pp. 212–41), Baldissera's appendix concerning the inscriptions (pp. 241–65), a bibliography and an index-cum-glossary.

The Introduction tells us neatly the story of research conducted on religious architecture in the Arabian Peninsula; the story is inevitably and depressingly brief, for so much remains to be done. The natural and built environment of Chapter 1 is a subject close to Costa's heart. The essay is succinct and offers an illuminating entremets before the main courses of Chapters 2 and 3 to follow. The division is in essence, on the one hand, the simple, even austere, mosque of very early Islam, square or rectangular, lacking minaret or any form of adornment. This is the Ibāḍī mosque of the Omani highlands (Chapter 2). On the other hand, the mosques of the coastal areas (Chapter 3), both Sunnī and Shī'ī, vary greatly in their nature and design.

In Chapter 4, 'Main aspects of the religious architecture of Oman', the highlight of the book, Costa deftly pulls all the strings together for a technical revision of his subject.

Baldissera's inscriptions follow the main text as an appendix. This is in general terms a workmanlike job, though offering up some strange renderings on occasions which are as much caused by slips in the English as by a misunderstanding of the texts of the inscriptions which are in the main Quranic anyway. It is very tempting to launch into a more nit-picking critique of the appendix, but this would sit ill with the short notice which this is meant to be and might well detract unjustly from what is a generally competent piece of work.

As we would expect, the book contains superb line drawings and plans. The quality of the paper permits clear and interesting black and white photographs, while the colour photographs are exquisite, sometimes breathtaking. And all this comes in a large, handsome paper-back format at the reasonable price of £36. The book immediately becomes an excellent pointer to further work in the field. With its publication too, Costa establishes himself as the superb cataloguer and the clear and articulate pioneering scholar of the religious architecture of Oman.

GRS

'Scienza e Islam'

edited by Giovanni Canova in Quaderni di Studi Arabi, *Studi e Testi 3 (1999), Herder, Venice. Pp. 111.*

'Dossier: Epigrafia araba'

edited by Eros Baldissera in Quaderni di Studi Arabi *16 (1998), Herder, Venice. Pp. 206.*

The third issue of 'Studi e Testi', a series of the Italian journal *Quaderni di Studi Arabi*, is devoted to 'Science and Islam' and gathers the proceedings of a workshop which was held at the University of Venice in 1999. This workshop was part of a project sponsored by the Centro Nazionale delle Ricerche (the Italian counterpart of the French CNRS) which focussed on the historical and cultural roots of the Islamic civilization in the Mediterranean. As the editor states in the introduction to the volume, many of the contributions reflect an understanding of science which goes beyond the Islamic definition of *'ilm*. Some articles discuss manifestations of popular culture which include geomancy and magic. Others analyse the development of scientific knowledge in the Arab-Islamic tradition by keeping an eye on its western counterpart. The overall contents of 'Scienza e Islam' suggest that the Islamic 'scientific spirit' was instrumental to fulfil basic human needs. Not only science was geared towards the acquisition of a particular type of knowledge for practical purposes, but it was also a means through which individuals gained access to the hidden meaning of the universe.

The first three articles by Anne Regourd, Angelo Scarabel and Ida Zilio-Grandi provide a clear example of the different meanings which scientific practice has assumed in the Arab-Islamic tradition. They set the terms of the debate on popular practices, *'ilm* and western science. Regourd (pp. 5–16) investigates the relationship between geomancy and the esoteric science of letters (*'ilm al-ḥurūf*), basing her study on the evidence provided by two practitioners from North Yemen. She argues that geomancy responds to the necessities of everyday life as a divinatory practice, but it is also concerned with universal truth. As the practice of 'decoding' natural signs is associated with the *'ilm al-ḥūrūf* (which is central to interpret the Qur'ān), geomancy is instrumental to understanding the attributes and workings of the Almighty. Regourd's case study highlights the parallel development of popular culture and *'ilm* for a holistic understanding of natural phenomena. The convergence of popular practices and Islamic beliefs is also implicit in Alexander Fodor's analysis of a nineteenth-century Iranian talismanic chart from the Ṭārīq Rāğab Museum of Kuwait (pp. 93–111). Fodor's linguistic analysis shows that this piece of magical-devotional literature displays a marked *ṣūfī* influence which is also reflected in some of the interesting figurative elements of the chart.

Scarabel discusses the place of blood in the Islamic tradition as an object of metaphysical speculation and scientific experience (pp. 17–19). He examines legal prescriptions which forbid the eating of dead animals and analyses the lexicon of blood in the *Lisān al-'arab* and in the *Tāj al-'arūs*. He concludes that blood is invested with a crucial metaphysical meaning as it is the bodily fluid which gathers the four elements constituting the universe. Yet, the terminology used for the word coagulation (*ğumūd*) suggests some understanding of the physiological phenomenon which is based on observation, a practice linked to modern medicine. Zilio-Grandi's contribution (pp. 31–46) provides an interesting example of the role played by experimental evidence in questioning an established corpus of knowledge. Her study of the famous treatise on precious stones and minerals by Aḥmad al-Tifāṣī (d. 1253) demonstrates that the Tunisian author made abundant use of Greek, Arab and oral sources. These sources, however, came to be under the vigilant scrutiny of al-Tifāṣī's personal observation and experience. Zilio-Grandi concludes that this treatise is an earlier example of a modern scientific tradition in Islam. She also emphasises the importance which al-Tifāṣī attributes to active experimentation based on traditional techniques.

Giovanni Canova's long piece on bees and honey (pp. 69–92) is a careful investigation into the representation of bees in the pre-Islamic/Bedouin tradition, Arab-Islamic popular culture and religious literature. He also discusses beekeeping in modern times and provides a very useful bibliography on the topic. This article is very interesting and informative but it does not clearly situate the topic between 'empirical knowledge, tradition and science' as suggested by its title. The contributions by Roberto Tottoli (pp. 47–58) and Antonella Ghersetti (pp. 59–68) show a similar reluctance to engage with conceptual debates. Totoli's erudite discussion of the literary genre of the *'āğā'ib* ends with the generic statement that: '… the literary purpose (of the *'āğā'ib*) is paralleled by a sort of scientific spirit which aimed at gathering these traditions for the sake of knowledge' (p. 58). Ghersetti raises the issue of how knowledge was legitimized by questioning the authorship and contents of a thirteenth-century treatise on female physiognomy. Although this treatise was attributed to the Greek rhetorician Polemon of Laodicea, Ghersetti shows that it was written by an unknown Arab author who was most concerned with erotic literature. The identification with Greek culture was often a pre-requisite for success in the Arab-Islamic world. Yet, when focussing on the mechanisms of transmission of a particular type of knowledge Ghersetti should have also discussed physiognomy as a scientific practice.

The sixteenth issue of the *Quarderni di Studi Arabi* is partly devoted to Arab epigraphy as an important instrument for the study of the history, societies and cultures of the Islamic lands. The first two contributions by Solange Ory (pp. 5–22), and by Ludvik Kalus and Frédérique Soudan (pp. 23–44), outline two interesting projects which are likely to be beneficial to many scholars in the field. Ory describes in detail a new computer software (EPIMAC) which provides an innovative cataloguing system for different types of inscriptions. For instance, scholars will be in a position to refine their research tools through advanced searches by theme and proper names. Kalus and Soudan provide an account of their new project under the name of *Thesaurus d'Épigraphie Islamique* which aims at cataloguing Arabic, Turkish and Persian inscriptions until the year 1000 a.h. This is an ambitious undertaking which will integrate the *Repertoire Chronologique d'Épigraphie Arabe* edited by the French Archeological Institute of Cairo, currently including Arabic inscriptions until the year 800 a.h.

The remaining articles on Arab epigraphy include studies of different types of inscriptions from Jordan, Iran and Oman. Frédéric Imbert (pp. 45–58) focuses on a series of inscriptions of Kufic graffiti which date back to the 2nd/3rd centuries of the Islamic era. He argues that these graffiti from Northern Jordan are likely to shed light on elements of popular religion and culture given that they come from the rural milieu. Sheila Blair (pp. 59–68) assesses the historical value of the inscription of an eleventh-century tomb tower which is located near Damghan (northern Iran). She analyses textual evidence on the site provided by later chronicles, particularly by al-Maqdisī. Giovanni Oman (pp. 69–88) discusses the distinguishing features of three types of Arabic writing known as square kufic. In the appendix to his article he analyses an inscription from the mausoleum of Pīr-i-Barkān in Iran. Eros Baldissera (pp. 89–124) studies the five tombstones of the mausoleum of Imam Aḥmad bin Sa'īd al-Būsa'īdī which is located in Rustāq (Oman). He also provides an interesting account of the Imam's life, based on local sources.

The contributions which are outside the section devoted to epigraphy are varied. Seeger Bonebakker and Alice Scott (pp. 125–141) use textual evidence to establish a link between Sayyidah Nafīsa, the early Muslim saint buried in Cairo, and Santa Nefissa, a Christian popular figure who, in sixteenth-century Italian poetry and prose, was mentioned as the protector of prostitution. Giuseppe Scattolin (pp. 143–163) and Giovanni Canova (pp. 189–196) focus on the *Dīwān* of Ibn al-Farīd and on the *Fatḥ al-Mulūk* of Diyārbī respectively. Vincenzo Strika (pp. 165–188) provides a cogent overview of prospects for partnership among the Mediterranean countries from the economic, political and cultural perspectives. Most notably, he explores the potential for the development of an 'Islamic alternative' to counterbalance the hegemonic role played by the countries of the northern shores of the Mediterranean.

Nelida Fuccaro, University of Exeter

Mehri Texts from Oman Based on the Field Materials of T.M. Johnstone

by Harry Stroomer, Harrassowitz Verlag: Wiesbaden Semitica Viva Band 22 1999, xxiii, 303 pp.

As the editor of the texts which are studied in this book reminds us (xiii), there are three major landmarks in the history of the study of the Modern South Arabian (MSA) languages: one, the early pioneering publications of the Austrian Südarabische Expedition in the first two decades of the twentieth century, associated with such names as Jahn, Müller, Hein and Bittner—and not forgetting the publications these spawned by such figures as Leslau and Wagner; two, the remarkable and extensive academic efforts of Tom Johnstone, whose life was so tragically cut short in 1983; and thirdly, the French connection, particularly the output of Marie-Claude Simeone-Senelle, who has admirably taken over the Johnstone baton and continues as the premier ambassadress of the field. The editor of the Mehri texts of this book, Harry Stroomer, modestly omits mention of the scholarly interest in MSA languages in his native Netherlands, where, thanks to his inspiration, a small, young group of scholars is beginning to emerge.

Certain misconceptions concerning the MSA languages, Mehri, Harsusi, Hobyot, Jibbali, Bathari and Soqotri, still manifest themselves. In particular, they are still frequently termed ‘dialects’, as if they are dialects of Arabic and not South Semitic languages in their own right. This is addressed by Stroomer (xiii).

In this book, Stroomer’s aim has been to publish the Mehri texts and English translations of more than one hundred documents, collected by Johnstone and deposited after his death in the Durham University Library. They were examined there in great detail in the 1990s by Anda Hofstede and figure in her subsequent publication, Description of the Johnstone Papers etc., *NAS* 4 (1997), 71–138, on pp. 77–8. These are the texts referred to in Johnstone’s *Mehri Lexicon* (London 1987, vii) (*ML*), for which they form the linguistic basis and for which ‘Alī Musallam, a Dhofari policeman, who worked with him for a year in London and also in Dubai in the late 1960s and ’70s, was the chief informant. Mehri, it should perhaps be mentioned, is numerically the greatest of the MSA languages, spoken as it is by about 100,000 people living on either side of the Yemen/Oman border.

After a brief preface and acknowledgements, Stroomer offers an easy-to-read and very informative introduction. He writes of the place of Mehri within the MSA languages and of past research. Considerable dialect variation occurs within the Mehri language and it should be noted that the texts studied represent Omani Mehri, whereas previous research, Austrian and more recently French, has been concentrated on Yemeni Mehri, the former varieties perhaps more archaic than the latter. The editor continues with a detailed description of the materials in the Johnstone collection. He has 106 texts in all in the book, 105 directly from the collection and one added by himself. The whole is published in the random order in which they can be found in the collection and were given headings by Johnstone such as folktale, beliefs, biographical story, snippet, tribal history and dialogue. Stroomer has, wherever possible, adhered to the transcriptions of the Johnstone *ML*, with two minor exceptions. The editor continues his introduction with mention of his explanatory notes, his translation policy (Johnstone’s own translations are used, but some gaps and errors have been dealt with by him). It is pointed out also that almost all the texts were also recorded on tape by Johnstone. The introduction draws to a close with a brief, but extremely useful, bibliography.

To return to Stroomer's brief preface (vii), it was an entirely pleasant surprise that it was suggested that, apart from the obvious interest to the Semitist, the Arabist and to scholars of folklore and ethnography, the published text might be *used* by a wider audience! With this in view, he proposes that, with 'a basic knowledge of Arabic morphology and lexicon', armed with a copy of Johnstone's *ML* and following his (Stroomer's) explanatory foot notes, one is ready to sample the texts provided. I think he is correct, though I would add much patience and application to his list. There is certainly no reason that this book could not be used as an advanced Mehri reader in an academic MSA languages course, for example, the type which Johnstone had in place at the School of Oriental and African Studies.

After some facsimiles of Johnstone's field notebook in his own hand and of a typescript and a transciption table, the texts proper begin. Each is numbered, given a title and a category, the text on the left hand side, the translation on the right. The text is annotated and footnotes, in the main references to the *ML*, added. The latter, much more frequent in the earlier texts, provide an excellent service to the reader who needs to be reminded that, for example, the word *kewṯēt* in text would require reference to the *ML*, root *k l ṯ*, *ḥaráwn* root *' r n*, to quote just two examples from the early pages.

It was suggested to me that I would not find great literature here. True, perhaps, although there is much to entertain and amuse, as well as inform. In fact those with only a passing acquaintance with medieval Arabic belles-lettres, or even of Aesop's fables, will soon feel at home here, for tales of intrigue, of jinn and spirits, of anthropomorphism and of sorcery abound. Bā Newās is both the hero and the villain in some of these: in Text 36, a force for good; in 65, one for evil. Such tales (e.g. nos 1, 4, 20, etc.), if a little convoluted, have much to recommend them. Of a *1001 Nights* standard they are perhaps not, but riveting none the less. There is poetry too and reminiscences, presumably Johnstone's informant thinking aloud, or describing facets of his life in London. Not surprisingly, one is left primarily with the strong atmosphere of stock culture, the camel and small livestock in particular, though the cattle of the Omani Nejd have a large part to play. One presumes too that many of these stories and anecdotes are of some antiquity.

The translations, for the most part Johnstone's, are literal and simple, very much in keeping with the originals. I find, however, some of the sexual terms rather prim and dated; two further minor points: there is a perfectly good English word, 'wadi'—'valley' is not always apt; the *wε̄l*, plural *ew'eyōl* (Text 30, lines 2, 4, 5 etc.) must be the mountain goat (*Hemitragus Jayakari*, Arabic *wa'l*, *aw'āl*), rather than the oryx. The latter cannot have been running around wild and hunted in the Arabian Peninsula for some centuries.

In sum, Stroomer has performed a very great service by the publication of this book on the major language of the MSA group. Yes, this will be of great value and interest to the Semitist and the Arabist, the anthropologist and ethnographer. But there is more; the book could well provide an Omani Mehri reader for interested scholars and it might well please folklorists everywhere. It is a credit to the editor and the discipline and yet another fine memorial to Tom Johnstone who had so much more to offer and who was taken from us much too soon.

GRS

Šams al-'ulūm wa-dawā' kalām al-'Arab min al-kulūm

by Našwān b. Sa'īd al-Ḥimyarī
edited by Ḥusayn b. 'Abdallāh al-'Amrī, Muṭahhar b. 'Alī al-Iryānī and Yūsuf Muḥammad 'Abdallāh, Dār al-Fikr al-Mu'āṣir: Beirut & Dār al-Fikr: Damascus 1999, 12 vols.

We have had to wait a very long time for a complete published edition of Našwān al-Ḥimyarī's lexicographical encyclopaedia *Šams al-'ulūm* and the reasons are several: its four parts are only rarely found conveniently together in MS form; there are abridgements which over the centuries have become mixed up with the original text; and, a rare phenomenon in the Arabic MS world, the number of MSS of the lexicon is very large. Persenius in his *The Manuscripts of Parts 1 and 2 of 'Shams al-'ulūm' by Nashwan al-Ḥimyarī* (Uppsala 1997, 40–84) describes no fewer than fifty-two of them. We have at last this beautiful hardback edition in twelve volumes edited by three of the Yemen's finest scholars, which has taken several years to produce.

Našwān b. Sa'īd al-Ḥimyarī died in 573/1178, just three years after completing *Šams al-'ulūm wa-dawā' kalam al-'Arab min al-kulūm* and, incidentally, four years after the Ayyubid conquest of the Yemen with a huge force of arms from Egypt. He is buried on a mountain known today as Ǧabal Abī Zayd in the district of Ḥaydān in the province of Ṣa'dah in the north of the Yemen. His tomb is still an object of visitation and it is believed that the four graves in the vicinity of his own are those of his sons. Among his literary works is *al-Qaṣīdah al-Ḥimyariyyah*. Persenius lists twenty-one such works in his *Manuscripts*, 20–2. *Šams al-'ulūm* is much more than another Arabic lexicon. Apart from its value in the fields of Qur'ān, *Ḥadīṯ*, *fiqh*, Islamic religious groups, biographies, genealogies, the Arabic language with full linguistic examples (*šawāhid*) from both poetry and prose, the heavenly bodies, botany, geology etc., it is a mine of information on pre-Islamic Yemen and Islamic Yemenite culture.

Naŝwān's presentation is as interesting as it is remarkable for a work at this stage of the historical development of Arabic lexicography. The work is divided into *bāb*s, each one representing a letter of the alphabet as the first radical of the root in question. The second and third radicals then appear in alphabetical order within the *bāb*. Thus, for example, *kataba*, would be found in *bāb al-kāf wa-al-tā' wa-mā ba'da-hā*. This is not quite the end, as each *bāb* begins with the heading *al-asmā'*, which includes nouns, adjectives and even particles constructed on the simple root, then nouns etc. with *ziyādāt* under the sub-heading *al-ziyādah*, and next comes the heading *al-af'āl*. The reader using this edition need not despair, however, if the above appears too daunting; he may simply refer to volume xii, *Fihris al-mawādd al-luğawiyyah* (445), where the thoughtful editors have provided an easy, modern, orthodox, first, second, third radical dictionary!

The editors' introduction covers the following ground: a biography of the compiler of *Šams al-'ulūm*, with a list of fifteen of his most famous writings, the work itself and its importance in the development of Arabic lexicography and its presentation, its strong points, three in number, first its historical information, second its geographical information and third its linguistic information, these three all much within the Yemeni context. There follows a section on those MSS of the work considered by the editors and their editorial policy. A total of four MSS from the Yemen were considered, four from Egypt and six from Europe and North America. The editors review all the literature on Našwān and partial editions of the *Šams*. They settle finally on the Escorial MS, which they reckon to be in two parts and numbered 34 and 603, as if they are two MSS. It is the oldest, they point out, and its scribe is the famous linguistic scholar, Ğumhūr b. 'Alī al-Hamdānī, who completed the copying of the MS in 626/1228, the first part, and 627/1229, the second. The editors state that it would seem that it is taken from the copy of the author himself. Their final argument is that the Escorial MS is the most complete.

Although the editors allow for comparisons with eight MSS and the abridgement *Ḍiyā' al-ḥulūm*, their concern is much more to ensure that the reader is able to make a correct interpretation of the text. Rather than producing a conventional *apparatus criticus*, therefore they set themselves the task of tracking down every possible reference and clarifying every possible doubtful expression which the text throws up. The result is quite remarkable, with often a large proportion of the page, even in a smaller font, devoted to their scholarly and extremely valuable footnotes.

Volume xii is devoted entirely to indices and there are no fewer than thirteen: Quranic references, *Ḥadīṯ*, personal names, religious groups, literary references, place names, plants, heavenly bodies, *fiqh*, proverbs and sayings, poetry, words defined in the lexicon and matters relating directly to the Yemen.

The reputation of the editors precedes them and they do not disappoint. With a lexicon in particular, the proof of the pudding is in the eating. These volumes are already making a difference for me in the endless task of interpretation which medieval Arabic texts demand. Anyone, certainly he or she working in the discipline of Yemenite studies, who fails to keep these handsome volumes very close at hand does so at his or her peril. While the work is of a standard which we have come to expect from the editors, they nevertheless deserve all our gratitude and praise for such a splendid effort.

GRS

Yemen Relations with European Countries
(Historical Background)*

Hussein A. Al-Amri

1. Early European Interest

At the beginning of the sixteenth century the Yemen shores and islands in the Red Sea, the Gulf of Aden and the Arabian Sea were an arena of conflict involving the Portuguese and the Ottoman fleets. The conflict was resolved in favour of the Ottomans after Albuquerque, the Viceroy of the King of Portugal in India, managed to occupy the island of Socotra in 1507. Having failed to occupy the port of Aden in March 1513, he seized the island of Kamarān off-shore of al-Ṣalīf and near the city of Hodeida. After 1517 Yemen became part of the Ottoman Empire for a hundred years and was visited by several European adventurers in the Orient. This was before the port of Mocha became an important trading centre at the beginning of the seventeenth century. European vessels competed for its use, and their ships, specializing in the trade of Yemeni coffee, docked there in great numbers. A number of monopolistic European companies competed fiercely to secure their share of Yemeni coffee, the most important being the East India companies of Holland, England and France.[1]

Perhaps the earliest information on Yemen available to the West in modern times was contained in a book written by Ludvico de Varthema who was the first European to visit Sana'ā'. His book was published in Rome in 1510 and gives his account and impressions of Sana'ā' which he describes as 'the beautiful city with high walls and spacious gardens'. He mentions that the city had five thousand dwellings at the time of his visit. While we recognize the

* Most of the contents of this paper draw on previously published works by the author.

historical significance of what de Varthema wrote, he, as in the case of other travellers in that era, fell into the trap of illusion and went on to describe as fact unfounded or non-existent legends. Some contemporary European researchers have ascribed this tendency to the possibility that the author had fallen prey to flawed information about the East. He may also have been repeating tales and legends he had heard from other travellers at the time.[2]

In the early chapters of Eric Macro's book *Yemen and the West*[3] are to be found precise and enchanting details about the early interests of the Europeans in Yemen from the beginning of the sixteenth century. At the beginning of this year (1998) the Dutch orientalist C.G. Brouwer published in Amsterdam a valuable documentary book on Mocha drawn from records of the Dutch East India Company between the years 1614 and 1640. This adds to previous writings by him on the subject.

2. The Dutch Commercial Activities

Dutch Commercial activity began in the early seventeenth century after the company's trading centre in Mocha had become one of the most important centres for trading in coffee which they exported to the company's branches in North Eastern India and Persia. Mocha coffee started to be sold in Amsterdam in 1661 but it took nearly another quarter of a century until the first coffee house served Yemeni Mocha coffee in Vienna. This was in the year 1685, two years after the failure of the Ottoman siege of Vienna. It appears that the Turks brought Yemeni coffee with them, since Yemen was part of the Ottoman Empire and Constantinople was a centre for importing Mocha coffee from Yemen which was later exported to other European markets. Although the Dutch had lost their position as a major power to the English by the end of the century, they remained represented in Mocha through an agency until 1724. This closed down in 1738, but Dutch vessels continued to sail into Mocha, albeit in decreasing numbers. The reason for this was that, by 1730, the European markets had become saturated with coffee which meant the Dutch had to bring in smaller quantities from Mocha. However they kept on the office of their commercial centre throughout the eighteenth century, despite the rarity of the appearance of their ships at the port of Mocha.[4]

The expanding coffee trade was not the only business activity of European companies and traders, as various types of spices and other commodities that were brought from the East to the West had produced large profits for the Europeans. This is borne out by a report written by P. Van Den Broecke, the most renowned of the early commanders of the Dutch commercial fleet which started to explore Southern Arabia in 1614. His report, written on 15 December 1616, states:

> The Mocha trade is of major importance for the company as large quantities of spices are sold there every year for cash and it is extremely lucrative, given the vast numbers of traders and vessels visiting the Port.[5]

Serious efforts of the Dutch to establish a commercial centre for the company began with the arrival in Aden of Broecke's ship on 30 August 1614. He was officially received by the Ottoman commander in Aden on 1 September 1614, but subsequently the latter banished Broecke and his companions to al-Šiḥr which they reached by ship on 19 September 1614. Broecke was obliged to meet the Ottoman governor in Sana'ā' in order to seek help with his business endeavours. This he was unable to secure before making a second trip from Ceylon, arriving at Mocha on 21 April 1616. From there he made for Sana'ā' through Ta'izz with five of his aides, accompanied by a group of Ottoman soldiers. He was received by the Ottoman governor of Sana'ā' Ja'far Pasha on 4 May 1616. However, the latter categorically refused to allow him to establish a permanent commercial station, since the Dutch did not possess a licence (*firmān*) from the Sultan. However, he gave Broecke and his companions permission to trade that season and reduced the tariffs which they had to pay. Nonetheless, he prohibited them from returning to Yemen without the required *firmān*.[6]

The various European companies had been representing conflicting interests and ambitions for the control of the East. Whereas British ambitions in the area evolved in the direction of politics instead of trade—military occupation becoming the last stage of this process in the nineteenth century—this was not the case in the relations of Yemen afterwards with the other European States.

The Ottoman presence in Yemen did not last longer than a hundred years and they were obliged to end it in October 1636. Following the Ottoman withdrawal, the Yemenis enjoyed nearly two centuries of political stability and central rule after unifying the country from its northern borders with the Hijaz to its southern frontiers with Oman under the early powerful imams of the al-Qāsim b. Muḥammad dynasty. The booming of trade in Yemeni coffee internationally, with its famous brand name 'Mocha', contributed substantially to the flourishing of the local economy and generated good income for the country and the state. The farmers, active as they were and with a history of agrarian experience behind them, went on to expand the planting of coffee trees in most valleys and terraces where the climate was temperate at altitudes as high as 3,400 to 6,800 feet. These areas consisted of the highlands near the Tihāma coast, the fertile and well watered valleys and streams of the Ibb and Ta'izz regions, also al-Ḥaymatayn, and Harāz to the west of Sana'ā' and Ānis to the south-west of the city. The crop also spread to Ḥağğah in the north. Besides coffee, farmers also cultivated vines whose grapes were renowned for the diversity of their types and species, some of which were dried and exported as raisins.

The business activities of European companies and traders were therefore not confined to coffee alone, but included spices, raisins, nuts, salt and other goods that were brought to the West from the East and from which they earned high profits.

3. Early Yemeni–French Relations

On 3 January 1708, the first two French vessels docked at the port of Mocha and the manager of the Dutch Commercial Centre played host to the French. In 1709 a commercial contract between the French and the Governor of Mocha was concluded, establishing a French Commercial Centre.[7]

In subsequent years French trading activity proceeded well. Several ships arrived at Mocha from St Malo in France and returned laden with coffee and other goods. Other French ships called at Mocha en route to or from India to take on board profitable cargoes.

On board one of those vessels arrived the first French Official Mission which included a physician among its members. The Mission paid a visit to Imam al-Mahdī Muḥammad b. Aḥmad (died 1718) in his capital al-Mawāhib to the east of Ḏamār at the beginning of February 1712. The French Orientalist Jean de la Roque published the results and impressions of the Mission's visit and its exaggerated description of al-Mahdī's court. Publication took place after four years of the Mission's visit under the title *Voyage en Arabie*, Paris 1716.[8] However, relations between France and the Yemeni authorities in Mocha came under strain after only a few years. This happened when the tax official (*'āmil*) of Mocha found out that the French, under the agreement with them in 1709, had been paying only 1¼ per cent tariff on exports and imports, whilst the other Europeans were paying 5 per cent. He resolved to raise the taxes levied on the French to the same level, causing offence to the French East India Company which deemed such action arbitrary and unjustified. The company then took punitive action, a French fleet consisting of four warships being ordered to shell Mocha in 1737. Consequently the local authorities were obliged to adhere to the agreement of 1709.[9]

French trading links with Mocha continued intermittently until the beginning of the nineteenth century within the framework of trade relations with Egypt after the latter became one of the most important French trading centres, exceeding the volume of Egypt's trade with England by twenty-five times. The French therefore, were able to impose a real European monopoly on the Egyptian trade. They also played a further role following the Napoleonic campaign in the autumn of 1798.

The Anglo–French competition to control trade and the strategic locations in the Red Sea constituted the onset of rivalry between them throughout the nineteenth century in both the Eastern and Western parts of the Arab World.[10]

4. Relations of other European Companies and the Mission of Niebuhr

Thus we find the European trade with Mocha at a record level in the third decade of the eighteenth century (1720–1730) as a result of the participation of many smaller European states such as the Ostend Company of Austria and the Swedish East India Company. The governments of the major powers, namely France, Britain and Holland had, despite their differences, forced the Austrian emperor to limit the extensive dealings of Ostend with Mocha.

To the Kingdom of Denmark, which had intermittent trading links with Mocha during the 17th century despite hostility from Holland, also participated in the period of flourishing trade in Mocha before it started to decline by the beginning of the middle of the eighteenth century.[11] Nevertheless the kingdom, under the reign of its enlightened dictator Emperor Fredrick the Fifth, supported and financed a scientific mission to Yemen whose work had a lasting impact. Through this historic mission, Denmark, its size notwithstanding, entered the record book of pioneering science, avoiding the practice of monopoly and political adventurism characterizing East–West relations in modern times. The Danish Mission to Yemen took place in the period 1761–1767 and its name was linked to one of its six members, the geodesist and engineer, C. Niebuhr. The memory of the mission is linked also to the reign of Imam al-Mahdī ‘Ābbās (died 1775).[12]

By the beginning of the nineteenth century, the economic and commercial situation had deteriorated and central state control from the capital had weakened. This adverse state of affairs facilitated the British occupation of Aden in 1839 which continued until 1967. The Ottomans also returned to Yemeni shores in 1849. After the opening of the Suez Canal in 1869, they were able to link Yemen with Istanbul following their entry into Sana‘ā’ on 25 April 1872. For 55 years Yemen became a province of the Ottoman Empire in the same way as other Arab provinces. Administratively as well as with regard to its relations with the outside world, it came under the control of the Ottomans until the end of the First World War when Yemen became the first independent Arab state.

If the first European visitor to Sana‘ā’ at the beginning of the sixteenth century was an Italian from Rome, as mentioned above, another Italian was the first prominent European visitor to the same city 416 years later in the twentieth century, namely Dr Gasbrini, the Viceroy of the King of Italy in Eritrea. This visit took place on 19 July 1926 and one of its results was the signing of the first Yemeni Treaty with any European or foreign power that recognized Yemen as an independent state. It ushered in special and distinctive ties between the two countries that have continued until the present time.[13]

In 1931 and after a long period of abeyance the Dutch Arabist D. van der Meulen was able to revive the old relations between Yemen and Holland when he visited Hadramawt and Sana'ā', followed by the first Yemeni Dutch agreement for friendship and trade in 1933.

On the other hand it was necessary to break out of the continued deadlock resulting from the British presence in Aden and so a treaty of friendship and mutual co-operation was signed with Britain on 11 February 1934, after lengthy negotiations undertaken in Sana'ā' by the British governor of Aden, Lt Colonel Bernard Reilly, known as the Treaty of Sana'ā'. This treaty recognized the *de facto* situation and acknowledged Imam Yaḥyā as King of Yemen. It also postponed dealing with 'the issue of the southern borders until negotiations to be carried out by them had been completed before the expiry of this Treaty', namely (after 40 years, in 1974!) 'in cordial manner and with full agreement without dispute or dissent.' (Article 3) The Treaty brought only temporary peace, for border incidents soon flared in al-Ṣubayḥah, Šabwah, Bayḥān, al-Ḍāli' and other areas within less than a year of its signing. 'The Treaty deliberately omitted any reference to the renouncing of territorial claims by either party.'[14]

The British memoranda and official secret reports[15] during and after that period show that the British grew more concerned about the activities of the official forces and tribes of Yemen against their presence in the area with the encouragement and blessing of Imam Yāḥyā 'because he never abandoned his belief in the legitimacy and historicity of Sana'ā' rule over all Yemeni territories including the Aden Protectorate, notwithstanding his signing of the Sana'ā' Treaty. In pursuit of his objectives, he also collaborated with Italy, arousing British foreboding expressed at the time in terms of the "Italian peril".'[16]

Diplomatic relations with Britain were not established until after the London talks in 1951, when a solution to the outstanding issues between the two countries was reached. It is worth referring here to the major world commercial activity of the port of Aden, which was a small town with a population not exceeding a thousand inhabitants at the time of occupation in 1839, half of them Yemenis and the rest Indians and Jews. It later became one of the biggest Yemeni cities and the largest port in the area, as well as a significant international centre linking East and West. Life in Aden until the British withdrawal in 1967 reflected on the cultural, social and political activities which made a significant impact on Yemeni life in one way or other.

Yemeni–Austrian Relations

After Niebuhr, the most important Austrian traveller in Southern Arabia was Edward Glaser (1855–1908), who made many important journeys in the eighties of the nineteenth century with the support of the Austrian National Academy of Research. We can say that before the First World War no special relations between Austria-Hungary and Yemen were recorded, since Yemen was regarded as a part of the Ottoman Empire. Therefore, the Austro-Hungarian Embassy in Constantinople was responsible also for the Yemen. In 1914 a Consulate was established in Hodeidah, but was closed a few months after the outbreak of the First World War. There are no relations recorded during the period 1918–1938.

Post Second World War diplomatic relations with the Yemen were established after 1970. The Republic of Yemen was within the competence of the Austrian embassy in Jeddah, afterwards Riyadh. After 1 May 1996 this competence was transferred from Riyadh to Muscat.

An embassy of Yemen was established in Vienna in 1990, especially in order to improve relations between the Yemen and the various UNO-offices in Vienna.

In January 1996 an Austrian honorary consulate was established in Sana‘ā’.

Although Yemen had signed treaties with other European powers in the thirties of the present century, its historical isolation under the rule of Imam Yaḥyā and his son Aḥmad until the launch of the revolution and the declaration of the Republican System in 1962 had prevented the progress of relations with the outside world. This was more than compensated for in the early seventies when diplomatic relations were restored with Germany following the crisis in the Arab-German relationship at that time. Germany, France, as well as Holland, with which diplomatic relations were established in 1983, were among the first European states to forge bilateral links with Yemen in the field of economic, cultural and technical co-operation.

Yemen relations were established with Norway at the same time as they were restored with Germany during the 1970s. By May 1975 an embassy was established with an exchange of non-resident ambassadors between the two countries. The ambassador of Norway in Riyadh became non-resident ambassador in Sana‘ā’ just as the Yemen ambassador in Bonn became non-resident ambassador in Oslo, and recently the Yemen Ambassador in London (the writer) paid an official visit and presented his Letters of Credence to His Majesty King Harald V of Norway on 27 October 1998.

It may be appropriate here to highlight the valuable roles played by the European Archaeological Missions working in Yemen. They number 23, from Germany, Italy, France, the UK, Holland, Russia and Switzerland as well as the two American and Canadian missions which are operating in several areas in the Republic.

The following is a list of those missions and the sites where they were operating during 1998/99. The list is based on data provided by the General Board for Antiquities and Museums in Sana'ā':

1. The German Archaeological Institute, in Bilqīs Throne, Mārib.
2. The German Archaeological Institute, in Bilqīs Shrine, Mārib.
3. The German Archaeological Institute, in Saber, Lahej.
4. The French Mission for Exploration in al-Šiḥr, Ḥaḍramawt.
5. The French Mission for Archaeological Survey in Safer, Mārib.
6. The French Mission for Archaeological Survey exploring in Bīr 'Ālī, Šabwah.
7. The Canadian Mission for Archaeological Survey and Exploration in Zabīd, Hodeida.
8. The American Mission for Survey and Exploration in Ḏamār.
9. The Archaeological Mission for the American Institute of Anthropology.
10. The British Mission for Exploration in al-Ḥāmid, Hodeida.
11. The Mission for Under Water Survey and Exploration in Bīr 'Ālī, Šabwah.
12. The American Archaeological Survey in al-Jawl, Ḥaḍramawt.
13. The American Archaeological Survey in Mahrah and Ḥaḍramawt.
14. The Russian Mission for Survey and Exploration in Bīr 'Ālī, Šabwah.
15. The Russian Archaeological Survey in Wādī Ḥaḍramawt.
16. The Italian Mission for Survey in Barāqiš, Mārib.
17. The German Mission for Exploration in Ṣirwāh, Mārib.
18. The Swiss-German Mission for Exploration in Wādī Markhah.
19. The Dutch Mission for Survey in Baynūn, Ḏamār.
20. The German Mission for Survey in Dhafar, Ibb.
21. The Dutch Mission for Maintenance in al-'Āmiriyyah, Radā', al-Bayḍā'.
22. The Dutch Mission for developing the National Museum.
23. The Mission for Developing al-Ahqaf Library, Tarīm, Ḥaḍramawt.

Notes

1. The Dutch East India Company was established in 1602 in the Netherlands for the purpose of trading with nations lying beyond the Cape of Good Hope. It enjoyed many advantages and entered into conflict with the English East India Company which had been established in 1599 and was able to break the Portuguese monopoly in the Indian Ocean. The Dutch company went out of business in 1799 following the increasingly dominant maritime and colonial role of the British Empire. The French East India Company was evolved in 1664 along the same lines as the English and Dutch Companies. (See *Yemen and the West*, 38.)

2. See our essay 'Sana'a in the Mirror of the West', *Majallat al-Ijtihād*, Beirut, Seventh Issue 1990, 281.
3. Eric Macro. 1978. *Yemen and the Western World*. Translated under the title (*al-Yaman wa-al-Gharb*).
4. Ibid. 31–35. Brouwer, C.G. and Caplanban. 1988.
5. *Yemen at the beginning of the seventeenth century; extracts from the Dutch documents pertaining to the economic history of Southern Arabia 1614–1630*. The Dutch orientalist C.G. Brouwer published in the same year an interesting research paper in English about the activities of the Dutch East India Company in Yemen 1614–1655, Amsterdam 1988. The author was kind enough to send me a copy of the book after I met him during a scientific visit he paid to Yemen in 1988.
6. Ibid. 23.
7. *al-Yaman wa-al-Gharb*, 39.
8. See Dr Yūsuf Shalhad, *Majallat al-Dirāsāt al-Yamaniyyah*, issue number 18, winter 1984, 67–80.
9. *al-Yaman wa-al-Gharb*, 40–41.
10. *al-Yaman wa-al-Gharb*, 59.
11. al-'Amrī, *Ittiṣāl al-Yaman bi-al-Gharb*, 65.
12. See *Mi'at 'ām min tārīkh al-Yaman* (2nd edition), 29–32; also *Tārīkh al-Yaman al-ḥadīth wa-al-mu'āṣir*, 140.
13. See al-'Amri, *al-Yaman wa-al-Manār*, 145–148. See also the text of the Treaty in the first issue of the newspaper *al-Īmān*, Sana'a, October 1926.
14. Eric Macro, *Yemen and the West*, 125–127.
15. There are numerous documents of this kind, see for example index of their numbers and topics in the years 1934–1938 in the British Archive (The Public Records Office).

    FO Index: 1934–38: 804, 873, 664–1937: 17, 656. 1938: 15–16, 581–582.

    See also index to: 'Green or Secret Papers'. 1933–1939: 161, 231, 133, 277.

    See also R.J. Gain, *Aden under British rule*, London, 1975, 294–351.
16. See the previous footnote, Macro, *Yemen and the West*; see the chapter of the same title, 130–138.

Carving and Recarving: Three Rasulid Gravestones Revisited[1]

Elizabeth Lambourn

The marble carving of Cambay in Gujarat has always been much sought after. At the time of its active production, gravestones and architectural carvings were ordered by patrons around the Indian Ocean, from the east coast of Africa to Java in Indonesia. In the 14th/19th century these carvings were coveted in their turn by western travellers and some found their way into western collections. The Sociedade de Geografia de Lisboa in Portugal has a Cambay headstone brought from Goa;[2] the Museum für Völkerkunde in Berlin holds part of a cenotaph panel recovered from the site of Kilwa in present-day Tanzania (Chittick 1974: ii, 262, and plates 106 a & b). However, probably the best known examples of Cambay carving in western collections are the three gravestones recovered from the site of Dhofar in southern Omàn and held in the Victoria and Albert Museum in London since the early 1930s.[3] The three stones belong to two graves. Two stones, a headstone and a footstone, belong to the grave of al-Malik al-Wāṯiq Nūr al-Dīn Ibrāhīm ibn al-Malik al-Muẓaffar, the son of the Rasulid Sultan of Yemen who served as governor of Dhofar from 692/1292 until his death on 20 Muḥarram 711/8 June 1311 (Plates 1 and 2). The third belongs to one Shaykh Muḥammad ibn Abī Bakr, who died on 1 Ḏū al Ḥijjah 714/ 7 March 1315 (Plate 3).[4] The Shaykh Muḥammad ibn Abī Bakr of this headstone has been identified with a certain Shaykh Abū Bakr who is mentioned in Ibn Baṭṭūṭah's account of his visit to Dhofar in 730/1329 (Guest 1935: 409).[5]

The stones in the Victoria and Albert Museum have been published three times since they entered the museum, first in an article on the history of Dhofar written by R. Guest in 1935 (Guest 1935: 408–410) and twice subsequently by Venetia Porter (Porter 1987: 235 and 252, Appendix nos. 52–54; and Porter 1988). Having been so thoroughly published one might ask what more there is

Plate 1. *Left Side:* Headstone of al-Wāṯiq (d. 711/1311), face with recarved epitaph (acc. no. A12 1933) *Right Side:* Footstone of al-Wāṯiq (d. 711/1311), reverse (acc. no. A13 1933). (Photograph courtesy of the Victoria and Albert Museum, London)

Plate 2. Left Side: Headstone of al-Wāṯiq (d. 711/1311), reverse (acc. no. A12 1933) *Right Side:* Footstone of al-Wāṯiq (d. 711/1311), face (acc. no. A13 1933). (Photograph courtesy of the Victoria and Albert Museum, London)

Plate 3. Headstone of Shaykh Muḥammad al-Damīrī (d. 714/1315) (acc. no. A5 1932). (Photograph courtesy of the Victoria and Albert Museum, London)

left to say about them and indeed, the fundamentals remain unchanged. However, the three gravestones still have a great deal of information to reveal. Until now the Victoria and Albert stones have largely been studied for the light they shed on Rasulid history and involvement in Oman. Less attention has been paid to their place within the corpus of Cambay marble carving from which they originate, because this corpus was itself poorly known. New research on the marble carving of Cambay (Lambourn 1999) means that we can now examine the Victoria and Albert Museum stones within this context. The three stones also provide a great deal of physical evidence for the history of their manufacture and use, this category of information has barely been exploited and contributes new data about the recarving and reuse of these stones at Dhofar.

Cambay Marble Production and Export

For a period of some five centuries—between the late 4th/10th and the early tenth/sixteenth century—Cambay was the premier port of western India and the second city of Gujarat. Cambay lay at the heart of a complex network of trade routes that ran across northern India and the Indian Ocean, reaching as far as China. Traveller's accounts and surviving inscriptions conjure the picture of a cosmopolitan port, home to merchants and traders from all over India, Asia and the countries bordering the Indian Ocean. It was also an extremely fine city, with rich traditions of domestic and religious architecture as emerges from Ibn Baṭṭūṭah's description of the early 1340s: 'Cambay is one of the most beautiful cities as regards the artistic architecture of its houses and the construction of its mosques'. He adds that the port had 'beautiful houses and wonderful mosques' (Ibn Baṭṭūṭah 1976: 172).[6] Although little of this architecture has survived, Cambay has preserved large numbers of grave memorials, foundation inscriptions and architectural carvings and from these it is clear that not only were the 'wonderful mosques' of Cambay furnished with fine marble *miḥrab*s and foundation inscriptions, but that its cemeteries were filled with fine marble cenotaphs and gravestones. The three gravestones in the Victoria and Albert Museum belong to this body of carving.

All the three stones in the Victoria and Albert Museum belong to a well-known Cambay type. Undoubtedly the most distinctive feature of all three gravestones is the high-relief carving at the top of the stone, of a lamp between two halved banana plants or plantains. Whilst lamp motifs enjoyed a widespread popularity in the funerary context throughout the Islamic world at this period, this particular rendering of the motif—the high-relief carving and the two split-plantains—are unique to Cambay and characterize the gravestones produced during the first half of the 8th/14th century.[7] The slightly etiolated and spidery *naskh* of the majority of inscriptions on all three stones also correlates with that of inscriptions and gravestones produced at Cambay during the same half century. Other smaller details indicate the decade of manufacture or design; unsurprisingly the first decade of the 8th/14th century, which corresponds with the dates of 711/1311 and 714/1315 given in the epitaphs. The simple pointed arches of all three examples affiliate them with the gravestones of one al-Ǧawzī al-Ǧazrī (d. 707/1307) (Plate 4) and a certain freed-slave named Miṣbāḥ (d. 709/1309), which are both preserved at Cambay.

The Indian origin of Shaykh Muḥammad's and al-Wāṯiq's gravestones was identified early on by Guest, although their origin in Cambay was not pinpointed until the 1980s by Venetia Porter (Porter 1988: 34). In fact, the commission of these gravestones for Dhofar belongs to a broader phenomenon of the export of Cambay carving around the Indian Ocean.[8] Isolated finds and publications can now be put together to illustrate the export of Cambay marble from as far east as Gresik in Java, where three marble cenotaphs were brought from Cambay in the early ninth/fifteenth century (Cabaton 1911),[9] to Kilwa in Tanzania in the west, where two halves of an 8th/14th century Cambay cenotaph panel were discovered (Chittick 1974: ii, 262). Gravestones were by far the most common carved items to be shipped out of Cambay although a *miḥrab* has been found at Lar in southern Iran (Howard 1976) and a *miḥrab* and portal facing have been identified at Mogadishu in Somalia.[10] In a number of instances contemporary histories or other inscriptions confirm that these carvings were originally manufactured for patrons outside Cambay, and therefore that the distribution of these headstones and cenotaphs is not simply the result of later spoliation.[11] No such doubts exist for the Dhofar graves since we know that al-Wāṯiq was the Rasulid governor of Dhofar, and it seems possible to identify the Shaykh Muḥammad of the other epitaph with the Shaykh Abū Bakr whose shrine Ibn Baṭṭūṭah visited at Dhofar (Guest 1935: 409).

Though the export of carving never constituted the mainstay of Cambay production, it was a regular phenomenon between the late 7th/13th and the mid-9th/15th centuries. The reasons for this are easy enough to see. The carvings produced at Cambay rank among the finest produced anywhere in the Islamic world, and were certainly the finest graves available in western India between the 7th/13th–8th/14th centuries. The purity of the white marble and its fine polish, the refinement of its carving and design must have elicited the attention and admiration of all those who saw it. Cambay's status as the premier port of western India ensured that a maximum number of people saw such carving in its mosques and cemeteries, whilst its port location made the shipment of this carving exceptionally easy. Not surprisingly, a number of people decided to order carvings themselves and shipped them abroad. The carved marble of Cambay must have been especially prized in Dhofar since the only stone available locally was coarse and unattractive. Although Dhofar had easy access to

Plate 4. Headstone of al-Ǧawzī al-Ǧazrī (d. 707/1307), shrine of Parvaz Shah, Cambay. (Photograph author's own)

limestone from a limestone shelf some two to six metres thick that runs the whole length of the coastal plain, this stone is granular and friable, making it unsuitable for detailed carving, and it also weathers badly.[12] In many cases the rough surface was 'used as a key for a gypsum plaster finish' that disguised these defects and traces of this finish are still found on some of the columns of the Great Mosque at Dhofar (Costa 1979:116). Since inscriptions could not be disguised in this manner, the local Dhofari gravestones are rather coarse.[13]

This new context establishes that the finds of Cambay gravestones at Dhofar are far from unique, but this is not the end of their story. In his monumental study of the art of stone carving, Peter Rockwell works from the premise that every stone carving is a document that can tell the story of its own manufacture.[14] Of all the gravestones exported from Cambay, the three stones in the Victoria and Albert Museum tell some of the most unusual stories.

Shaykh Muḥammad's Headstone

The headstone of Shaykh Muḥammad provides a rare example of a grave memorial ordered for export during the lifetime of its patron and completed after his death.

At first glance Shaykh Muḥammad's headstone corresponds seamlessly with contemporary headstones still at Cambay. However, a second look at the carving in the area of the epitaph (Plate 3) reveals two distinct styles of script and carving technique. The first four lines, giving the name, titles and general blessings, are carved in the technique and style characteristic of 8th/14th century Cambay. However, the last two lines—significantly, those containing the date of his death—are carved quite differently. The carving of these panels is shallow and soft-edged, quite distinct from the sharp-edged and deep *champlevé* typical of the rest of the carving and all other Cambay inscriptions. The *naskh* in these two lines is also rather angular and with words arranged in horizontal tiers, a strong contrast to the slightly spidery *naskh* with occasional *riqā'* flourishes and the diagonal overlap of the other panels. The contrast with the sophistication and skill of the other inscription panels on the same tombstone is extreme and there is no doubt that these two panels were written and carved by craftsmen from very different backgrounds.

Venetia Porter has already explained this discrepancy, suggesting that the grave memorial was manufactured and partly inscribed in Cambay, presumably while Shaykh Muḥammad was still alive, and then completed in Dhofar after his death. The shallow carving and angular script of these last two lines certainly do not correspond to any contemporary carving from Cambay. Indeed, their shallowness and angularity suggest that they were executed by stone carvers more accustomed to a soft stone, such as the local Dhofari limestone, rather than a hard stone such as marble. Shaykh Muḥammad's gravestone is a rare example in Cambay carving of a gravestone produced in advance, during the lifetime of the person it was intended for, and then completed upon their death. Although this practice was probably quite common, no physical evidence of this has survived on the gravestones manufactured for local patrons at Cambay since they were undoubtedly completed by the same atelier and thus maintained stylistic cohesion. In the case of the other exported stones, the stylistic unity of their epitaphs suggests that they were exported with their epitaphs completed, and therefore after the death of the individual they commemorate.

Another area of Shaykh Muḥammad's gravestone also shows discrepancies in the style of its carving and suggests an interesting glitch in the production of his headstone. The third line of the epitaph contains the shaykh's *nisbah,* currently read as al-Damrīnī or al-Damrānī. This area is awkwardly carved and uses a somewhat angular script compared to the rest of his name. Furthermore, several letters—the *dāl*, the *rā'* and the final *yā'*—all have foliate terminals, a feature not found in the *naskh* commonly used at Cambay. However, all these features characterize the script and carving of the last two lines of his epitaph which we know were completed later in Dhofar. Together, these details suggest that the *nisbah* had to be left blank for completion or correction when the gravestone reached Dhofar, probably because it was not clearly understood when the epitaph was prepared at Cambay.

This is also the occasion to propose an alternative reading of Shaykh Muḥammad's *nisbah*, readings of which have varied considerably because of the clumsily carving in this area. An initial *dāl* followed by a *mīm* are clear and distinct, as is the final *yā'*, but the intermediate letters are hard to decipher. So far two options have been envisaged, Damrīnī (given by Guest) and Damrānī (given by Venetia Porter). The problem with these two options is that the letters present do not correspond to either reading. Close observation of this area suggests that the intermediate letters are a *yā* and a *rā'*, giving the final reading al-Damīrī, i.e. from Damīrah, one of two small towns bearing the same name located near Samannud in the Nile Delta in Egypt.[15] The Rasulids had close and regular contacts with Mamluk Egypt at this period and these connections may have encouraged the arrival of an Egyptian shaykh at Dhofar.

Al-Wāṯiq's Gravestone Pair

The gravestones of al-Wāṯiq have been identified and discussed as a pair since their arrival at the Victoria and Albert Museum in the 1930s (Plates 1 and 2). Like Shaykh Muḥammad's headstone, the two stones carry panels carved in a divergent style and technique; one of these panels, the headstone, carries the epitaph whilst the footstone is inscribed with the *fātiḥah*. Here too the carving is shallower and softer than elsewhere, and the *naskh* is angular, with contamination from foliated and interlaced Kufic visible in certain letters. The text is also arranged differently, in horizontal tiers rather than the diagonal overlap seen in the other inscription panels. The shallow carving technique and style of script, as well as the identity of the person they finally commemorated (al-Wāṯiq the Rasulid governor of Dhofar), suggest that this carving was executed in Dhofar by local limestone carvers. Following the example of Shaykh Muḥammad's headstone, the first assumption is that al-Wāṯiq's stones were also ordered before his death, only this time with the entire epitaph left blank for completion in Dhofar. However, the physical evidence of al-Wāṯiq's two stones suggests a far stranger tale.

The most obvious difference between al-Wāṯiq's and Shaykh Muḥammad's gravestones is that the panels on al-Wāṯiq's two stones are carved on a different plane from the main body of inscriptions. Alone, this feature might be seen as no more than a stylistic device to emphasize the central panels, as seen, for example, on the well-known headstone of 'Umar al-Kāzarūnī (d. 734/1333) at Cambay. However, in combination with the different technique and script this detail suggests that the two panels are actually recarved areas. They are recessed because an earlier text was cut back to give a fresh surface so that a new epitaph, al-Wāṯiq's, could be inserted on one stone and the *fātiḥah* on the other.

Examples of recutting are relatively common in Cambay carving, though they have not generally been noted. Perhaps one of the clearest examples is an early 8th/14th century headstone that was recarved for a certain Ḫwājah Ǧalāl al-Dīn Gīlānī who died in 979/1571 (Plate 5a).[16] The script and decorative carving of the headstone identify it as belonging to a group produced at Cambay between ca. 713/1314 and 730/1330, yet the date of the epitaph makes this dating quite impossible at first glance. However, here also, the style of carving, the script and the plane of carving in the area of the epitaph are quite different from the majority of inscriptions on the stone (Plate 5b). The epitaph is written in a small and awkward *naskh*, with two lines of text per panel instead of one, and the inscription surface within these two panels is noticeably deeper than the rest of the inscriptions. Clearly an early 8th/14th century headstone was re-used, its original epitaph was cut back and the new 10th/16th century epitaph was inserted. In the case of Ǧalāl al-Dīn's headstone the appropriation is quite coarsely executed, not simply in terms of carving technique and script, but even in terms of how the headstone was obtained. The manner in which the Quranic verses of the outer inscription band are cut off at the base suggests that those involved in the recarving did not even take the pains to dig out the headstone they wished to reuse, but simply sawed it off at ground level with little regard for the integrity of the inscriptions.[17] By comparison, the adaptation of 'al-Wāṯiq's' stones is relatively sophisticated but the principle remains the

Plate 5a. Recarved 14th-century headstone, recarved for Ǧalāl al-Dīn Gīlānī (d. 979/1571) Lal Mahalla, Cambay. (Photograph author's own)

Plate 5b. Detail of recarved epitaph, grave of Ǧalāl al-Dīn Gīlānī (d. 979/1571, Lal Mahalla, Cambay. (Photograph author's own)

same.[18] We are fortunate to have one Cambay headstone that has survived in mid-recarving process. On the headstone in the Sociedade de Geografia in Lisbon the bottom four panels of the original epitaph have been cut back, but they never received a new Muslim epitaph. In the end, the plain reverse of the stone was used for a Portuguese Christian epitaph, that of one Rui Freire who died in AD 1562 (Perez 1997: plates on 61 and 63).

Traces of the earlier inscriptions cut back for al-Wāṯiq's epitaph and the *fātiḥah* can still be made out on both stones in the left-hand borders of both panels (Plate 1, left hand stone). At Cambay carvers frequently extended the terminals of letters, and sometimes several letters, into the border surrounding the inscription panel. These terminals or letters were not carved in relief, but were simply incised in outline, as for example at the end of the second line of

Shaykh Muḥammad's epitaph where the final *yā'* of the word Abī and the final *rā'* of Bakr are rendered in incised outline on the border or the panel (Plate 3). As a consequence the borders of many Cambay inscriptions are peppered with small incision marks. When the two panels were cut back on al-Wāṯiq's stones, this fringe of incised terminals and letters remained on the left-hand borders and can still be made out today. These small incisions prove that workmen in Dhofar did not simply carve a blank area, as with Shaykh Muḥammad's epitaph, but had to first cut back existing inscriptions. The necessity of cutting out and levelling an earlier inscription explains why both panels are recessed into the stone.

The evidence reviewed above demonstrates that the tombstone pair currently discussed as the gravestones of al-Wāṯiq was not originally commissioned from Cambay for his grave, but was opportunistically appropriated for it. The pattern of incisions in the left-hand border and the blank panel remaining at the base of both stones further suggest that the gravestones recut for al-Wāṯiq's grave were not fully inscribed when they were appropriated. Just as Shaykh Muḥammad's gravestone was delivered with its epitaph half completed, these two stones appear to have reached Dhofar with the first lines of their epitaphs already carved but with the final panels intended for the date of death left blank.

Moreover, it appears that the two stones recarved for al-Wāṯiq's grave were never even designed as a pair. Analysis of the programme of inscriptions on both stones proves that they were originally made for two separate graves.

The Quranic Verses on 'al-Wātiq's' Gravestone 'Pair'

The two gravestones that finally commemorated al-Wāṯiq's grave work well together as a pair, but they are not a perfect pair and differ subtly in terms of size, shape and decoration. Paradoxically, it is the only area in which they do resemble each other closely—their programme of Quranic verses—that demonstrates conclusively that they were never manufactured as a pair. The two headstones repeat six out of the eleven Quranic passages they carry (see Figs 1 and 2, and Table 1 below).

No purpose-carved gravestone pair would have repeated the same Quranic citations in this manner and the only conclusion is that al-Wāṯiq's grave memorial was assembled from two gravestones intended for two different graves. One headstone was recarved with the new epitaph, the other headstone was recarved with the *fātiḥah* and became a footstone.

The example of Shaykh Muḥammad's gravestone suggests that other people at the Rasulid court may well have ordered Cambay gravestones during their lifetimes and that two of these stones were subsequently appropriated for the governor's grave. But with the original epitaphs gone and no further

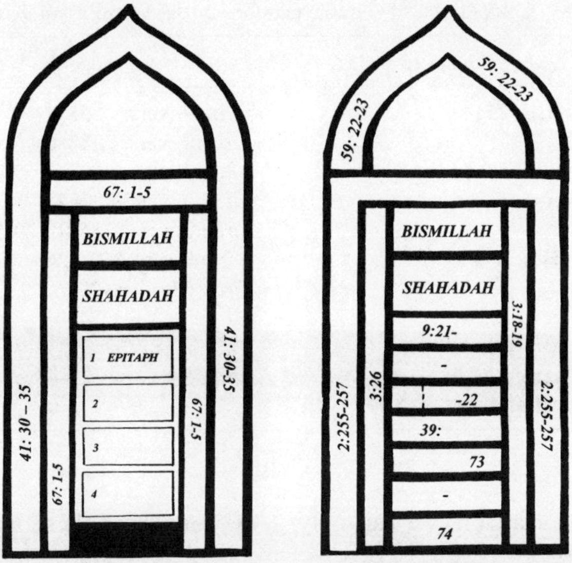

Figure 1. Quranic verses on al-Wāṯiq's headstone (d. 711/1311), face and reverse. Victoria and Albert Museum, acc. no. A12 1933. (Drawing author's own)

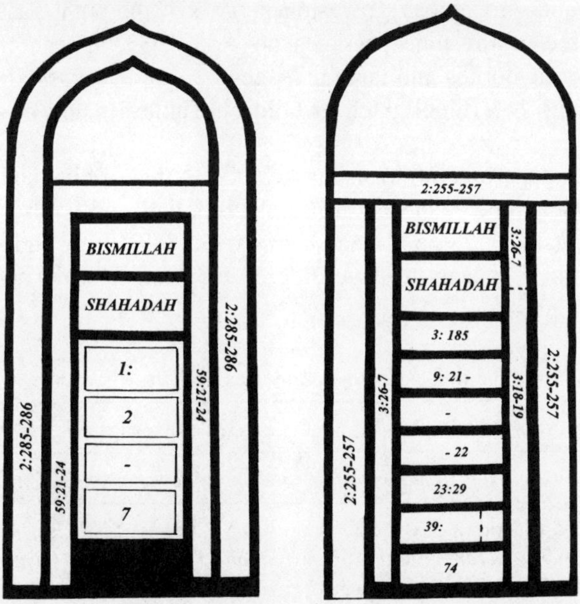

Figure 2. Quranic verses on al-Wāṯiq's footstone (d. 711/1311), face and reverse. Victoria and Albert Museum, acc. no. A13 1933. (Drawing author's own)

Table 1. Coincidence of Quranic citations on 'al-Wātiq's' tombstones.[19]

Fig. 1 (V & A acc. no. A12 1933)	*Fig. 2 (V & A acc. no. A13 1933)*[20]
sūrah 2, verses 255–7	*sūrah* 2, verses 255–7
	sūrah 2, verses 285–6
sūrah 3, verses 18–9	*sūrah* 3, verses 18–9
sūrah 3, verse 26	*sūrah* 3, verses 26–7
	sūrah 3, verse 185 (or 29:57)[21]
sūrah 9 verses 21–2	*sūrah* 9 verses 21–2
	sūrah 23, verse 29
sūrah 39, verses 73–4	*sūrah* 39, verse 74
sūrah 41, verses 30–5	
sūrah 59, verses 22–3	*sūrah* 59, verses 21–4
sūrah 67, verses 1–5	

documentation available we can only guess for whom these two headstones were destined.

The mystery of who originally purchased these stones is all the more tantalizing since they present unusual programmes of inscription and interesting formal details. Nearly half the Quranic passages on both headstones are not commonly found on Cambay gravestones. Two of the eight passages on A12 1933, and three of the nine passages on A13 1933, appear only rarely on Cambay grave memorials and three passages—*sūrah* 3, verses 26 or 26–7, and *sūrah* 67, verses 1–5 (highlighted in bold on Table 2 below)—are unique to these graves.

This Quranic repertory contrasts markedly with that of Shaykh Muḥammad's headstone, which adheres closely to Cambay models and is inscribed with the Throne verse (*sūrah* 2:255–7) and *sūrah*s, 3:18–9, 9:21 and 59:22. Thus, although the latter appears to have ordered his headstone during his lifetime,

Table 2. Uncommon and non-standard Quranic passages on 'al-Watiq's' tombstone pair

Fig. 1 (V & A acc. no. A12 1933)		*Fig. 2 (V & A acc. no. A13 1933)*	
Cambay repertory	*Non-Cambay*	*Cambay repertory*	*Non Cambay*
sūrah 2, verses 255–7	***sūrah* 3, verse 26**	*sūrah* 2, verses 255–7	*sūrah* 2, verses 285–6
sūrah 3, verses 18–9	*sūrah* 39, verses 73–4	*sūrah* 3, verses 18–9	***sūrah* 3, verses 26–7**
sūrah 9, verses 21–2	*sūrah* 41, verses 30–5	*sūrah* 3, verse 185[22]	*sūrah* 23, verse 29
sūrah 59, verses 22–3	***sūrah* 67, verses 1–5**	*sūrah* 9, verses 21–2	*sūrah* 39, verse 74
		sūrah 59, verses 21–4	

there is no evidence that he personalized the programme of inscriptions on his grave, as was sometimes the case at Cambay.

Most of the non-standard extracts on 'al-Wāṯiq's' gravestones have an obvious funerary symbolism or usage that makes them appropriate to this context. *Sūrah* 39, verse 74; *sūrah* 41, verses 30–5, and *sūrah* 67, verses 1–5, all deal with the Garden of Paradise or the seven heavens. *Sūrah* 67, verses 1–5, makes specific mention of the lamps that adorn the lower heaven, a neat reference perhaps to the major decorative motifs of the gravestone. *Sūrah* 3, verses 26–7, is again entirely appropriate in a funerary context since it speaks of God's all encompassing power, including that over life and death, 'Thou bringest the Living out of the Dead; and Thou bringest the Dead out of the Living.' These selections may reflect the personal taste of the person or persons who commissioned these headstones, or may reflect another tradition of funerary epigraphy. Unfortunately, it is difficult at present to know whether this relates to local Dhofari or Rasulid taste, because this material is incompletely documented.[23] But the idea of a local influence on the epigraphic programme finds some support in an analysis of the form of the gravestones. Both tombstones are free-standing headstones, inscribed and decorated on *both* faces and on their sides, which carry a running flower scroll. In his preliminary survey of Islamic epigraphy at Dhofar Giovanni Oman noted that local Dhofari tombstones were all inscribed on the front, rear and sides of the stone, something that he had not encountered elsewhere and which matches perfectly the two headstones discussed here. Since no double-sided headstones have been documented so far amongst the production at Cambay, this may suggest that our two headstones were commissioned to meet with local Dhofari taste.[24]

The Recarving and Appropriation of Cambay Marble

The analysis of the so-called gravestone pair of al-Wāṯiq reveals a complex history of manufacture and reuse. Although it robs us of one of the most illustrious patrons of Cambay carving known so far—the Rasulid governor of Dhofar—it also adds new data to one of the less known aspects of this production, namely its recarving and appropriation after manufacture. Although a number of Muslim friends and acquaintances have been able to inform me that they have seen recarving of this type in contemporary Muslim cemeteries, this practice has not been widely documented in Islamic funerary epigraphy and has certainly not been recognized at Cambay.

Yet examples of recarving are relatively common at Cambay, and the cases of al-Gīlānī and the Lisbon headstone have already been cited. In general, this recarving appears to fit into two categories. In the first half of the 9th/15th century carvers at the port re-inscribed old 8th/14th century graves for export to patrons in Sri Lanka and Sumatra. Since Cambay still had a thriving marble carving industry at this period, evidenced by numerous tombstones still at Cambay, this recarving appears to have been a labour-saving device. However, by the 10th/16th century the production of fine marble carving had all but ceased at Cambay and consequently stone carvers resorted to adapting old gravestones and inserting fresh epitaphs because such fine work could no longer be accomplished.

The Cambay graves made for export rarely appear to have been touched once they reached their final destination, and most have remained in situ on the graves and in the shrines for which they were originally made and with their original epitaphs intact. 'Al-Wāṯiq's' stones now provide another example of Cambay graves recut by craftsmen outside Cambay, and this only a couple of years after their manufacture. It is only a pity that we do not know more about the later history of these three gravestones, when and why they were taken from Dhofar and how they finally reached the Victoria and Albert Museum, since this would truly complete our understanding of their life-history.

Bibliography

Archaeological Survey of India, 1887–ongoing. *Annual Reports on Indian Epigraphy*. Delhi.

Ibn Baṭṭūṭa *Tuḥfat al-nuẓẓār fī gharā'ib al-amṣār wa-'ajā'ib al-asfār*, ed. and transl. Defrémery and Sanguinetti 1914–26: *Voyages d'Ibn Batoutah* (4 vols.). Paris.

Ibn Baṭṭūṭah *Travels* transl. Gibb 1914–26: Ibn Baṭṭūṭah, *Travels in Asia and Africa, AD 1325–1354*, translated by Gibb, H.A.R. London: Hakluyt Society.

Ibn Baṭṭūṭah *The Rehla* transl. Husain 1976: Ibn Baṭṭūṭah, *The Rehla of Ibn Battuta (India, Maldive Islands and Ceylon)*, translated by Husain, M. Baroda.

Cabaton, A. 1911. L'Epitaphe de Malik Ibrahim à Gresik. *Revue du Monde Musulman* 13: 257–260 and plate facing p. 249.

Cerulli, E. 1957. *Somalia Scritti Editi ed Inediti* (2 vols). Rome.

Chittick, N. 1974. *Kilwa. An Islamic Trading City on the East African Coast* (2 vols). Nairobi: The British Institute in East Africa Memoir Number Five.

Costa, P.M. 1979. The Study of the City of Zafar (al-Balid). *Journal of Oman Studies* 5: 111–50.

Desai, Z.A. 1961. Arabic Inscriptions of the Rajput Period in Gujarat. *Epigraphia Indica Arabic and Persian Supplement*: 1–24.

Desai, Z.A., 1971. Some Fourteenth Century Epitaphs from Cambay in Gujarat. *Epigraphia Indica Arabic and Persian Supplement*: 1–58.

Garlake, P.S. 1966. *The Early Islamic Architecture of the East African Coast*. Oxford.

Guest, R. 1935. Zufar in the Middle Ages. *Islamic Culture* 9: 402–10.

Howard, R. 1976. The Lar Mihrab. *Art and Archaeology Research Papers* 9: 24–5.

Inzerillo, M. 1980. *Le Moschee di Mogadiscio: Contributo alla Conoscenza dell'Architettura Islamica*. Palermo.

Kopf, L. 1999. 'al-Damīrī'. *Encyclopaedia of Islam*, 2nd edit.
Lambourn, E. 1999. A Collection of Merits Gathered from Different Sources. The Islamic Marble Carving and Architecture of Cambay in Gujarat between 1200 and 1350 AD. PhD. thesis. University of London.
Lambourn, E. 1999b. The Decoration of the Fakhr al-Din mosque. Fakhr al-Din mosque in Mogadishu and other pieces of gujorati marble carving on the East African Coast. *Azania* 34: 61–86.
Lewcock, R. and Smith, G.R. 1974. Three Medieval Mosques in the Yemen—A Preliminary Survey. *Oriental Art* 20, 1: 75–86 and 20, 2: 192–203.
Misra, S.C. 1982. *The Rise of Muslim Power in Gujarat. A History of Gujarat from 1298 to 1442*. New Delhi.
Oman, G. 1983. Preliminary Epigraphic Survey of Islamic Material in Dhofar. *Journal of Oman Studies* 6: 227–89.
Oman, G. 1989. Arabic-Islamic Epigraphy in Dhofar in the Sultanate of Oman. In Costa, P.M. and Tosi, M. (eds), *Oman Studies. Papers on the Archaeology and History of Oman*. Rome: IsMEO, 193–99.
Perez, R.M. *et al.* 1997. *Histórias de Goa*. Lisbon.
Porter, V. 1987. The Art of the Rasulids. in Daum, W. (ed.), *Yemen 3000 Years of Art and Civilisation in Arabia Felix*. Innsbruck and Frankfurt/Main, 232–53.
Porter, V. 1988. Three Rasulid Tombstones from Zafar. *Journal of the Royal Asiatic Society:* 32–7.
al-Radi, S. 1997. *The 'Amiriya in Rada'. The History and Restoration of a Sixteenth-century Madrasa in the Yemen*. Oxford: Oxford Studies in Islamic Art XIII.
Reggio Governo della Somalia, 1934. *Museo della Garesa—Catalogo*. Mogadishu.
Rockwell, P. 1993. *The Art of Stoneworking: a Reference Guide*. Cambridge.
Sadek, N. 1996. Patronage and Architecture in Rasulid Yemen, 626–858/1229–1454 AD. PhD. thesis. University of Toronto.
Sadek, N. 1993. In the Queen of Sheba's Footsteps: Women Patrons in Rasulid Yemen. *Asian Art* 6 no. 2: 15–27.
Smith, G.R. 1988. The Rasulids in Dhofar in the VIIth-VIIIth/XIII-XIVth Centuries. *Journal of the Royal Asiatic Society:* 26–32.
Tichelman, G. L. 1940. Een Marmeren Praalgraf te Koeta Kareuëng (Nordkust van Atjèh). *Culturël Indie* II: 205–11.

Notes

1. My thanks go to Venetia Porter for her feedback and encouragement during the writing of this article. The material presented here is taken from my PhD thesis and was also delivered under the title 'Exotic stones: three Indian tombstones from Rasulid Dhofar' at the 1998 *Seminar for Arabian Studies* in London.
2. Accession no. AB–957. See Perez 1997: 243, CAT. no. 165 and plates on pages 61 and 63.
3. Accession numbers A12 1933 and A 13 1933. See Smith, 1988 for an account of the Rasulid conquest of Dhofar.
4. Accession number A5 1932.

5. Guest cites Ibn Baṭṭūṭah 1914–26: ii, 201. Ibn Baṭṭūṭah apparently visited the shrine of this *shaykh* and also met his sons.
6. For the Arabic original see Ibn Baṭṭūṭah, 1914–26, iv, p.53. According to Misra's calculations Ibn Baṭṭūṭah arrived in Cambay in 743/1342 (Misra 1982: 216).
7. The first examples are found on the headstones of Ḥasan al-'Irāqī (d. 699/1299) at Somnath Patan in Saurashtra (*ARIE* 1954–55, insc. C 168 and one plate of the rubbing) and Sulaymān al-Bammī (d. 699/1300) at Cambay (Desai 1961: 5–7, insc. I, plate I (a)). The last headstone to carry this motif records the death of one bint Muḥammad Anṣarī who died in 746/1345 (Desai 1971: 52–53, insc. XXVI and plate XIII (b)).
8. For a full study of the export of Cambay marble carving during the late 13th and 14th centuries see Lambourn 1999, Part VI.
9. The graves at Gresik are widely published.
10. Reggio Governo della Somalia 1934: 69–70, no. 14 and plate on page 74; Cerulli 1957: i, 9–10, insc. XIII and Fig. V; Garlake 1966, Fig. 65; and Inzerillo 1980, plates 27 and 28; and Lambourn 1999b. The Manṣūriyyah *madrasah* at Juban in the Yemen, built in 887/1482, incorporates eight alabaster pillars that display evidently western Indian features such as the hanging bell and chain, floral garlands and leaf designs (al-Radi 1997, figs 6 and 52). A recent analysis of these columns by al-Radi has sought parallels in a variety of Indian Islamic architectural traditions, from Delhi, via Gujarat and Khandesh to the Deccan, (al-Radi 1997: 100–1). However, whilst the closest parallels appear to be with Gujarat, there is no evidence so far to suggest that these columns belong to the production of Cambay.
11. Other examples can be confirmed at Somnath Patan in Saurashtra, where earlier inscriptions demonstrate that the family of Ḥasan al-'Irāqī (d. 699/1299) (*ARIE* 1954–5, insc. C 168) had been settled in the port for several generations before his death, or the cenotaph and headstone of a daughter of the Sultan of Samudera-Pasai in north Sumatra (d. 831/1428) whose ancestors are commemorated by nearby gravestones and mentioned in local histories (see Tichelman 1940).
12. The geological situation at Dhofar has also been well investigated by Paolo Costa. Costa points out that 'shallow quarries are visible everywhere in the plain between Raysut and Taqa and many of them appear to have been exploited in ancient times' (Costa 1979: 112).
13. See illustrations in Oman 1989.
14. Rockwell 1993.
15. For the biography of one of the most famous persons to bear this *nisbah*, see Kopf 1999.
16. The headstone has not been published before but is recorded in the *ARIE* 1959–60, insc. D 102.
17. Adding to the crudity with which this memorial was assembled, the 14th century headstone in fact fronts a cenotaph assembled from plain uncarved blocks and the remains of a 15th century cenotaph.
18. Another example of this phenomenon is a headstone preserved in the Qadi Mosque at Cambay. Whilst the design of the headstone and the style of script suggest a date of manufacture somewhere in the first half of the 15th century AD, the heavily recessed epitaph is carved in a different script and records the death of one Sa'd

Allāh *'urf* Bihārī in 916/1511. The inscription is unpublished but listed in *ARIE* 1959–60, insc. D 114.

19. The Quranic verses are here cited following the numbering system adopted from 1924 onwards in the Cairo editions of the Quran, not according to Fleugel's Leipzig edition of 1841.
20. This tombstone is also inscribed with *sūrah* 1, verses 2–7, but this extract was carved in Dhofar and therefore does not belong to the original repertory of inscriptions executed in Cambay style and technique.
21. The phrase *kullu nafasin dā'iqat ul-mawt* appears in both verses and so may be considered to derive from either *sūrah*.
22. Or *sūrah* 29, verse 57.
23. The 14th century epitaphs of Dhofar have not been published in detail, and we have only a general idea of the texts they use (Oman 1989: 198). From a preliminary survey, these seem quite unexceptional, although significantly different from Cambay; Dr Giovanni Oman noted a preference for *sūrah* 3, verse 185 and *sūrah* 55, verses 26–7. There is also very little data on the broader field of Rasulid epigraphy in the Yemen, only a small number of later graves survive in Ta'izz. These are the cenotaphs of the Rasulid Sultans al-Ashraf II (reg. 799–803/1377–1400) and al-Nāṣir Aḥmad (reg. 803–27/1400–24), they are in the main tomb chamber of the Ashrafiyyah *madrasah* in Ta'izz. For an overview of Rasulid architecture and these cenotaphs in particular, see Sadek 1996: 219–21, also Lewcock and Smith 1974: 75–86 and 192–203. For a monographic study of another Rasulid *madrasah*, the 'Āmiriyyah *madrasah* at Radā', see al-Radi 1997.
24. Although a majority of headstones are built up into the walls of existing structures and so cannot be examined in full, all the seven late 13th and 14th century headstones that have remained unattached to a wall are carved on one side only. These are the headstones of al-Takrītī in Kerala (*ARIE* 1965–6, insc. D 95 and one plate of the rubbing); al-Āstarābādī (Desai 1961: 17–8, insc. VI, plate III (b)); Sulaymān al-Bammī (Desai 1961: 5–7, insc. I, plate I (a)); the fragmentary headstone preserved in Naib Mahalla at Cambay (unpublished but listed in *ARIE* 1959–60, insc. D 106 and Lambourn 1999, Cat. No. 40); the Lisbon headstone already mentioned; grave III at Chandi Said Syarif near Lok'seumawe in Sumatra (unpublished) and the recarved headstone of Ǧalāl al-Dīn Gīlānī at Cambay. However, local Dhofari grave conventions use a pair of head- and footstones to mark a male grave, and three stones, a head- and footstone pair with a third stone erected between these two, to indicate a female burial which would suggest that both headstones are lacking their footstones (Oman 1989).

The Politics of Protection in the Gulf: The Arab Rulers and the British Resident in the Nineteenth Century*

James Onley

> If Great Britain has become, in any sense, the arbiter and guardian of the Gulf, it has not been through a restless ambition urging her on to the control of the waste places of the earth, but in obedience to the calls that have been made upon her in the past to enforce peace between warring tribes, to give a free course to trade, to hold back the arm of the marauder and the oppressor, to stand between the slave-dealer and his victim.
>
> Confidential Foreign Office memorandum, 1908[1]

Was Britain's role as 'arbiter and guardian of the Gulf' one it assumed in response to appeals from the Gulf Arabs, as the imperial memorandum claims? Or was British protection imposed on the Gulf Arabs, as some historians are now arguing? To address this highly contentious issue, this study considers British involvement in the Gulf in relation to the political system of nineteenth-century Eastern Arabia. What was the nature of Britain's relationship with the Gulf rulers from an Arab perspective? How did Britain's Political Resident in the Gulf fit into the regional political system? Through the process of answering

---

* This article is based on research conducted in Bahrain, funded by the Bahrain-British Foundation; in London at the Oriental and India Office Collections (OIOC) of the British Library, funded partly by the Society for Arabian Studies; and in Oxford at the Middle East Centre of St. Antony's College. For reading drafts of this article and offering helpful comments, I am indebted to James Piscatori, Frauke Heard-Bey, Ahmad Al-Shahi and Gloria Onley. For helpful discussions on the article's subject, I would also like to thank Paul Dresch, Jill Crystal, Ali Akbar Bushiri, Nelida Fuccaro, Yoav Alon and Samer El-Karanshawy.

these questions, this study shows that Anglo–Arab relations cannot be explained solely by reference to the Anglo–Arab treaties, but that a detailed examination of the Gulf rulers' involvement in the politics of protection is necessary to provide a realistic evaluation of what Britain's presence meant in the Gulf.

1. Historical Background

British India's initial interest in Eastern Arabia grew out of its need to protect its ships and subjects in Arabian waters. From 1797 onward, maritime toll-levying and raiding by Arabs of the lower Gulf—similar to bedouin practices along desert trade routes—increasingly threatened British Indian shipping.[2] To put an end to these practices, which they considered extortion and piracy, in 1806 the British blockaded a fleet of dhows belonging to the Qawāsim (singular Qāsimī), who they believed to be responsible, and in 1809 and 1819 sent naval expeditions against Qasimi ports on the southeast Persian coast and on the 'Pirate Coast', as they termed the Coast of Oman (the present-day U.A.E). After the second expedition, the British were able to impose an anti-piracy treaty—known as the General Treaty of 1820—on the rulers and governors of the Pirate Coast. The Rulers of Bahrain, who wished to avoid maritime toll-paying, were admitted to the Treaty at their request. To manage British India's relations with these rulers, supervise the enforcement of the General Treaty, and protect British India's ships and subjects in Arabian waters, the British created the post of Political Agent for the Lower Gulf, headquartered on Qishm Island in the Strait of Hormuz. Two years later, in 1822, the British transferred this post to Bushire on the southwest Persian coast and amalgamated it with the much older post of Bushire Resident. The new post of 'Resident in the Persian Gulf'—'Political Resident in the Persian Gulf' (PRPG) after the 1850s—was responsible for Britain's relations with the entire Gulf region.[3] To support the Resident in his role, the British assigned a naval squadron to the Gulf to patrol its waters—a system known as 'watch and cruise'. The Gulf Squadron was under the command of the 'Senior Naval Officer in the Persian Gulf' (SNOPG) and was headquartered at the entrance to the Gulf, first on Qishm Island (1821–63, 1869–79) and then on neighbouring Henjam Island (1879–1935).[4]

After the imposition of the General Treaty, Gulf rulers consented to other treaties over the course of the century. The most important of these were the Maritime Truces, which established the Pax Britannica in the Gulf. The first Maritime Truce, signed in 1835 by the rulers of Abu Dhabi, Dubai, 'Ajman and the Qāsīmi empire (Sharjah, Umm al-Qaiwain, Ras al-Khaimah, Rams, Dibba, Khor Fakkan, Fujairah, Kalba, Mughu, Lingah and Qishm Island), was an experimental ban on maritime warfare during the pearling season. The Truce was a great success and a second Truce was arranged the following year, which the newly-independent Ruler of Umm al-Qaiwain also signed. After a series of annual twelve-month truces and a ten-year Truce in 1843, the rulers signed a Perpetual Maritime Truce in 1853. In recognition of the shaikhdoms' membership in the Maritime Truce, the British referred to them as the 'Trucial States' and to the Coast of Oman as the 'Trucial Coast'.[5] The British eventually invited the rulers of Bahrain and Qatar to join the Truce in 1861 and 1916 respectively. Under the terms of the Truce, the Gulf rulers gave up their right to wage war by sea in return for British protection against maritime aggression. This arrangement, known as the 'trucial system', cast Britain in the role of 'arbiter and guardian of the Gulf'. Later on, the rulers also signed Exclusive Agreements (Bahrain in 1880, the Trucial States in 1892, Kuwait in 1899, Najd and Hasa in 1915, Qatar in 1916) binding them into exclusive treaty relations with, and ceding control of their external affairs to, the British Government.[6] Although these states were still foreign territory and their rulers remained as heads of state, their status vis-à-vis the Government of India placed them within the sphere of Britain's Indian Empire.[7]

2. The State of the Debate

The Gulf's best-known historians, J.G. Lorimer and J.B. Kelly, paint a positive picture of Britain's role as 'arbiter and guardian of the Gulf'.[8] Kelly concludes his *Britain and the Persian Gulf, 1795–1880* by commenting that Britain's position in the Gulf rested, above all, 'upon the exertions and sacrifices of the men who brought peace, justice, and the rule of law to the Gulf in the nineteenth century, and in so doing wrote one of the most honourable pages in the history of the British Empire.'[9]

Since the 1980s, however, a different view of Britain's role in the Gulf, represented by the works of Khaldoun Al-Naqeeb, Jacqueline Ismael, Abdullah Taryam and the Ruler of Sharjah, Shaikh Sultan bin Muhammad al-Qasimi, has emerged in the historiography.[10] Al-Qasimi, for example, argues in *The Myth of Arab Piracy in the Gulf* that the works of Lorimer and Kelly

> emphasize a complete misunderstanding of the history of the area and the factors involved. The people of the Gulf were normal people with normal human ambitions. ... The only abnormal factor was the introduction of a foreign people whose aim was to dominate and exploit. The intruders were the forces of British imperialism, who knew very well and often testified that the indigenous people of the Gulf were only interested in the peaceful pursuits of pearl diving and trading.[11]

He contends that Kelly's account agrees with Lorimer's because 'Kelly's purpose was to support rather than challenge Lorimer's work. In a sense he was more royalist than the king and his adoption of the imperialist point of view was almost more unquestioning than that of the imperialistic functionaries themselves.'[12] Sultan al-Qasimi believes that historians who present Britain's role in the Gulf as a positive one have a hidden, imperial agenda. They 'want us to believe', says al-Qasimi, 'that the Arabs of the Gulf were saved ... by the benevolent efforts of the British East India Company, whose intervention in the Gulf was for the sole purpose of preserving law and order [and that the] resulting British domination of the Gulf for almost two centuries was a responsibility thrust upon the British almost against their will.'[13]

Did the Gulf Arabs truly benefit from British hegemony or were they merely exploited by it? Was British protection imposed on the Gulf Arabs, or was the role of protector imposed on the British? This study attempts to resolve the argument between these opposing points of view by examining the politics of protection in the Gulf.

3. The Study's Approach

The history of Anglo–Arab relations in the Gulf has been overshadowed by the general assumption that all the Anglo–Arab treaties were imposed by Britain. Lorimer and Kelly have rationalized the imposition as necessary acts of benevolence; Sultan al-Qasimi and others have described it as imperialistic domination. This study challenges the assumption of imposition by considering Britain's presence in the Gulf from the perspective of the nineteenth-century Gulf Arab rulers. It draws on a number of historical, political and anthropological studies of Eastern Arabia to define the political reality of these rulers and their shaikhdoms. It examines the economic, military and social foundations of Gulf rulership to show how Eastern Arabian politics were shaped by the ever-present need for protection and the Arabian custom of protection-seeking. That Gulf rulers sought out protector-protégé relationships as a survival strategy is apparent from the well-documented history of Bahrain, in this respect a typical Gulf shaikhdom. The history of Bahrain's involvement with other regional powers is the key to understanding Bahrain's evolving relationship with Britain and throws new light on the role of Britain in the Gulf in the nineteenth century.

4. The Economic Foundations of Rulership

Fierce competition between and within ruling families for control of the limited economic resources in the Gulf created an atmosphere of uncertainty and insecurity.[14] The possession of scarce resources carried with it the endless problem of protection. It created what one Gulf Resident described as 'a condition wherein every man's hand was ever prone to be raised against his neighbour.'[15]

As a result, the need for protection dominated and shaped regional politics more than any other factor.

Eastern Arabia's harsh environment constrained lucrative economic activity along the coast to the exportation of pearls and dates, the importation of goods from abroad, shipping, and ship-building.[16] Economic activities of any note were limited to twenty-five coastal towns—Kuwait, Qatif, Dammām (then on Dammām Island), 'Uqayr, Manamah, Muharraq, Zubarah, Khor Ḥassān (now Khuwayr), Ḥuwaylah, Bid' (now a district of Doha[17]), Wakrah, Abu Dhabi, Dubai, Sharjah, 'Ajman, Umm al-Qaiwain, Ras al-Khaimah, Rams, Dibba, Khor Fakkan, Fujairah, Sohar, Matrah, Muscat and Sur—each of which had its own cycle of prosperity and decline within the nineteenth century.[18] Throughout the nineteenth century, the majority of these towns were controlled by just three ruling families: the Āl Khalifah of Bahrain, the Qawāsim of the Coast of Oman, and the Āl Bū Sa'īd of Muscat. The locations of the towns can be seen on Map 1, below.

In the first half of the nineteenth century, Bahrain competed with Kuwait as Eastern Arabia's second busiest port after Muscat. In the 1870s, under the stability of Shaikh 'Īsā bin 'Alī Āl Khalifah's rule (1869–1923), Bahrain rivalled and then replaced Muscat in this regard. Writing in 1874, Lieutenant-Colonel Edward Ross (Resident 1872–91) noted: 'The chief ports and centres of trade in the Gulf are Bushire, Lingah, Bundar Abbas, and Bahrein. Bahrein is conveniently situated to be an *entrepôt* for the Arabia trade and is much used as such. The commercial importance of these islands is not inconsiderable. With the exception of the Islands of Bahrein, the trade of the Arab ports is comparatively petty.'[19] To illustrate Ross' observation, compare Bahrain's imports/exports of 1874 with those of Muscat and the Trucial States in Table 1, below.[20]

Table 1. Bahrain, Muscat and Trucial States Imports/Exports during 1874.

	Imports in 1874		*Exports in 1874*	
Shaikhdom	*Rupees*	*Pounds*	*Rupees*	*Pounds*
Bahrain	3,144,295	314,429	2,952,650	295,265
Muscat	3,167,672[21]	316,767	1,623,024[22]	162,302
Trucial States[23]	2,276,500	227,650	1,364,500	136,450

Bahrain's imports were virtually identical to Muscat's, while its exports nearly equalled those of the other seven states combined: Rs 2,987,524 (£298,752).[24] Clearly, Bahrain's function as an entrepôt was of considerable importance to its economy.

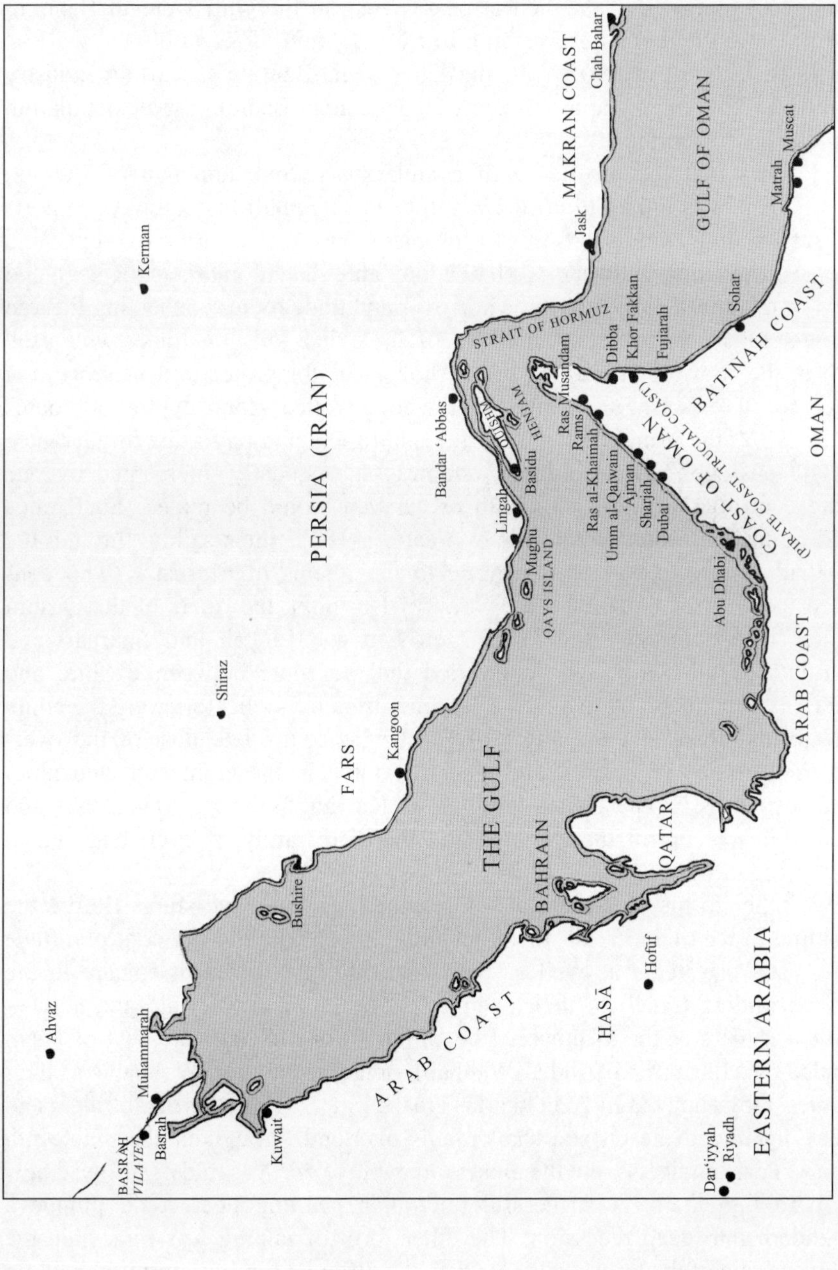

Map 1. The locations of towns of economic note.

A shaikhdom's most vulnerable source of income was its pearling fleets. Before oil, the pearling industry was the Gulf's largest single income source and its biggest employer.[25] The richest pearl banks in the Gulf were in Bahraini waters. These yielded an estimated profit for Bahrain of Rs 4,000,000 in 1873 and Rs 16,100,000 in 1905.[26] In the latter year, Bahrain's pearling industry employed 17,500 men—approximately 70 per cent of Bahrain's male population over the age of fourteen.[27]

It follows that the prosperity of a Gulf shaikhdom, and that of Bahrain in particular, was linked to a ruler's ability to safeguard his commercial ports and surrounding waters. A further problem was the security of ships and caravans travelling between a shaikhdom and distant markets. Rulers and tribes who controlled the maritime and overland trade routes connecting Eastern Arabia's towns with distant markets often levied tolls on those who used them in the form of *ẖūwah* (a 'brotherhood fee' for protection) or *ğuwayzah* (a fee for free passage). A merchant who travelled along controlled routes had to call at the principal towns of the controllers and pay a fee to guarantee his safe passage.[28] If he did not, and was subsequently intercepted by one of the controller's patrols, his ship or caravan would be raided. Such raids could be fatal. Before the anti-piracy treaty of 1820, ships sailing through the Gulf had to pay *ẖūwah* or *ğuwayzah* to the imams of Muscat[29] (who controlled the Gulf of Oman and the Strait of Hormuz), the rulers of the Qāsimī empire (who controlled the lower Gulf between Lingah and Sharjah) and the rulers of the Ka'b (who controlled the sea route between Bushire and Basra). The mainland equivalents of the maritime toll-collectors were the amirs of Najd and Hasa and the amirs of Ḥā'il who controlled most of the overland trade routes of Eastern and Central Arabia in the eighteenth and nineteenth centuries.[30] The ruling families of Kuwait, Bahrain, Abu Dhabi and Dubai did not control these routes and therefore rarely, if ever, engaged in toll-levying.

Two other forms of raiding also threatened caravans and ships. Before the Maritime Truce of 1835, all rulers, including those who did not control a trade route, used privateers as well as their own military forces to engage in the wartime raiding (*ğazū*) of their enemies.[31] As the amirs of Najd and Hasa—political leaders of the Wahhabis (the Unitarian or *Muwaḥḥidūn* sect of Islam founded by Muḥammad 'Abd al-Wahhāb)—regarded all non-Wahhabis as their enemies, they engaged in *ğazū* to a far greater extent than other Arab rulers and repeatedly raided the coastal shaikhdoms overland throughout the nineteenth century. Pearling fleets were the most vulnerable to *ğazū*, as raiders always knew where to find them. A successful raid on a pearling fleet could plunge a shaikhdom into deep recession. The other form of raiding was piracy, in the usual meaning of the term. To the British, the different kinds of maritime raiding were all piracy. And it is apparent that they all interfered with the economic well-being of the Gulf shaikhdoms.

While Gulf rulers profited directly from shipping and pearling through their own extensive involvement in them, they also obtained revenue by taxing subjects who engaged in these trades. The collection of taxes carried with it a responsibility to protect the taxpayers.[32] For general merchants and their cargo fleets, taxes took the form of customs duties. For pearl merchants and their pearling fleets, they took the form of a pearl-boat tax. In return for these taxes, before the Maritime Truce, the rulers stationed war dhows in their ports and at the pearling banks to provide protection. If a ruler could not protect his merchants and their fleets (especially their pearling fleets) from raiding and extortion, or if he made excessive financial demands on them, the merchants would often migrate to other shaikhdoms.[33] The threat of migration gave the merchants some political leverage to limit the power of the rulers and discourage them from levying an arbitrary general tax (known as *šūfah*) or confiscating their property.[34] As Lieutenant Arnold Kemball (Assistant Resident 1841–52) observed in 1845, 'the loss of authority and revenue consequent on their secession … act … as a salutary check on the tyranny and oppression of the respective chiefs.'[35] The option of migration was also exercised by tribes under the rulers' protection and control.[36]

The provision of protection could also generate revenue in the form of tribute from submissive tribes (tribute relations will be discussed in more detail in Section 7). The Āl Khalifah of Bahrain collected tribute from a large number of tribes in Qatar between the 1760s and 1860s. The amount of tribute they received before the mid-nineteenth century is unknown, but by the 1860s they were collecting Ks 9,000 (Rs 3,600) annually.[37] This was not high by Arabian standards; the Amir of Ḥā'il, for example, collected £40,000 (Rs 400,000) from his dependants in 1876.[38] Therefore, although there was a decline in status and prestige when the Āl Khalifah lost most of their tributary network in Qatar in 1871, Bahrain's economy was not affected.

What clearly emerges from this overview of the Gulf shaikhdoms' economy is the high vulnerability of the main sources of income to raiding, the extent to which raiding could interfere with the economic well-being of a shaikhdom, and the resulting importance of protection. The next section examines how the Gulf rulers were able to provide the necessary protection.

5. The Military Foundations of Rulership

Without military power, a ruler could not protect and maintain the economic well-being and political integrity of his shaikhdom. Henry Rosenfeld has observed in Arabia 'an interlocking hierarchical social structure status-scale …

based on military power and the ability to control certain territory and groups and maintain independence from other groups.'[39] In other words, the greater a ruler's military strength, the more territory and economic resources he could control, and the higher his status in regional politics. Borders naturally fluctuated according to rulers' military abilities. If a ruler was succeeded by one of significantly greater or lesser ability, there were often territorial consequences. There are countless examples of village shaikhs asserting their independence and of town rulers taking villages under their control.[40] The majority of Gulf Arab rulers lacked the resources they needed to guarantee the constant security of their shaikhdoms. Their personal military forces were small, leaving the rulers vulnerable to antagonistic regional powers, or alliances formed against them.[41]

In 1905, for example, Lorimer estimated the Āl Khalifah to have 540 armed retainers or *fidāwīyah* (singular *fidāwī*) in full-time service in Bahrain, only 200 of whom had rifles.[42] Most were recruited from the Na'īm tribe in Qatar and the Dawawdah clan of the Banī Khālid tribe in Hasa.[43] Numbers were higher in the years before British protection. In the late 1820s, for example, the British estimated the Āl Khalifah to employ around 1,100 *fidāwīyah* and, in an emergency, to have the potential of mustering a further 18–20,000 tribesmen capable of bearing arms.[44] Military forces in the full-time employ of Gulf rulers in the nineteenth century ranged in size from 200 to 2,000 men.[45] All rulers relied upon tribal alliances either to redress the balance when faced by a stronger enemy, or to gain an advantage over an enemy of equal strength.[46] The rulers of Bahrain, for example, maintained an alliance with the Na'īm from c.1766 to 1937—the Na'īm providing the Ruler with warriors in times of need, the Ruler providing the Na'īm with reciprocal military support and subsidies to secure their loyalty.[47] Lorimer estimated the Na'īm to have, at most, 400 fighting men in 1905, of whom less than half were generally present in Bahrain at any one time.[48] Alliances did not always work, of course, nor did they always last. In the ever-changing political environment of the Gulf, rulers were quick to seize advantages and abandon liabilities with the result that alliances themselves were ever-shifting.[49] One's allies were often fair weather friends. The consistent loyalty of the Na'īm to the Āl Khalifah was quite exceptional, as was the enduring friendship of the Āl Ṣabāḥ—the only branch of the 'Utūb tribal confederation, to which the Āl Khalifah belonged, never to take up arms against the rulers of Bahrain.

6. The Social Foundations of Rulership

Money and arms enabled a shaikh to rise above the position of tribal leader and become a ruler, but he could not do this without first securing: (1) support from family members; (2) approval from the affluent merchants and leaders of tribal sections; and (3) legitimacy in the eyes of his people. The first two conditions are self-explanatory, so attention here will be given mainly to legitimacy.[50] A ruler normally gained legitimacy through his own personal attributes and through observing the social obligations of rulership. Harold Dickson identifies four social foundations of rulership in his celebrated *Arab of the Desert* (1949).[51]

The first consisted of the ruler's personal attributes. He is expected to be a wise, eloquent, persuasive, able and courageous leader. As Paul Harrison puts it: 'The ablest ruler is the man wanted and the one who is eventually secured.'[52] But these qualities alone are not enough. To be a successful ruler, a shaikh must have *ḥaẓẓ* (luck). In the highly adversarial environment of the Gulf, a ruler's *ḥaẓẓ* was considered essential for a tribe's prosperity. 'The Badawin has no use for a man having courage and leadership in plenty if *hadh* is lacking', notes Dickson. 'A lucky general is what the tribesman wants in war, and, still more important, he wants a lucky shaikh in peace, for to him the whole daily round and welfare of the tribe is bound up in this word *hadh*.'[53] If a ruler could guarantee victory on the battlefield, his subjects would place great confidence in him as a protector. Conversely, a ruler unlucky in war would soon find himself without allies. Beyond this, a shaikh's rulership also depended upon his respect for the opinion of the important and influential men who commanded large political followings within his shaikhdom. A ruler always had the option of imposing his will, but this undermined his influence and legitimacy. He would quickly lose the support and loyalty of his most important followers. A ruler must consult with those who matter, therefore, before undertaking a new policy or embarking on a course of action. Once a decision was reached, however, leadership lay with the ruler. So long as the ruler adheres to the conditions of the decision, his orders must be obeyed.[54]

The second requirement is that a ruler is expected to be a 'father to his people', with all the responsibilities that entails.[55] For the majority of his subjects, these responsibilities originate from the payment and collection of tax or tribute. When a person pays tax to his ruler, that ruler becomes responsible for his protection (physically as well as diplomatically) from all quarters, as if he were the payer's father. Likewise, the ruler is expected to know his people as if they were his own family.[56] At least this is the ideal against which his rulership is measured. The payer-payee relationship will be discussed in more detail in Sections 7–9.

The third requirement, and related to the second, is that a ruler is expected to keep an open house. As a 'father' of his people, he must be accessible to them.[57] This is the purpose of the ruler's majlis, a regular, often daily, council held at his residence. The practice is comparable to the European custom of holding court, except that majlis is informal and access is unrestricted. Literally anyone with an enquiry, a request, or a case may attend majlis to present it to the ruler.[58] Once he has settled a case, the ruler is also responsible for its enforcement.[59] The position of arbiter is a prestigious one in Arabian society. The settling of cases reinforces a ruler's legitimacy in the eyes of his subjects.[60]

The fourth requirement, and related to the third, is that a ruler is expected to be generous.[61] Tremendous importance is attached to a ruler's reputation for generosity. The greater his generosity, the greater his popularity, the greater his legitimacy, and the greater his influence.[62] The obligation to hold an open house placed the ruler in the additional role of host (*muḍayyif*). Dickson notes that 'a guest (*ḍayf*) is a very sacred person indeed, and the unwritten laws of hospitality lay down that such a person … be entertained, fed and looked after in a fitting manner, and to the best of the host's power.'[63] A *muḍayyif* was also obligated to protect his *ḍayf* and treat him with honour and respect.[64] Understandably, it is important for the ruler of a shaikhdom to be known as its most generous host. A ruler must hold feasts, distribute gifts, and grant favours to those who visit him. This belief is reflected in a saying of the Shammar tribe of Najd: *al-amīr sayf wa mansaf* (the amir is someone who owns a sword and gives food), meaning the true ruler is someone who commands coercive force and is generous.[65] 'No name has a more unworthy meaning', explains Dickson, 'or leaves a nastier taste in the mouth of the Badawin, than the epithet *bakhil*, or "stingy one". Once this name *bakhil* sticks to a chief, his influence is at an end.'[66] As noted above, a ruler's subjects expect assistance and protection in return for their taxes. In return for assistance and protection, a ruler is entitled to their loyalty.[67] A ruler's reputation for generosity counts most with those who pay no tax: the shaikhs of his family and his tribal allies. In return for their loyalty, he must spend lavishly on them, paying them salaries and subsidies.[68] Madawi Al-Rasheed argues that rulers 'maintained a tradition of subsidizing these shaikhs through the continuous distribution of cash and gifts of rice, coffee, sugar, camels, and weapons. These gifts acted as a bribe to maintain the allegiance of the shaikhs, who remained to a great extent autonomous.'[69] As Lieutenant Arnold Kemball (Assistant Resident 1841–52) noted in 1845: 'Of so great importance is [the Bedouin tribes'] alliance or forbearance considered by the maritime chieftains, that these … find it their best policy to conciliate them by repeated and considerable presents.'[70] Payments to secure loyalty accounted for the majority of a ruler's expenses, as is evident from the British estimate from 1905 of the expenses of Shaikh 'Īsā bin 'Alī of Bahrain (Ruler 1869–1923) in Table 2, below.[71] Most of the Rs 56,000 Shaikh 'Īsā spent on subsidies and presents went to the Na'īm tribe. Colonel Edward Ross (Resident 1872–91) observed in 1877 that, 'were he to offend the Naim by withholding presents or preventing their visiting Bahrein, the result would probably be that they would unite with the Beni Hajir in forming a hostile coalition against

Table 2. British estimate from 1905 of the expenses of Shaikh ʻĪsā bin ʻAlī of Bahrain (Ruler 1869–1923)

Expenses	*Portion*	*Rupees*	*Pounds*
personal expenses (including salaries of *fidāwīyah*)	33.3%	100,000	6,666
family allowances to the Āl Khalifah	33.3%	100,000	6,666
subsidies and presents to bedouin	18.7%	56,000	3,733
special expenses (marriages, journeys, etc.)	10.0%	30,000	2,000
administration expenses	4.7%	14,000	933
	100%	Rs 300,000	£20,000

him.'[72] Without payments, the Shaikh could not have obtained the one hundred armed retainers (*fidāwīyah*) from the Naʻīm he employed that year.[73] Money enabled a ruler to reward or bribe people for their loyalty, most importantly his *fidāwīyah*, who enforced his will, and his fellow shaikhs.

The principal difference between the leading shaikh of a tribe and the ruling shaikh of a shaikhdom was the latter's command of *fidāwīyah*. While both shaikhs had authority derived from their leadership qualities and social status, only the latter had the coercive power to collect taxes and tribute, enforce laws, and punish criminals.[74] Both led, but only the latter ruled. Only the latter had the ability to control enough people and territory to constitute a shaikhdom or amirate. The key to rulership was the consistent loyalty of one's people, but even the ablest leader could not secure this without money. That no shaikh could rule his people without a command of economic power explains why all rulerships were town-based, at the heart of economic activity in the Gulf.[75] A town fort, therefore, symbolized both control of a town and the rulership of a shaikh. It also symbolized the difference between a ruler of a shaikhdom and a leader of a tribe, who lived in a tent. Peter Lienhardt explains that, 'when rulers have been overthrown, the seizing of the fort has often been the main stepping stone to power.'[76] The British, too, drew upon the symbolism of forts to great effect. If a ruler seriously breached the terms of the General Treaty or Maritime Truce and then ignored the Resident's instructions for reparation, the Resident usually threatened to bombard the ruler's fort. In the rare instances when the Resident was forced to follow through on his threat, the ruler suffered a powerful blow to his rulership. In the case of Shaikh Muḥammad bin Khalifah of Bahrain (Ruler 1843–68), it symbolized the end of his rulership.

The rulers, Peter Lienhardt tells us, 'held their power in order to do a job for the people, keeping order and managing defence, and were not there either by any absolute right or by brute force'.[77] Nor were they 'regarded as being indispensable for the conduct of the affairs of their people'.[78] Therefore a ruler who ignored his social obligations, or fulfilled them poorly, risked both the loss of important and affluent members of his shaikhdom to migration and the loss of his rulership to a rival member of his family.[79]

7. The Collection and Payment of Tribute

Sections 4–6 have explained the economic, military and social foundations of rulership, the causes of regional instability, and a shaikhdom's ever-present need for protection. This, and the remaining sections, examine the implications these factors had for the regional political system and for Britain's involvement in the Gulf.

If a ruler faced the impending attack of a much stronger enemy, he would typically seek the protection of a regional power to ward off the threat. These protectors gave guarantees of defence in return for subservience or the relinquishment of some degree of independence. The protégé's payment of tribute symbolized this and had a transforming effect.[80] The protector regarded his tributary as a part of his own tribe.[81] Similarly, the protector regarded his tributary's territory as *his* territory, but with one important distinction. The protector considered such land, especially if it was at some distance from his shaikhdom, to be a 'dependency' rather than a part of his shaikhdom. The protector usually left the governing of his dependency to the local ruler or tribal leader who had submitted to his authority.[82] When he did, the only noticeable difference between an independent shaikhdom and a dependency apart from the tribute payments was that the dependants or protégés owed allegiance to their protector as if they were his own subjects. Indeed, he considered them his subjects.

Custom dictated the amount of tribute an individual protégé should pay his protector, if he were to pay any at all.[83] Custom did not dictate what a protégé ruler should pay, however, although he was usually able to negotiate the payment. If the parties failed to agree on the amount, they would often enlist a neutral ruler to arbitrate. Tribute was normally paid annually and could take many forms: a fixed sum of money; a share of the annual customs revenue; a share of the agricultural produce (mainly dates); a certain number of horses, camels, etc.; provision of men for military service; and even *zakāt* (enjoined Islamic alms that, in the Sunni interpretation, Muslim officials normally collect from Muslim subjects).[84] Tribute was typically imposed as *ẖūwah*. In its original form, *ẖūwah* was a 'brotherhood fee' paid voluntarily by the weak to the strong in return for protection.[85] The protector became, in effect, his protégé's big brother, with all the responsibilities that entailed.

A would-be attacker's forceful imposition of *ẖūwah* as a 'protection tax' on an opponent, however, symbolized not brotherly relations but political domination.[86] Militarily-strong rulers would often threaten to attack weaker rulers with the intention of tribute collection, not military conquest. The same tactic was employed by those who controlled Arabia's trade routes and imposed tolls (often as *ẖūwah*) on those who used them. If the ruler of a shaikhdom, captain of a ship, or leader of a caravan refused to pay tribute to a would-be attacker, he risked military conquest or raiding. Payment in this context depended largely upon the payer's belief in the likelihood of attack. There had to be a threat, or a perceived future threat; no threat, no tribute. From a Western perspective this looked like extortion—an Arabian form of protection-racketeering. But there was one important difference: the 'extortionist' assumed responsibility for the complete protection of his 'victim'. Where actual war was involved, tribute could have the positive effect of transforming an adversarial relationship into a protective one, and was the customary method of settling a conflict. Paul Harrison observed in 1924 that 'the amount of tribute extorted is simply the measure of the balance reached between [the] two contending forces.'[87]

Henry Rosenfeld tells us how a group's increased power typically resulted in 'increased tribute payments, tributary groups and honour', while decreased power meant 'less ability to receive tribute, less recognition and, as the group itself becomes tributary, [a] gradual reduction on the status scale of honour.'[88] Madawi Al-Rasheed elaborates on this analysis:

> The inter-connection between military power and economic power was a cyclical process. The two factors, power and tribute, were interdependent; the alteration of one factor automatically affected the other. The more power the amirs had, the more they were able to collect tribute. Equally, more tribute meant more power. The reverse of the cycle was also possible. Less military power meant no effective control over trade, pilgrims, and subjects, consequently, less tribute. Any decrease in tribute meant less subsidies, less loyalty, and a diminished ability to invest in the means of coercion. As a result, the amirs' power would inevitably be affected and would tend to decrease.[89]

Tribute payment created what Rosenfeld calls the 'web of overlordship and the recognition of a hierarchy of dominance' in Arabia.[90] Personal honour and status relations were at the centre of Arabian politics in the nineteenth century, as they are today. Just as one speaks of 'status relations' and not 'class relations' at the personal level in Arabia,[91] so are regional relations a reflection of status relations between rulers vis-à-vis their military power. Iraq's financial demands on Kuwait in the months preceding the August 1990 invasion, for example, resemble the familiar pattern of tribute-collection followed by Gulf Arab rulers in the nineteenth century.

8. The Āl Khalifah's Tribute Relations

The long history of the Āl Khalifah's tribute relations with the imams of Muscat and the amirs of Najd, and with their own dependent tribes in Qatar, illustrates the centrality of the tribute system in Arabian power politics. It also provides the best context for understanding how their political relations with the British Government evolved into a protégé-protector relationship.[92]

The Āl Khalifah had an extensive tributary network in Qatar (see Table 3, below). The Āl Khalifah collected tribute from these tribes, but often had to pay tribute themselves to the imams of Muscat or the amirs of Najd.

Table 3. The Āl Khalifah's dependants and dependencies in Qatar, c.1766–1871[93]

Tribes	*Locations*
Āl Bū 'Aynayn	Bid', Ḥuwaylah, Ruways, Fuwayriṭ and Wakrah?[94]
'Ağmān	Bid' and Wakrah
Āl Bin 'Alī	Fuwayriṭ, Ḥuwaylah and Bid'
'Amāmarah	Bid'? and Wakrah?
Kalb	Ḥuwaylah
Kibīsah	Khor Ḥassān
Āl Bū Kuwārah	Sumaysimah, Fuwayriṭ, Ḥuwaylah, Ruways, Abu Ẓulūf and Ḍa'ā'in?
Ma'āḍīḍ (Āl Thānī)	Fuwayriṭ, Bid', Wakrah? and Lūsayl?
Mahandah	Khor Šaqīq? and Ḏaẖīrah?
Manāna'ah	Abu Ẓulūf
Āl Musallam	Ḥuwaylah, Bid', Fuwayriṭ? and Wakrah?
Na'īm 1	interior of eastern and northern Qatar
Na'īm 2	interior of western Qatar and Zubarah
Sādah	Ruways
Sūdān	Bid' and Fuwayriṭ

In 1799, the Imam of Muscat, Sayyid Sulṭān (1792–1804), attacked Bahrain on the pretext that Bahraini ships were failing to pay him *ẖūwah* or *ğuwayzah* for their passage through the Strait of Hormuz. The Āl Khalifah managed to repel his attack.[95] In 1800, he threatened another attack, this time demanding that the Āl Khalifah pay him tribute. The Rulers of Bahrain, Shaikhs Salmān bin Aḥmad (1796–1825) and 'Abd Allāh bin Aḥmad Āl Khalifah (1796–1843), initially sought the protection of the Persian Governor of Bushire, but this came to nothing. Eventually the Rulers yielded to Sayyid Sulṭān and agreed to pay him tribute. Within the year, however, they repudiated the agreement. Soon after, Sayyid Sulṭān made good his threat and attacked Bahrain with the assistance of the Governor of Bushire, forcing the Āl Khalifah to escape to Zubarah and Kuwait. Before Sayyid Sulṭān returned to Muscat, he installed his twelve-year-old son, Sālim, as Governor of Bahrain and placed a garrison at ʻArād Fort on Muharraq Island. The Rulers turned to the Wahhabi Amir of Najd, ʻAbd al-ʻAzīz bin Muḥammad Āl Suʻūd (1765–1803), for assistance to regain Bahrain. The Amir agreed, but only if they paid him tribute and recognized his authority. They accepted the Amir's terms and the next year they successfully retook Bahrain with Wahhabi assistance. One of the conditions of the arrangement, however, was that Zubarah would be given over to the Wahhabis and that the Rulers of Bahrain would send members of their families to reside in the town as a guarantee for their loyalty.

The Āl Khalifah continued with this arrangement and paid tribute to the Wahhabis until 1805, when they sought the protection of the new Imam of Muscat, Sayyid Badr bin Saif Al-Bu-Saʻīd (r. 1804–7), to throw off the Wahhabi yoke. Sayyid Badr arrived at Zubarah with a war fleet to protect the Rulers while they evacuated their families to Bahrain. The Rulers then proposed to Captain David Seton (British Resident in Muscat, 1800–09) that they and Sayyid Badr would be able to keep the Wahhabis at bay in the Gulf if the British Government of Bombay would promise the occasional assistance of one or two British gunboats. This was the first recorded instance of the Āl Khalifah requesting British protection. Seton forwarded their proposal with his favourable recommendation in the light of the Government's anti-Wahhabi stance. The Governor of Bombay rejected the request, however, not wanting to become involved in the political affairs of Bahrain. It would be another thirty-four years before the British began to respond favourably to the Āl Khalifah's requests for protection. Their request refused, the Āl Khalifah continued to pay Sayyid Badr tribute until the following year, when they were able to repudiate their agreement with him and reassert their independence.

In 1809, a powerful enemy and former ally of the Āl Khalifah, Shaikh Raḥmah bin Ǧābir, Ruler of the Āl Ǧalāhimah, allied himself with the Amir of Najd, Suʻūd bin ʻAbd al-ʻAzīz Āl Suʻūd (1803–14), so as better to pursue his vendetta against the Āl Khalifah. Later that year, the Wahhabis occupied Zubarah. The next year, Amir Suʻūd and Shaikh Raḥmah sent a fleet of forty dhows to Bahrain and captured the island. Amir Suʻūd installed a garrison at ʻArād Fort on Muharraq Island and summoned the Rulers of Bahrain to either Darʻiyyah or Riyadh (accounts differ), where they were detained as hostages.[96] Amir Suʻūd then appointed a *wakīl* (agent), ʻAbd Allāh bin ʻUfayṣān, to supervise the government of Bahrain, Zubarah and Qatif. Members of the Āl Khalifah were appointed governors of Bahrain and Zubarah and made to pay tribute to the *wakīl*. Shaikh ʻAbd al-Raḥmān bin Rāšid Āl Khalifah, a cousin of the two exiled Rulers, escaped to Muscat and asked Sayyid Sa'īd bin Ahmed Al-Bu-Sa'īd (r. 1807–56) for assistance. The following year, in 1811, Shaikh 'Abd al-Raḥmān returned to Bahrain with a military force led by the Imam. The force inflicted a serious naval defeat on the Āl Ǧalāhimah, captured the *wakīl* and expelled the Wahhabi garrison from Bahrain.[97] Amir Su'ūd later permitted the two Rulers to return to Bahrain after they had sworn allegiance to him.[98]

Upon their return to Bahrain, the Rulers resumed their tribute payments to the Imam of Muscat for five years, until 1816, when they again sought Wahhabi protection and a military alliance with the Qawāsim to throw off the hold of Muscat for a fifth time. Shaikh Raḥmah Āl Ǧalāhimah then sought the protection of Sayyid Sa'īd so as to be able to resume his vendetta against the Āl Khalifah. Later that year, Sayyid Sa'īd and Shaikh Raḥmah attacked Bahrain, but the Āl Khalifah succeeded in repelling them with the support of the Wahhabis and the Qawāsim. The Qawāsim were Wahhabi dependants at the time and therefore an ally of the Āl Khalifah. The following years did not fare well for the Āl Khalifah's protector and ally, however. In 1817, Wahhabi forces withdrew from the Gulf to battle an invading Egyptian army in Najd. They did not return to the Gulf in force until the late 1820s. In December 1819, the British launched their anti-piracy expedition against the Qawāsim, destroying much of the Qāsimī fleet by early January 1820.

Sayyid Sa'īd took advantage of this turn of events and threatened to attack Bahrain in January 1820. The Āl Khalifah, without protectors or allies, had no choice but to offer full submission. They agreed to pay MTD (Maria Theresa Dollars) 30,000 in tribute annually to the Imam, on condition that he release the prisoners and property he had captured from the Āl Khalifah. The parties asked the Bushire Resident, Captain William Bruce (1804–22), to guarantee the agreement, but he refused. It would be many years before the Resident would finally agree to play the role of guarantor in the Gulf. The parties went ahead with the agreement, but the Āl Khalifah paid only MTD 12,000 of the tribute before they, once again, repudiated the agreement the following year. In 1822, Sayyid Sa'īd again prepared to attack Bahrain, but the Governor of Bombay sent letters to both parties urging them to settle the matter peacefully. He suggested that the Āl Khalifah should pay the tribute only if it had been a regular and long-established custom, otherwise Sayyid Sa'īd should withdraw his demands. Sayyid Sa'īd called off his attack. In 1823, Shaikh 'Abd Allāh (Ruler 1796–1843) asked Captain John MacLeod (Resident 1822–23), during his visit to Bahrain, if the General Treaty of 1820, which the Shaikh had signed three years before, entitled him to British protection. MacLeod informed him that it did not.

In 1828, a rumour spread that Sayyid Sa'īd was once again preparing to attack Bahrain. When Captain David Wilson (Resident 1827–31) questioned Sayyid

Sa‘īd about this, he denied it and even sent presents to the Rulers of Bahrain. Shaikh ‘Abd Allāh was suspicious and asked Wilson to intervene, but he declined, not wanting to become unnecessarily involved in Bahraini affairs. In October, Sayyid Sa‘īd launched his attack on Bahrain, joined by a force led by Shaikh Ṭaḥnūn bin Šaẖbūṭ Al-Nahyan of Abu Dhabi (Ruler 1818–33). The Āl Khalifah managed to rout the combined force, however, and Sayyid Sa‘īd narrowly escaped with his life. Shaikh ‘Abd Allāh again addressed Captain Wilson, complaining that Shaikh Ṭaḥnūn had broken the terms of the General Treaty of 1820 and requesting his intervention. Wilson again declined the Shaikh's request, pointing out that the treaty banned only piracy, not open and declared warfare. It would be another seven years before the trucial system (1835–1971) banned maritime warfare between its members, and another thirty-three before Bahrain joined it.

The following year, in 1829, Sayyid Sa‘īd sent out hints that he intended to launch yet another attack on Bahrain (the seventh Muscati attack since 1799). At this point, Captain Wilson offered to mediate between the two parties. This is the first recorded instance of the Gulf Resident offering to play such a role in regional politics, a role he would come to play more frequently as the century progressed. Both sides readily accepted Wilson's offer, but the negotiations came to a standstill when Wilson rejected Shaikh ‘Abd Allāh and Sayyid Sa‘īd's condition that he guarantee any settlement they agreed upon. Eventually, the Ruler of Bushire, Shaikh Muḥammad bin Nāṣir al-Maḏkūr, mediated a peace settlement among Sayyid Sa‘īd, Shaikh Ṭaḥnūn of Abu Dhabi and Shaikh ‘Abd Allāh, guaranteeing the peace between them. Sayyid Sa‘īd dropped his demands for tribute, in return for which all three parties agreed not to interfere in the affairs of the others and to come to each other's aid if attacked by a fourth party. Sayyid Sa‘īd and his successors never reasserted their tributary claims over Bahrain again.

In 1830, the Amir of Najd and Hasa, Turkī bin ‘Abd Allāh Āl Su‘ūd (1823–34), demanded that Shaikh ‘Abd Allāh pay him *zakāt* plus an additional MTD 40,000 as compensation for horses supposedly left behind in Bahrain when the Wahhabis had withdrawn from the Gulf thirteen years before. Amir Turkī also demanded that the Shaikh surrender the fort on Dammām Island, which the Āl Khalifah had captured from the Āl Ǧalāhimah in 1826. Shaikh ‘Abd Allāh immediately sent word to Captain Wilson in Bushire, requesting his mediation and protection, but Wilson refused the Shaikh's request. Shaikh ‘Abd Allāh then sent a *wakīl* to Amir Turkī in Riyadh to negotiate a settlement. Shaikh ‘Abd Allāh agreed to pay *zakāt* and acknowledge his overlordship in return for the Amir's promise to protect Bahrain. He refused to surrender the fort, however, because of the Amir's intention to hand it over to Shaikh Raḥmah Āl Ǧalāhimah's son, Bašīr, who was then a Wahhabi protégé. The Amir dropped the issue of Dammām in consideration of the Shaikh's submission and settled Shaikh Bašīr on neighbouring Tārūt Island opposite Qatif instead. This naturally aroused Shaikh 'Abd Allāh's suspicions.

In 1833, Shaikh Bašīr threw off his allegiance to the Wahhabi Amir and sought the protection and assistance of Sayyid Sa'īd in Muscat to further his vendetta against the Āl Khalifah. In 1834, Shaikh 'Abd Allāh renounced his allegiance to the Amir and blockaded the Wahhabi ports of Qatif and 'Uqayr, on the shore opposite Bahrain, and occupied Tārūt Island. In May, the Shaikh's nephew and co-Ruler, Shaikh Khalifah bin Salmān (1825–34), died. Shaikh 'Abd Allāh prevented Shaikh Khalifah's son, Muḥammad, from taking his father's place and assumed the sole rulership of Bahrain. But Shaikh 'Abd Allāh was a weak Ruler. His governors, all sons and near relations, flouted his authority. Soon their misgovernment and abuses began to unsettle the shaikhdom and its dependencies. Things had deteriorated so much by 1836 that Shaikh 'Abd Allāh took the unusual step of informing the head of the merchant community of Manamah, in the presence of the Resident's Native Agent in Bahrain, Hajji Muḥammad 'Alī Ṣafar (1833–42), that he could no longer protect the merchants or provide them with redress. A rapid depopulation of merchants followed and the shaikhdom's economy declined. These factors seriously undermined the economic and social foundations of the Āl Khalifah's power and influence. That year, the Persian Prince-Governor of Fars, in Shiraz, took advantage of the deteriorating situation and threatened to attack Bahrain unless Shaikh 'Abd Allāh acknowledged Persian authority and paid him tribute. Unable to organize a united front to this new threat, the Shaikh had no option but to return, for a fifth time, to the Wahhabi fold for protection. Amir Fayṣal bin Turkī Āl Su'ūd (1834–37, 1843–65) promised to supply troops for the protection of Bahrain in return for Shaikh 'Abd Allāh's submission, payment of a nominal tribute of MTD 2,000, and termination of his blockade of Qatif and 'Uqayr.

In 1837, Wahhabi influence again receded from the Gulf in the face of yet another Egyptian army and Shaikh 'Abd Allāh ceased to pay tribute. By January 1839, the Egyptian army had occupied the principal ports and towns of Hasa. The Commander of the army, Khurshid Pasha, immediately despatched a *wakīl* to Bahrain to tell Shaikh 'Abd Allāh that he was expected to pay Khurshid the tribute he had previously paid the Wahhabi Amir of Najd and Hasa. The Shaikh declared he could not do this because he was under Persian protection. He then sent a letter to the Prince-Governor of Fars in Shiraz asking for his protection and stating that he was willing to pay tribute. The Prince-Governor soon sent a *wakīl* to Bahrain to present the Shaikh with a *ẖil'ah* (robe of honour) and to collect the tribute he had been promised. By this time, however, it had become clear to Shaikh 'Abd Allāh that the Persians did not have the naval force necessary to protect Bahrain. The Shaikh changed his mind and paid Khurshid the MTD 2,000 in tribute he had demanded. The tribute payments lasted only two years, however, for the Egyptian army withdrew from Hasa the following summer.

In 1842, civil war broke out between two factions of the Āl Khalifah in Bahrain. The following year, in 1843, Shaikh ʻAbd Allāh was ousted from his rulership by his great-nephew, Shaikh Muḥammad bin Khalifah (Ruler 1843–68), whom he had prevented from assuming the joint rulership of Bahrain seven years before. The same year, Amir Fayṣal returned to power after the Egyptian withdrawal from Arabia. He called upon the new Ruler of Bahrain to acknowledge Wahhabi authority for a sixth time and to resume tribute payments, with arrears. Shaikh Muḥammad agreed to the Amir's demand, but subsequently failed to deliver up the tribute. After two years of non-payment, the Wahhabis had had enough. When Shaikh ʻAbd Allāh turned to the Wahhabis in 1845 to help him regain his rulership of Bahrain, they supported his cause. In October, the Wahhabi Governor of Qatif began preparing for an attack on Bahrain in conjunction with Shaikh ʻAbd Allāh. However, Shaikh Muḥammad discovered the plan and placed Qatif and ʻUqayr under blockade. The Governor of Qatif asked the Resident, Major Samuel Hennell (1838–41, 1843–52), for assistance, threatening to resort to piracy if he did not. Hennell responded by despatching two gunboats to Qatif as a warning to the Governor.[99]

In October 1846, the Governor of Qatif asked Hennell for permission to call upon the rulers of the Coast of Oman to assist him against Shaikh Muḥammad, but Hennell refused his request, explaining that the rulers were prevented by the Maritime Truce from waging war by sea. The following month, Shaikh Muḥammad made a similar request to Hennell, which was likewise refused.[100] The blockade continued, therefore, until early 1847, when one of Shaikh Muḥammad's allies, the ʻAmayr tribe, left him and went over to the Wahhabis. This tipped the balance in favour of the Wahhabis and Shaikh Muḥammad decided to enter into negotiations. In August he agreed to acknowledge Amir Fayṣal's authority for a seventh time and pay MTD 4,000 (approximately Rs 8,000)[101] annually as *zakāt*, in return for which Amir Fayṣal promised not to aid and abet Shaikh ʻAbd Allāh and his sons (then residing on Wahhabi-controlled Dammām Island) in their bid to retake Bahrain. He also promised to refrain from attacking Shaikh Muḥammad's tribal dependants in Qatar. The tribute Shaikh Muḥammad collected from these tribes defrayed the cost of his tribute to the Wahhabi Amir.

Angered by this arrangement, Shaikh ʻAbd Allāh left Dammām, seeking alliances elsewhere. He first sought the help of the Āl Bin ʻAlī tribe and, later, the Imam of Muscat. Twice, in May 1847 and again in February 1849, Shaikh Muḥammad asked Hennell for protection against attacks by Shaikh ʻAbd Allāh's allies. The British Government refused both requests as it did not want to become unnecessarily entangled in Bahraini affairs. Shortly after Shaikh Muḥammad's second request, however, Shaikh 'Abd Allāh died and with him the principal threat to Shaikh Muḥammad's rulership.[102]

In 1850, Shaikh Muḥammad stopped his tribute payments to Amir Fayṣal and the Amir began to threaten Bahrain once more. This time, Shaikh Muḥammad opened correspondence with the Ottoman Sharif of Mecca, asking to be placed under Ottoman protection and offering to pay tribute. In April 1851, Amir Fayṣal occupied the Āl Khalifah's dependencies in eastern Qatar and sent Shaikh Muḥammad excessive demands for tribute. A few months later, the dependent tribes renounced their allegiance to Shaikh Muḥammad and joined the Wahhabi fold. At this point, Shaikh Muḥammad asked for Hennell's intervention, but Hennell replied that he could do nothing until he received instructions from India. When Hennell learned of Shaikh Muḥammad's offer of tribute to the Ottoman Porte the following month, however, he decided not to wait. The British Government, he knew, would not welcome the establishment of Ottoman authority over Bahrain, as this would inhibit the General Treaty's enforcement in Bahraini waters. In early July he sent the Gulf Squadron to Bahrain with orders to defend the island from the Wahhabis, thus neutralizing the Shaikh's need for Ottoman protection. When the Squadron arrived at Bahrain, Shaikh Muḥammad came on board the Commander's boat and expressed great satisfaction at the Squadron's arrival to protect Bahrain.[103] In August, Hennell sent a letter to Amir Fayṣal warning him that the Gulf Squadron would not permit him to invade Bahrain.[104] A few weeks later, at Hennell's encouragement, Shaikh Muḥammad finally agreed to resume his tribute payments of MTD 4,000 to the Amir. The Shaikh lifted his blockade of Qatif, Wahhabi forces withdrew from Qatar and the Gulf Squadron departed Bahraini waters.[105]

Not long after Shaikh 'Abd Allāh's death in 1849, Shaikh Muḥammad bin Khalifah learned that the former Ruler's eldest son, Muḥammad bin 'Abd Allāh, desired the rulership of Bahrain and was actively seeking support from Gulf rulers towards this end. Thus, when Amir Fayṣal permitted Shaikh Muḥammad bin 'Abd Allāh and his brothers to settle within his domain on Dammām Island in 1852, Shaikh Muḥammad bin Khalifah was naturally alarmed. He complained bitterly to the Amir and ceased his tribute payments in protest. The new Resident, Captain Arnold Kemball (1852–55), managed to persuade the Shaikh to resume the payments, however, and the impending conflict was avoided.[106] The following year, the Shaikh appealed to the Imam of Muscat for support, but he was not interested. The Shaikh then turned to the Ottoman Viceroy of Egypt for support. The Viceroy sent a *wakīl* to Bahrain to discuss the situation, but nothing came of it as the Viceroy was in no position to offer the Shaikh any material assistance. The next year, in 1854, the Ottoman *Mutaṣarrif* (Governor) of Basra informed the Shaikh that if he wished to place himself under Ottoman protection, he should apply to him. Amir Fayṣal learned of the Shaikh's activities and punished him by launching an attack upon Bahrain in July, but the Shaikh's forces managed to repel the attack. In retaliation, Shaikh Muḥammad sent his fleet to blockade Dammām and Qatif. When Kemball learned of the attack, he immediately set sail for Bahrain with the Gulf Squadron to prevent a second assault. Over the following ten months, Kemball managed to mediate a settlement between Shaikh Muḥammad and Amir Fayṣal, whereby the Shaikh would continue to pay the tribute, but Kemball refused to guarantee the settlement's enforcement personally. Despite this, the settlement lasted for four years.[107]

In 1859, Shaikh Muḥammad again ceased his payments to Amir Fayṣal. That summer the Amir gave instructions to Shaikh Muḥammad bin 'Abd Allāh (still residing on Dammām Island) and the Governor of Qatif to begin preparations to invade Bahrain. In September, the Resident, Captain Felix Jones (1855–62), heard of the impending invasion, wrote to the Amir to call off the attack and sent some gunboats across to Bahrain. One of the gunboat commanders met Shaikh Muḥammad and warned him not to attack. The Shaikh replied that, since Britain intended to defend Bahrain, he would call off the invasion. Despite the Shaikh's assurances, Jones recognized that the threat posed by the exiled Āl 'Abd Allāh branch of the Āl Khalifah to the Āl Salmān branch was undermining regional stability. He accordingly recommended to his superiors in India that Shaikh Muḥammad bin 'Abd Allāh be declared an enemy of the peace and be forbidden to reside any closer to Bahrain than Kuwait or the Persian coast. The Government agreed with Jones' recommendation and, in February 1860, authorized him to eject Shaikh Muḥammad from Dammām, which he finally did in November 1861.[108]

Despite Britain's *de facto* assumption of responsibility for the defence of Bahrain, Shaikh Muḥammad remained unsatisfied. J.B. Kelly offers the most plausible explanation for the Shaikh's unhappiness:

> Implicit in the protection afforded Muhammad ibn Khalifah by the British Government against the Wahhabis was an understanding that he himself should not disturb the peace of the Gulf, and, in particular, that he should do nothing to provoke the Amir Faisal. This restraint on his conduct was not to Muhammad ibn Khalifah's taste: now that Muhammad ibn 'Abd Allah and his followers at Dammam had been rendered harmless by the British intervention of September 1859, Muhammad ibn Khalifah wanted to push his advantage to the limit and crush the fugitives completely.[109]

This explains why Shaikh Muḥammad subsequently tried to break free of his commitments to his new-found protector by simultaneously seeking Persian and Ottoman protection. In 1859, the Shaikh sent formal requests to the Prince-Governor of Fars and the Ottoman *Vali* (Governor-General) of Baghdad to place

Bahrain under the protection of their respective governments. The Persians responded by sending a *wakīl* to Bahrain in March 1860 to present the Shaikh with a royal proclamation (*firmān*) and jewelled sword from the Shah, and a robe of honour (*ẖil'ah*) from the Prince-Governor of Fars. Shaikh Muḥammad responded by publicly announcing Bahrain to be a dependency of Persia, raising the Persian flag on his fort, and writing to the Shah and Prince-Governor declaring his allegiance and promising to pay tribute. The following month, however, an Ottoman *wakīl* arrived from Baghdad. The Shaikh told him he had already declared his allegiance to the Shah, but would renounce it if the Ottoman Porte could offer him better terms and greater protection than Persia. After two days of negotiations, the Ottoman *wakīl* convinced the Shaikh that he had more to gain by being an Ottoman subject. The Shaikh accordingly renounced his allegiance to the Shah, hauled down the Persian flag on his fort, raised the Ottoman flag, and presented the *wakīl* with a letter for the *Vali* of Baghdad promising to pay MTD 7,000 in tribute annually. The Ottoman *wakīl* then returned to Baghdad. The Persian *wakīl* refused to acknowledge the Shaikh's change of allegiance, however, and remained in Bahrain. As both *wakīl*s had been unaccompanied by military force, Jones ignored Shaikh Muḥammad's double dealings, regarded Bahrain as still independent and continued to hold the Shaikh to his treaty commitments to the British Government.[110]

During this time, Shaikh Muḥammad also tried to release himself from the restrictions of British protection by violating the norms of behaviour expected of a protégé: he began insulting Jones; insulting and threatening Jones' Native Agent in Bahrain, Hajji Jāsim (1842–62); bullying and extorting money from the British-Indian merchant community in Manamah; and raiding ships at Qatif and Dammām in open defiance of the General Treaty. In response, Jones despatched a gunboat to lie at anchor off the coast of Bahrain throughout the summer and autumn as a check on the Shaikh's activities.[111] In early May 1861, Shaikh Muḥammad intensified his efforts. He blockaded Qatif and Dammām and increased his raiding of local shipping. He also increased his oppression of the British Indian merchant community, forcing many to flee. His *fidāwīyah* harassed, insulted and threatened Hajji Jāsim.[112]

When Jones heard of these recent developments, he sailed to Bahrain with the full Gulf Squadron. He arrived on 18 May and immediately sent a letter to the Shaikh reminding him of his commitments under the General Treaty of 1820, demanding that he call off the blockade, and assuring him that the Gulf Squadron would protect Bahrain against a Wahhabi invasion.[113] The Shaikh consulted the Persian *wakīl*, asking if the Persian Government was willing to help him resist the British. The *wakīl* lied, telling him that a French warship was on its way to support him. Encouraged, the Shaikh chose to wait for the arrival of the ship, to continue his blockade and raiding, and to ignore Jones.

Jones waited patiently for a week, during which time he had two meetings with the Ruler's brother and Governor of Manamah, Shaikh 'Ali bin Khalifah (c.1843–68). During these meetings, the Shaikh explained to Jones that 'Protection is imperative.' It was the Āl Khalifah's paramount concern. That said, he disliked his brother's association with the Persians, believing it to be counterproductive.[114] After eight days of waiting, Jones instructed the Squadron Commander to take action.[115] On 28 May, Jones directed his Native Agent and all British-Indian subjects, whose protection he was responsible for, to evacuate Bahrain and warned Shaikh Muḥammad against pillaging the possessions they left behind.[116] During the evacuation, however, the Shaikh's men seized and threatened the *nakhodah*s (skippers) of the dhows taking the Indians to safety.[117] The Squadron Commander responded quickly by seizing two of Shaikh Muḥammad's war dhows blockading Qatif. This had the desired effect: the Shaikh capitulated and later withdrew his blockade.

Jones realized that the only way to hold the Shaikh to his treaty commitments to the British Government in future would be to allow Bahrain to become a member of the Perpetual Maritime Truce. He believed the reasons for previously excluding Bahrain to be 'scarcely valid'. The exclusion of Bahrain from the Truce, 'has been highly detrimental to our policy for some time past. Treaties though not infallible with Arab tribes, no more than with other nations, have with them an importance which it is unwise to neglect.'[118] He accordingly drew up a Friendly Convention binding the Shaikh to abstain from all maritime warfare on condition of protection from similar aggressions. The Convention further provided for the protection of British subjects in Bahrain from attack and extortion.[119] He summoned Shaikh 'Alī aboard his ship and presented him with the Convention, which the Shaikh delivered to Shaikh Muḥammad and the elder shaikhs of the Āl Khalifah for their consideration. The elders and Shaikh 'Alī expressed 'great satisfaction' with the Convention and Shaikh Muḥammad 'observe[d] nothing but what is right and just for the interests of all parties'.[120] They signed the Convention on 31 May 1861, making Bahrain a British-protected state. After the signing, Jones returned one of Shaikh Muḥammad's dhows, but retained the other as a guarantee for future behaviour.[121]

As Bahrain could be defended by naval means alone, its incorporation into the trucial system was to have two serious consequences. The first was for the Āl Khalifah's tributary relations with the tribes of Qatar. Although their dependants were also now subject to the trucial system, Qatar could not be defended solely by sea. Jones therefore encouraged Shaikh Muḥammad to keep paying tribute to Amir Fayṣal to secure Qatar from mainland attack, which he did. What Shaikh Muḥammad does not seem to have realised, however, is that British maritime protection of his dependants included protection from maritime aggressions by *him*.

The second consequence was for Shaikh Muḥammad's rulership. So long as the British Government chose to extend its maritime protection to the Ruler's territorial possessions, the Ruler was obligated to abstain from maritime aggression. However, it was not a case of British protection lasting only so long as the Ruler chose to observe the Truce. A treaty violation would not result in Britain withdrawing its protection from the Ruler's territory, although it might result in Britain withdrawing its protection from the Ruler. The British Government made its conditional protection of the Ruler's position quite clear to Shaikh Muḥammad's successors, as typified by this policy statement from 1874: 'so long as [the Chief of Bahrein] adheres to his Treaty obligations the British Government will protect him: but if such protection is to be accorded him, he must not be the aggressor, or undertake measures which will involve him in complications.'[122]

These consequences of the trucial system did not became apparent until 1867, when a dispute erupted between the Āl Khalifah and their dependants over the amount of tribute they were asked to pay. The Governor in Wakrah, Shaikh Aḥmad Āl Khalifah, handled the situation badly and the tribes rebelled, forcing him to flee with his family and belongings to Khor Ḥassān. The Governor returned in October 1867 with the Ruler of Bahrain, the Ruler's brother, Shaikh 'Ali, and the Ruler of Abu Dhabi, Shaikh Zāyid bin Khalifah Al-Nahyan (1855–1909), at the head of a combined force of 3,700 armed men and 94 dhows. They raided Wakrah, Bid', Doha and other ports, taking away an estimated MTD 200,000 (Rs 400,000) in booty. The following June, the Qatari tribes sailed to Bahrain to avenge the raid, but were intercepted off the northern Qatari coast by a Bahraini war fleet. A bloody battle ensued in which around sixty dhows were sunk and 1,000 men killed.

The Resident, Colonel Lewis Pelly (1862–72), naturally regarded these conflicts as a gross violation of the Perpetual Maritime Truce. As the Government of India had disbanded the Gulf Squadron (along with the Indian Navy) four years previously, Pelly's ability to enforce reparation was severely limited. He attempted to do it through correspondence alone, but Shaikh Muḥammad and Shaikh Zāyid evaded the issue, confident that Pelly could do nothing. In early June 1868, nearly a year after the raid on Qatar, the Government of Bombay finally promised to send three gunboats to the Gulf so Pelly could settle this outstanding issue. In mid-August, shortly before the arrival of the gunboats, Pelly sent the Rulers a verbal warning through their *wakīl*s at Bushire, which he later repeated in a letter to Shaikh Muḥammad:

> you have mistaken the moderation and forbearance of the British Government for an absence of force, and an inability to fulfil its functions as arbitrator of the maritime truce. The British Indian Government have at length most reluctantly found themselves compelled to resolve that your conduct calls for exemplary punishment ...[123]

When Shaikh Muḥammad received this warning, he fled to Khor Ḥassān to escape punishment.

A few days later, when the gunboats arrived at Bushire, Pelly set sail for the Arab coast, calling first at Wakrah and then at Bahrain. When Pelly arrived off the coast of Muharraq on 6 September, he found Shaikh ʻAlī in temporary charge of the shaikhdom. Shaikh ʻAlī sent a *wakīl* to Pelly, informing him that the treaty violations were entirely the fault of Shaikh Muḥammad and that ʻthere was no alternative other than the ruin of [Bahrain], or the removal of Shaikh Mahomed from power'.[124] Later that day, Shaikh ʻAlī joined Pelly onboard ship with an assembly of Bahrain's senior shaikhs. They told Pelly that they considered Shaikh Muḥammad to have forfeited his rulership and asked for time to propose ʻan arrangement under which all the demands and interests could be satisfied.'[125] Pelly agreed and the shaikhs departed. After two days of consultations, they returned and handed Pelly the text of a declaration terminating Shaikh Muḥammad's rulership and entrusting Shaikh ʻAlī to act in his place.[126] It further stated that Shaikh ʻAlī would pay an initial fine of MTD 25,000 (Rs 50,000) and return all booty to Qatar. This would be followed by three further annual payments of the same amount. All payments were to be given to the victims of the raid. Pelly accepted the declaration, but insisted on the destruction of Shaikh Muḥammad's fort (on a small island off the coast of Muharraq) and his war dhows as a symbolic destruction of his rulership. Pelly explains how he ʻtook the Gunboats *Clyde* and *Hugh Rose* up the creek which leads to Moharraq Fort, and, anchoring those vessels within 300 yards of the walls, destroyed both fort and cannon, and burnt Mahomed's three war craft lying immediately under the walls of the fort.' The fort, he discovered, ʻwas of solid stone and required considerable pounding from the 10-inch guns of the *Clyde* and *Hugh Rose*'.[127] In a further symbolic act, Pelly sent the *Clyde* ʻto lie at anchor under Shaikh Ali's fort [in Manamah], thus affording him the benefit of our moral support and recognition.'[128]

Pelly then departed with the two remaining gunboats, the *Hugh Rose* and *Vigilant*, to meet with the Āl Khalifah's dependants at Qatar. He obtained from them a promise to return to their former relations with the Āl Khalifah. In an effort to prevent future disputes, he then imposed a new tribute arrangement on the Āl Khalifah and their dependants—an arrangement which provides an interesting example of how complex the tribute system could become. The shaikhs of the Āl Bū ʻAynayn, Kalb, Āl Bū Kuwārah, Maʻāḍīḍ (Āl Thānī), Mahandah, Āl Musallam, Naʻīm and Sūdān of eastern and northern Qatar were to pay Ks 4,000 (Rs 1,600) to the Naʻīm of western Qatar on behalf of Shaikh ʻAlī and a further Ks 5,000 (Rs 2,000) to the Resident, who was to transmit it to Shaikh ʻAlī. The Ks 4,000 would keep the Naʻīm loyal to Shaikh ʻAlī who, in turn, would ensure that the Naʻīm did not attack the tribes of eastern and northern

Qatar. Shaikh ʿAlī was to hand over the Ks 5,000 he received to the Amir of Najd and Hasa who, in turn, would promise not to attack the Āl Khalifah's dependants in Qatar.[129] Pelly's imposed arrangement was fundamentally flawed, however. The basis of tribute relations was a protector's ability to both protect and punish his protégés—an ability the Ruler of Bahrain now lacked because of the Maritime Truce. The new arrangement would not last for long.

In December 1870, civil war broke out in the Amirate of Najd and Hasa. The Amir, ʿAbd Allāh bin Fayṣal Al Suʿūd, appealed to the Ottoman *Vali* of Baghdad, Midhat Pasha, for help. In April 1871, Midhat Pasha sent a military expedition to Hasa to restore order, declaring Hasa and Najd to be part of the Ottoman Empire. By June, Ottoman forces were in control of Qatif and Dammām. In early July, the Commander of the Ottoman expedition, Nafiz Pasha, despatched a steamer to accompany the Ruler of Kuwait, ʿAbd Allāh bin Ṣabāḥ Āl Ṣabāḥ (1866–92), to Bidʿ in order to persuade the Governor of Bidʿ to acknowledge Ottoman suzerainty. Shaikh ʿAbd Allāh failed to persuade the Governor, but he won over the Governor's son, Shaikh Qāsim bin Muḥammad Āl Thānī. Qāsim was given four Ottoman flags. He raised one over his own fort in Bidʿ, sent a second to his father, a third to the Governor of Khor Šaqīq and a fourth to the Governor of ʿUdayd. When their annual tribute to the Ruler of Bahrain became due later that year, the tribal leaders withheld their payment. The Āl Khalifah were prevented from launching a punitive expedition against their Qatari dependants by the Maritime Truce, but the Wahhabis were now free to raid Qatar, which they soon did. In January 1872, Midhat Pasha despatched an infantry battalion to Bidʿ to defend eastern Qatar and to establish a garrison. After repulsing the Wahhabi raiders, the battalion re-embarked a few weeks later, leaving behind a garrison of 100 troops with field guns.[130] This marked the end of the Āl Khalifah's tributary relations with eastern and northern Qatar and soon threatened their tributary relations with western Qatar.

In July 1873, a rumour reached the Ruler of Bahrain, Shaikh ʿĪsā bin ʿAlī (1869–1923), that an Ottoman official had arrived in Zubarah with an escort of 100 soldiers and had asked the Shaikh of the branch of the Naʿīm tribe living there to become an Ottoman subject. The Resident, Colonel Edward Ross (1872–91), sent his Assistant, Major Charles Grant, to investigate. Shaikh ʿĪsā told Grant that the Naʿīm, as his subjects, were entitled to British protection from the Ottomans. Grant discovered that the Ottoman visit had indeed taken place, although he dismissed the alleged purpose of the visit as 'mere coffee-room gossip'.[131] Nevertheless, the implications were clear. While Britain was not obligated to protect the Ruler's mainland dependencies from attack by land, there would still be a serious risk of confrontation with the Ottoman authorities if Britain acknowledged the Ruler's right to protect the Naʿīm. Deliberations passed between India and Bushire on the issue. By the end of the year, the

Indian Foreign Department, anxious to avoid such a confrontation, settled upon a policy of denying recognition of these dependencies and of forbidding the Ruler to defend them either militarily or politically.[132]

While the British Government would continue to defend Bahrain, it would only support the Ruler's position in Bahrain so long as he continued to observe the treaties and uphold the Pax Britannica.[133] Thus prevented from affording protection to his dependants in western Qatar, the Ruler's authority there became merely nominal. In 1878, his enemies attacked Zubarah, destroying the town and scattering its inhabitants. Had the Resident permitted the Ruler to defend Zubarah, the town might have been saved and his authority preserved. To bolster his authority and influence with the shaikhs of the Na'īm, the Ruler increased his subsidies to their leading shaikhs. He continued to pay these subsidies until 1937, when the Āl Thānī of eastern Qatar defeated the Na'īm in battle, bringing the whole of Qatar under their control. The Na'īm migrated to Bahrain soon after, thus bringing to a close 171 years of Āl Khalifah overlordship in Qatar.[134]

9. Protection-seeking and the Protector-protégé Relationship

Hitherto, historians have explained the relations between, and the protection-seeking tactics of, the Gulf Arab rulers as a result of rational calculations of self-interest and shrewd pragmatism. No historical explanation has yet taken into account Arabian political culture. The tribute system of Eastern Arabia was based upon the Arabian custom of protection-seeking. Its norms and obligations and the resulting protector-protégé relationship provided the rulers with an effective survival strategy in the face of Arabia's ever-shifting power dynamics. In so far as the need for protection weighed heavily upon the minds of the rulers, these customary norms and obligations shaped the conduct of regional relations—including, in time, Anglo–Arab relations.

As political relations between the shaikhdoms were really relations between individual shaikhs, studies of protection-seeking customs at the individual level are relevant to the study of regional political relations in the Gulf. Paul Dresch has examined how protection operates on a personal level in South Arabia.[135] The same practices are described in Harold Dickson's study of Eastern Arabia, although his analysis is not as extensive.[136] Just as personal honour was central to regional political relations, so too was it central to the politics of protection.

If someone requests protection, honour demands that protection be given.[137] Once this happens, Dresch notes, the protégé (*al-daẖīl* or *al-ğār*) is 'on the honour' (*fī wağhi-hi*) of his protector (*muğawwir*).[138] The protégé is henceforth in his charge and must be defended by him.[139] Protégés of the same protector are forbidden to offend or attack each other, just as all others—including the protector himself—are forbidden to violate the protection placed over them.[140] For a protector to offend his own protégé is the greatest disgrace of all.[141] This law of entering another's protection, known as *daḫālah* (entering), is a sacred and honoured custom in Arabia.[142] One claims *daḫālah* by saying *anā daḫīlak* or *anā daḫīl 'ala Allāh wa-'alayk* (I am your protégé, I enter upon God's pardon and yours).[143] Dresch describes this as entering the 'personal peace' of another. Every tribesman has a 'peace' by virtue of his personal honour.[144] If a protégé offends someone else, especially a fellow protégé, or otherwise behaves badly, he violates this 'peace' and insults the honour (*wağh*) of his protector. When this happens, the protector may justifiably take action against his protégé or revoke his protection. The penalties for violating *daḫālah* and insulting a person's honour are severe.[145] The onus is on the protector to exact compensation or take revenge on behalf of the victim. If he cannot, he must personally compensate the victim out of his own pocket. Only compensation or revenge will wipe out the disgrace to the protector and restore the honour of his protégé. If a third party offends someone living in the 'peace' of another and escapes being penalized, he has not only affronted the protector's honour, but also disgraced him by revealing his inadequacy as a protector. In this system of protection, a protégé is answerable to his protector who, in turn, is answerable to the public for the actions of his protégé. If one has a claim against a protégé, he must go to the protector, not the protégé.[146] This effectively casts the protector in the secondary roles of mediator, arbiter and guarantor of settlements. If one side breaks a settlement, the settlement's guarantor must intervene on the side of the victim.[147] These norms and expectations eventually shaped Anglo–Arab relations.

Dresch notes that one may become the protégé of another without demeaning himself. The protégé has a 'peace' of his own and one day the protector may be in need of it.[148] A ruler who seeks protection, however, loses some of his personal honour and prestige, as Rosenfeld's comments above suggest. Protégés of rulers—be they individuals, tribes, or other rulers—normally paid tribute to their protector.[149] In this sense, protégés become like a ruler's own subjects, from whom he collects taxes such as *zakāt*. In both cases the payee is obligated to protect the payer.

If a ruler was unable to secure, or unwilling to accept, the protection of a regional power, or an alliance with a less powerful ruler, and faced certain defeat in battle against his enemy, he had one last resort. It was acceptable for him to place himself under his enemy's protection as a form of reluctant nominal subservience. This was a political compromise preferable to outright military defeat. A skilful ruler might even use such a temporary submission to his advantage. This practice may originate from the tactic Bedouin warriors resorted to in the face of certain death in battle, whereby the supplicant says to his enemy, *yā fulān anā fī wağh-ak* (O so-and-so, I place myself under your protection/on your honour). If he gets the reply, *inta fī wağhī, sallim silāḥak* (You are under my protection/on my honour, hand over your arms), the supplicant is safe. The protector must then defend the supplicant with his life until the battle, and possibly the war, is over. The supplicant becomes, effectively, a prisoner of war and is not free to go on his way.[150]

For a ruler, there was little advantage in surrendering after the commencement of hostilities; only his life would be spared. It was far better for him to offer submission before battle, then his rulership would be spared as well. If he did this, he became a protégé and was required to pay tribute as a sign of submission and political subordination. Henceforth, the ruler's shaikhdom was considered a dependency of his protector, as discussed in Section 7. The ruler became, in effect, a governor who ruled on behalf of his protector.[151] Unlike a military conquest, a submission was not normally followed by military occupation, although the protector might send a political agent (*wakīl* or *mu'tamad*) to reside at the ruler's court, making the ruler's submission largely symbolic and the incorporation often nominal. This was for a good reason. For, as Frauke Heard-Bey notes, a tribe under the protection of a more powerful tribe typically rebelled if its protector imposed its own governor.[152] A protector would normally send a *wakīl* or impose his own governor in only two circumstances, therefore: (1) if he was distrustful enough of his protégé; or (2) if the dependency had a mixed tribal population and no ruler, making problematic the appointment of one of the local tribal leaders to the governorship. If the dependency was inhabited or dominated by only one tribe, the protector was well advised to leave the administration in the hands of the ruler or leader of that tribe.[153] With his rulership intact, a submissive ruler or tribal leader would pay tribute and bide his time until he was able to reassert his independence, often by securing the protection of another regional power or an alliance with a less powerful ruler or tribal leader. For powerful rulers and tribes, these submissions were often nominal and always temporary, lasting no more than a few years. For weak rulers and tribes, submission involved a greater loss of autonomy and tended to be more permanent, lasting for decades or even generations, as did the tribute payments.

Frauke Heard-Bey also explains how the greater the geographical distance between a governor and his ruler, the greater the governor's independence, and the less his ruler's personal influence was felt in the town, district or dependency under the governor's supervision.[154] Another factor was a ruler's choice of governor. The stronger the bonds of trust between governor and ruler, the more a ruler could delegate authority without the risk of secession. 'This is the reason', says Heard-Bey, 'why most Rulers put a brother or a son in charge of an important dependency, but this was not always a sure safeguard against secessionist movements, either led by the *wali* [governor] or perpetrated by the inhabitants themselves.'[155]

10. The Āl Khalifah's Rule of Qatar and Bahrain

The centrality of protection and the implications it had for Gulf rulership and Anglo–Arab relations are well illustrated by the Āl Khalifah's rule of Qatar and Bahrain. Three patterns in particular emerge: the identification of rulerships and governorships with forts or fortified buildings (see Map 2), the remarkable autonomy of governors, and the high turnover of allies and protectors. Historical accounts of the first 35 years of Āl Khalifah rule in Bahrain vary widely. What follows is a synthesis of the various accounts.

When the Āl Khalifah made Zubarah the capital of their new shaikhdom in 1766, they constructed Marayr Fort to protect the town and solidify their rulership on the west coast of Qatar.[156] After his conquest of Bahrain in 1782–83, Shaikh Aḥmad bin Khalifah '*al-Fātiḥ*' (Ruler 1783–96) appointed Shaikh 'Alī bin Fāris Āl Khalifah, a close relative, Governor of Bahrain.[157] Shaikh 'Alī resided in Dīwān Fort in Manamah (also known as Manamah Fort, the present-day Police Fort), then on the southern outskirts of Manamah.[158] Shaikh Aḥmad also placed Bahrain Fort—five kilometres west of Manamah at the former commercial centre of Bahrain—in the care of one of his military commanders, a protégé tribal leader named 'Ağāğ.[159] Between 1783 and 1796, the capital of the Āl Khalifah shaikhdom alternated between Zubarah, where Shaikh Aḥmad resided during the winter, and Dīwān Fort in Manamah, where he lived during the summer.[160]

When Shaikh Aḥmad died in 1796 in Manamah, his sons, Salmān and 'Abd Allāh were residing in Zubarah.[161] They assumed joint rulership of the shaikhdom, with the elder son, Salmān, holding most of the power.[162] At the time, Zubarah was under siege by the Wahhabis and Salmān made the decision to evacuate to Bahrain.[163] By 1800, Salmān had most likely moved to Muharraq, where he almost certainly had command of 'Arād Fort.[164] 'Abd Allāh may have initially moved to Manamah, taking up residence in Dīwān Fort, but by 1819 he was living in Muharraq.[165] In 1816, Salmān retired from active rulership and moved to Rifā' Fort at some distance from Muharraq at the centre of Bahrain Island.[166] Thereafter, 'Abd Allāh became the *de facto* Ruler of Bahrain.[167]

'Abd Allāh's rise to power was symbolized by his construction of Abū Māhir Fort (also known as Muharraq Fort) upon the ruins of a much older fort on Abū Māhir Island. Abū Māhir was an ideal fortress island, just off the shore of Muharraq town but connected to it at low tide by a sand bar. The fort stood on the island's southern tip, at the end of a sandy point jutting out into Bahrain's

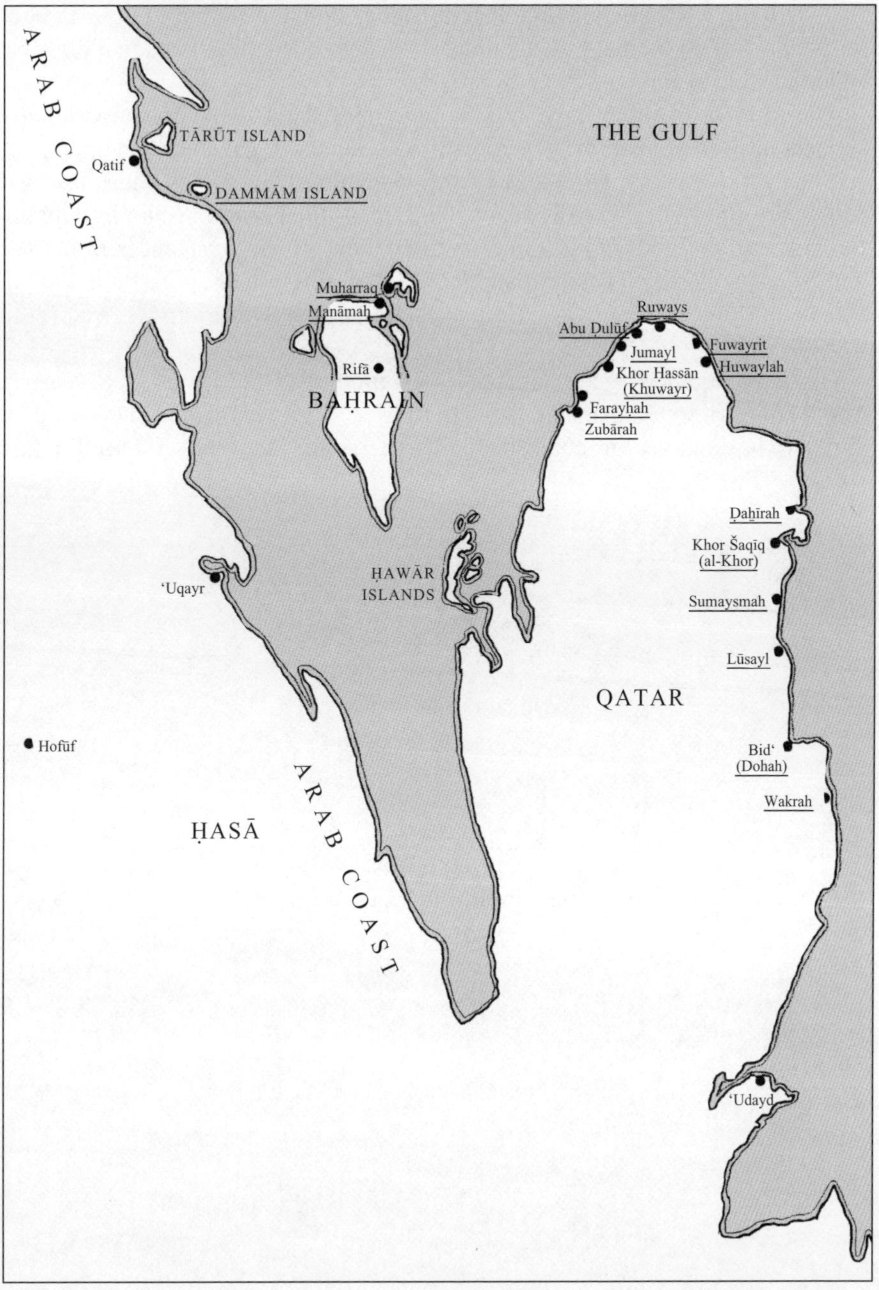

Map 2. The locations of towns (underlined) governed by the Āl Khalifah or their protégés.

main harbour, Khor al-Qulay'ah. It commanded both the entrance of the harbour and Muharraq's principal water source, an underwater spring, making it the most important fort in Bahrain.[168]

After the Āl Khalifah moved to Bahrain, the island shaikhdom was rapidly divided into a number of governorships, with each governor occupying or building his own fort. Drawings of the main forts, comparing their size and design, are shown in Figure 1, below. Once their rule became secure in Bahrain, the Āl Khalifah rulers and governors shifted their primary residences from their forts to *qaṣr*s (fortified palaces) and *bayt*s (mansions), such as Qaṣr Khalifah in Manamah (built c.1829), Qaṣr Rifāʿ in Rifāʿ and Bayt ʿĪsā in Muharraq (built c.1820–30s).[169]

The most populous governorships in Bahrain were the towns of Muharraq, Abū Māhir, Ḥidd, Manamah, ʿAwālī, Rifāʿ and Buḍayyiʿ, and the island of Sitrah (whose governor controlled a large coastal area on eastern Bahrain

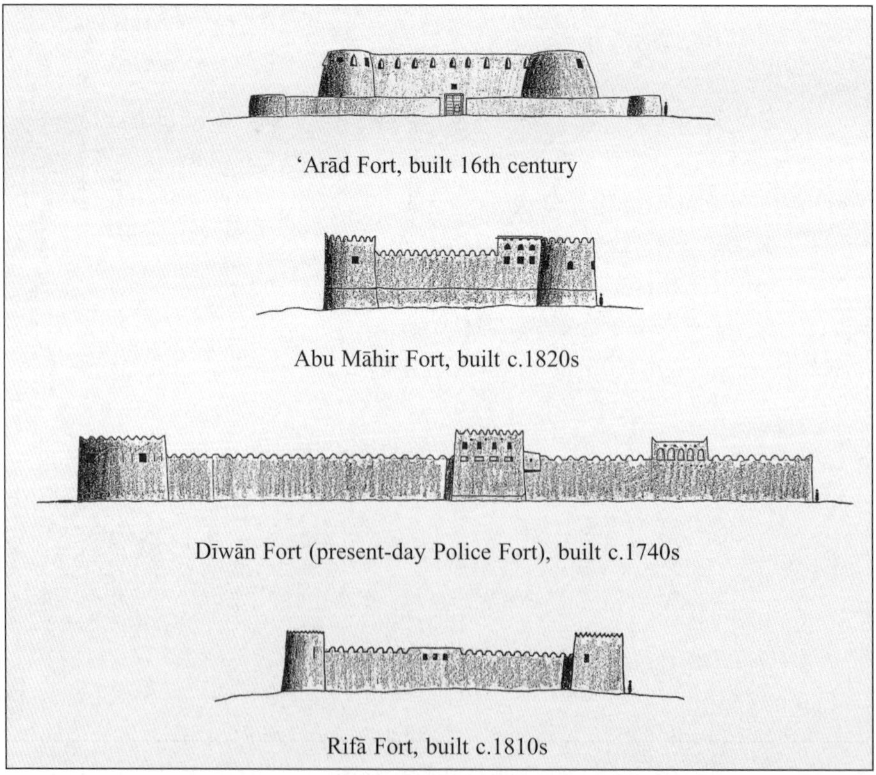

Figure 1. The main forts of Bahrain (scale indicated by the man beside each fort).

Island). There were many more governorships of villages and rural estates. Captain George Brucks of the Indian Navy, who visited Bahrain in 1827, noted that there were about 50 forts or fortified buildings in different parts of the islands, suggesting the existence of an equal number of governorships.[170] Many of these were held by members of the Āl Khalifah, including the Ruler himself. Fuad Khuri has identified 29 towns, villages and rural estates personally governed by eleven Āl Khalifah shaikhs in the late nineteenth century.[171] Other governorships were held by protégé tribal leaders or high-ranking *fidāwīyah*.[172] The Āl Khalifah and their governors ruled an island population, estimated at 60,000 in 1827 and 100,000 in 1905,[173] composed mostly of *Baḥārinah* (the Shi'i Arabs of Bahrain) and tribes from Qatar, Hasa and Najd; as well as several thousand *Hawalah* (Arabs from Persia[174]); several thousand *Mawālī* (African slaves and former slaves); and a few hundred '*Ağam* (expatriate Persians), *Bania*s (Hindu merchants from India) and *Khojah*s (Isma'ili merchants from western India).[175]

The governors had a high degree of autonomy and collected their own taxes.[176] Rulers had only a loose control over their governors. When Lieutenant John MacLeod (Resident 1822–23) visited Bahrain in January 1823, for instance, he observed that 'the authority of the Shaikhs of Bahrain in their own dominions did not appear to be so absolute as might have been expected'.[177] This seems to have been a common state of affairs throughout much of Eastern Arabia, a point reflected in the ambivalence of the words for 'governor' and 'ruler' used by most ruling families. Before independence, the Āl Khalifah used the title of *amīr* (meaning commander, ruler, chief and prince) for their governors of towns, while the ruling families of the Trucial States used the title of *wālī* (governor). Both groups of families used the title of *ḥākim* (meaning both governor and ruler) for their rulers.[178] Upon independence, the rulers of Bahrain, Kuwait and Qatar adopted the title of amir, while the rulers of the United Arab Emirates, paradoxically, retained the title of *ḥākim*. The Āl Su'ūd of Najd and the Āl Rašīd of Ḥā'il used the title of amir for their rulers in the nineteenth century, while today the Āl Su'ūd use it only for their provincial governors.[179] British officials generally used the title of 'chief' in the nineteenth century and 'ruler' from the 1910s onward. In the interests of clarity, when referring to Gulf shaikhdoms, this study has employed the titles of Ruler (for *ḥakim*, amir and chief) and governor (for *wālī* and *amīr*).

Beyond the Bahrain islands, the Āl Khalifah directly governed at various time at least seven of their dependencies: the island of Dammām off the coast of Hasa, and the towns of Zubarah, Khor Ḥassān, Ruways, Ḥuwaylah, Bid' and Wakrah, in Qatar. The locations of these towns can be seen on Map 3, below. Zubarah, on Qatar's western coast, was directly governed by the Āl Khalifah for 103 years; first by the rulers themselves from 1766 to 1796, and

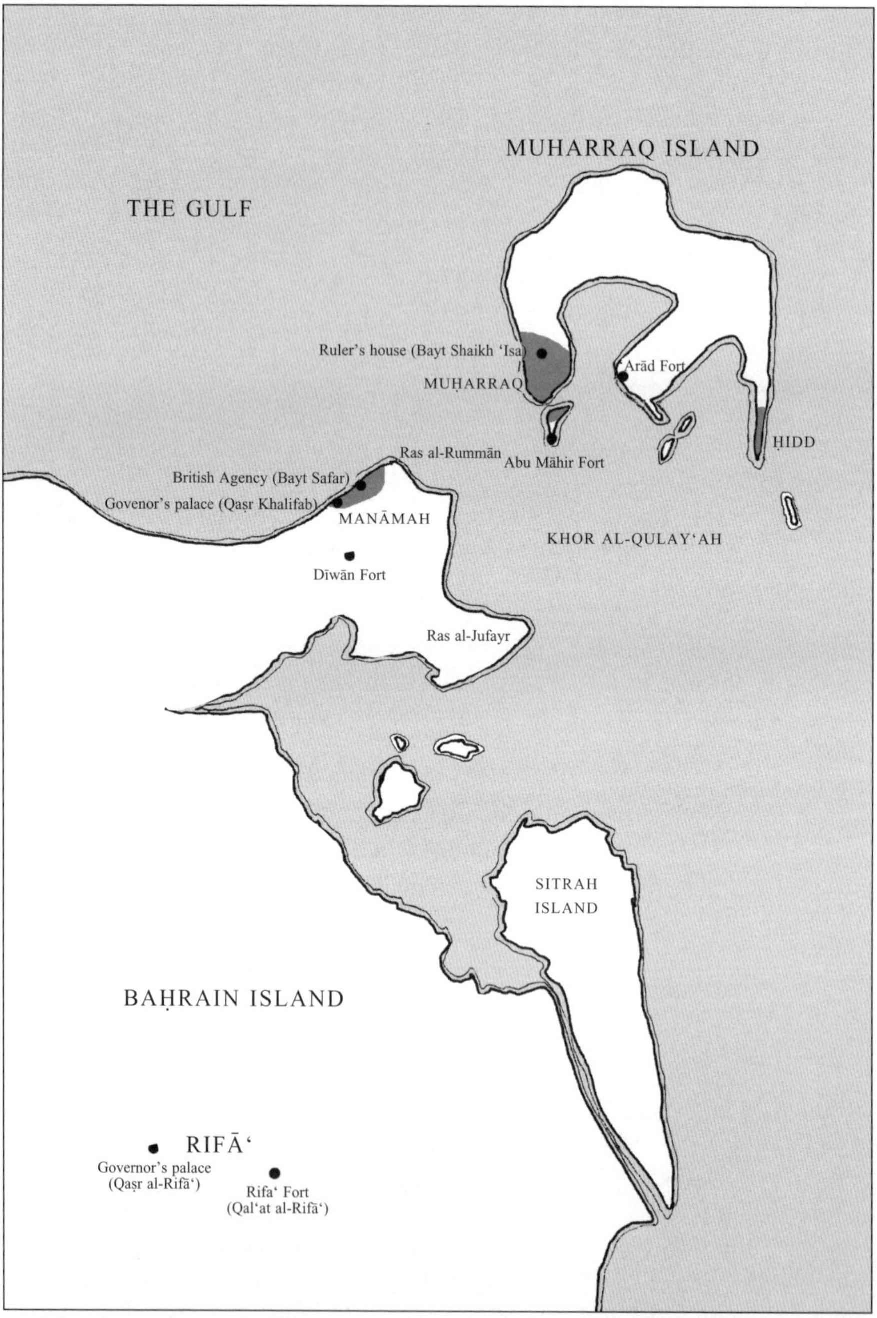

Map 3. Locations of the main forts and buildings of Baḥrain.

Table 4. Occasions when the Āl Khalifah sought military alliances[180]

Allies	*Dates*
1. Āl Ṣabāḥ rulers of Kuwait	1770, 1782–83, 1811, 1843[181]
2. Āl Ǧalāhimah shaikhs of Ruways and Qays Island	1782–83, 1842[182]
3. Āl Bin 'Alī shaikhs of Qays Island and Bid'	1842, 1847
4. Na'īm shaikhs of Qatar	c.1766–1937
5. Qāsimī rulers of Sharjah and Ras al-Khaimah	1816–1819, 1843, 1867
6. Āl Maktūm Ruler of Dubai	1843
7. Banī Hāğir tribe of Hasa	1843, 1869
8. Āl Nahyān rulers of Abu Dhabi	1829, 1867

Occasions when the Āl Khalifah sought or accepted protection[183]

Protectors	*Dates*
1. Banī Khalid rulers of Hasa	1716–95
2. Persian prince-governors of Fars	c.1784–89, 1839, 1843, 1859–60
3. Persian Governor of Bushire	1799
4. Wahhabi (Su'ūdī) amirs of Najd and Hasa	1801–05, 1810–11, 1816–17, 1830–33, 1836, 1843, 1847–50, 1851–55, 1856–9 1861–65, 1867–71
5. Āl Bū Sa'īd imams of Muscat	1800, 1801, 1805–06, 1811–16, 1820–1821, 1829
6. Commander of the Egyptian army in Hasa	1839–40
7. Ottoman Viceroy of Egypt	1853
8. Ottoman Sharif of Mecca	1853
9. Ottoman *Vali* of Baghdad	1859–60
10. British Residents in the Gulf	1805, 1823, 1830, 1838, 1839, 1842, 1843, 1844, 1846, 1847, 1848, 1849, 1851, 1854, 1859, 1861, 1869, 1872, 1873, 1874, 1875, 1878, 1879, 1880, 1881, 1887, 1888, 1892, 1895

then intermittently by a series of family members until 1869. The governorships of the Āl Khalifah's remaining dependencies in Qatar were all held by protégé tribal leaders, the most well-known being Shaikh Muḥammad bin Thānī, the Āl Khalifah's Governor of Bid' (1847–71), who later became the first independent Ruler of Qatar (1871–76).

The governing of a ruler's shaikhdom and dependencies by a number of semi-autonomous governors, some of whom might be rivals for the rulership, meant that a ruler's authority rested, not only on a general acceptance of his rule and his command of economic resources and armed retainers, but ultimately on his superior ability to protect his subjects and dependants. A ruler's presumed or actual skill at forging military alliances, and devising effective protection-seeking tactics when his shaikhdom and dependencies were threatened, was what kept him in power over his governors. The internal structure of his shaikhdom and dependencies thus motivated him to obtain the most powerful protector he could—hence the frequent appeals of the rulers of Bahrain for British protection.

The protection of the Āl Khalifah's shaikhdom and dependencies from antagonistic regional powers was an on-going problem for the rulers of Bahrain. Often they lacked sufficient military resources and were forced to seek or accept outside support (see Table 4, above). The Āl Khalifah may have had an unusually high number of protectors, but they were by no means unusual in having been protégés. All the ruling families of the Gulf today have been the protégés of regional and extra-regional powers in the past. In the nineteenth and twentieth century, most of them sought British protection. The reason was simple: the Resident had the greatest coercive power in the Gulf at his command: the Gulf Squadron. The Resident had a better chance than any other regional protector of punishing and exacting compensation from offenders. As a result, British protection was the least likely to be violated.

By allying with a powerful protector like the British Government, a ruler also reinforced his own position. If a ruler could create the impression amongst his family and governors that he alone had access to the Resident and that the beneficial connection would be lost without him, he gained security for his rulership against internal rivals.[184] In the act of protecting a shaikhdom, either militarily or politically, Britain also enhanced the political status of the ruler and his shaikhdom within the regional political system. British protection 'bestowed a legal status on the concept of "shaykhdom",' as J.E. Peterson puts it.[185] It also served as recognition of shaikhly families as sovereign governments, reinforcing their independence within the regional political system. Peter Lienhardt explains that British protection and recognition accorded the rulers 'a status higher than the traditional way of life had allowed them', reinforcing their authority within their shaikhdoms and dependencies.[186] The withdrawal of British protection and recognition from a shaikhdom or its dependencies, therefore, made a ruler vulnerable to a family coup d'état or a tribal secession respectively.

Despite the advantages British protection brought, it proved to be a double-edged sword for the rulers. It came at a high price: accountability to the Resident for any action he disapproved of. Accountability was common to both British and Arabian understandings of the protégé-protector relationship, of course, but the problem for the rulers was that the Resident was able to hold them thoroughly accountable. Once a Gulf Arab ruler obtained a promise of British protection, he disregarded it at his peril, as Shaikh 'Abd Allāh bin Aḥmad Āl Khalifah (Ruler 1796–1843) and Shaikh Muḥammad bin Khalifah Āl Khalifah (Ruler 1843–68) discovered at the cost of their rulerships.

11. The Protection-seeking Tactics of Shaikh 'Abd Allāh

The tactics of Shaikh 'Abd Allāh bin Aḥmad Āl Khalifah (Ruler of Bahrain 1796–1843) provide a good illustration of the complexities of protection-seeking in regional politics.

In November 1838, the Shaikh submitted a request to the Resident, Captain Samuel Hennell (1838–41, 1843–52), for British protection against an Egyptian army that had recently occupied Najd and was now pushing towards Hasa.[187] Hennell drew up a full report on the Egyptian threat to Bahrain and submitted it, along with Shaikh 'Abd Allāh's request, to his superiors in India. Approval for a formal commitment to protect Bahrain must come from the East India Company's Secret Committee of the Court of Directors in London, came the reply. Until the Court's views were known, the Company authorized Hennell to intervene militarily if the Egyptians invaded. The Commander of the Royal Navy squadron in the Gulf at the time, Rear-Admiral Sir Frederick Maitland, verbally informed Shaikh 'Abd Allāh of this temporary measure. Meanwhile, Hennell opened up diplomatic channels with the Commander of the Egyptian army, Khurshid Pasha, to discourage him from invading Bahrain.

By January 1839, the Egyptian army had occupied all the main ports of Hasa and Khurshid Pasha despatched a *wakīl* to Bahrain demanding tribute from Shaikh 'Abd Allāh. With the British response still pending, the Shaikh decided to hedge his bets. As mentioned above, he first sought Persian protection but, realizing that Persia could not protect him, changed his mind and placed himself under the protection of the Egyptian army. He chose this course of action instead of holding out for a formal commitment of British protection partly because of Khurshid's generous terms: the Commander would send no *wakīl* to reside in Bahrain and would abstain from interfering in Bahraini affairs. In return, Shaikh 'Abd Allāh must pay a yearly tribute of MTD 2,000. The Shaikh considered this 'a trifling and merely pecuniary sacrifice' for the 'virtual immunity from disturbance' he received in return.[188]

In July, Hennell received authority from London to offer only a verbal promise to the Shaikh of the temporary protection of the Royal Navy squadron in the Gulf. When Hennell made the offer to the Shaikh, he declined it, arguing that he could not repudiate his agreement with Khurshid Pasha for anything less than a formal, written promise of British protection. This seems to have been an attempt by the Shaikh to play Hennell off against Khurshid to obtain a more permanent form of protection for his rulership. The Shaikh may have had this end in mind when he submitted to Khurshid in the first place. In the end, his bid to turn Bahrain into a British protectorate was unsuccessful. Hennell had no authority to provide the Shaikh with a written promise of temporary defence, let alone permanent protection, and the Court of Directors in London considered a regular protectorate inexpedient.[189] Shaikh ʻAbd Allāh's bid for lasting security from his many foes and rivals had disastrous long-term consequences. Captain Hennell and Lieutenant Arnold Kemball (Assistant Resident 1841–52) considered Shaikh ʻAbd Allāh 'to have forfeited the friendship of the British Government' when the Shaikh chose Egyptian over British protection. The Secret Committee in London even discussed 'the possibility of his being displaced by a more favourably disposed Shaikh'.[190] Unfortunately for Shaikh ʻAbd Allāh, the Egyptian army withdrew from Hasa and Najd the following summer. Within a few years he would need military assistance again. This time, promises of British protection would not be forthcoming.

After the withdrawal of the Egyptian army in 1840, a group of concerned Ḥasawīyah (Arabs from Hasa) sent a representative to Shaikh ʻAbd Allāh with a proposition. Would he send his grand-nephew, Shaikh Muḥammad bin Khalifah, to the mainland to wrest the governorship of Hasa from Wahhabi hands? Khurshid Pasha had placed the current Wahhabi Amir, Khālid ibn Suʻūd (1837–41), in power after his conquest of Najd. The Ḥasawīyah thought ill of Amir Khālid and believed Āl Khalifah rule would be preferable to his.[191] Six years before, Shaikh ʻAbd Allāh had blocked his grand-nephew's assumption of the joint rulership of Bahrain after the death of the young Shaikh's father, Shaikh Khalifah bin Salmān (joint Ruler 1825–34). It appears that Shaikh Muḥammad believed his great-uncle was obliged to support the proposal of the Ḥasawīyah as compensation for this denial. But Shaikh ʻAbd Allāh did not agree and rejected the plan. A violent difference of opinion resulted between the Shaikh and his grand-nephew over the summer. Shaikh Muḥammad asked for British assistance to overthrow his great-uncle, but Captain Hennell declined to interfere in the affair and told the Shaikh he must settle his differences with the Ruler on his own.[192] Shaikh Muḥammad then left Bahrain for Khor Ḥassān, where he began organizing opposition to Shaikh ʻAbd Allāh. Shaikh Muḥammad returned to Bahrain in 1842 at the invitation of Shaikh ʻAbd Allāh in the hope of reconciling their differences, but his visit led only to confrontation. A dispute quickly broke out between Shaikh Muḥammad and one of Shaikh ʻAbd Allāh's sons, sparking the Bahraini civil war of 1842–43.[193] The camps divided, Shaikh Muḥammad gathering his supporters in Manamah and Shaikh ʻAbd Allāh gathering his in Muharraq. A military build-up ensued, with both sides recruiting Bedouin warriors from the mainland. Skirmishes between the two camps soon began, during which a brother of Shaikh Muḥammad and a grandson of Shaikh ʻAbd Allāh were killed. In June, Shaikh ʻAbd Allāh attacked and captured Manamah. Shaikh Muḥammad fled to the mainland.[194]

Back on the mainland, Shaikh Muḥammad sought Wahhabi support for an eventual counter-attack on Bahrain. He also enlisted the support of Shaikh Bašīr bin Raḥmah Āl Ǧalāhimah and Shaikh ʻĪsā bin Ṭarīf Āl Bin ʻAlī of Qays Island.[195] Shaikhs Bašīr and ʻĪsā seem to have feared the Resident's support of Shaikh ʻAbd Allāh, for they sought the permission of Lieutenant-Colonel Henry Robertson (officiating Resident 1842–43) before agreeing to join Shaikh Muḥammad, as mentioned briefly before. Recalling the Egyptian episode of 1839–40, Robertson had no interest in rescuing Shaikh ʻAbd Allāh's rulership. He sanctioned the Shaikhs' request to oust Shaikh ʻAbd Allāh from Bahrain.[196] In November 1842, Robertson despatched Lieutenant Kemball, his Assistant, to Bahrain to warn Shaikh ʻAbd Allāh about this. Robertson likely intended the warning as notice of the withdrawal of British support for the Shaikh's rulership. The Shaikh received Kemball's words with 'much surprise and apprehension'.[197] Resorting to a previous tactic, he threatened to seek the protection of the Wahhabi Amir, of whom the British disapproved.[198] But the threat fell on deaf ears. In February 1843 Shaikh ʻAbd Allāh again appealed to the Resident, but he did not reply. The Shaikh made his request for a third time the following month and the Resident finally issued a refusal.[199]

In March 1843 Shaikh Muḥammad recaptured Manamah. Shortly afterwards, the Qays Island shaikhs arrived in Manamah with several hundred armed men and preparations began for the final assault on Muharraq. The allies attacked Muharraq in April 1843 and overwhelmed Shaikh ʻAbd Allāh's forces. The Shaikh capitulated and was permitted to leave for exile on Dammām Island, where his son, Mubārak, was Governor.[200] Shaikh Muḥammad's allies, the Āl Ǧalāhimah and Āl Bin ʻAlī of Qays Island, then returned to Qatar, which they had left in 1826 and 1835 respectively, and settled at the Āl Khalifah's dependency of Bidʻ.

Over the summer Shaikh ʻAbd Allāh turned to Bushire, Dubai and Sharjah for military assistance to regain his rulership. Kemball, now acting Resident in Bushire (April-December 1843), refused the Shaikh's request and forbade the Rulers of Dubai and Sharjah to assist him.[201] While he indicated that the Maritime Truce had determined his decision, Kemball's real motive was obviously his dislike of the Shaikh.[202] In fact, the Maritime Truce barred members from maritime warfare against each other, not against outsiders like Bahrain. Kemball then offered to mediate in the dispute, although he would not guarantee any settlement reached. But Shaikh ʻAbd Allāh did not accept the offer.[203] His requests denied, Shaikh ʻAbd Allāh resorted to his previous tactics. During October 1843-March 1844 he attempted to play the Prince-Governor of Fars off against Kemball and later against Captain Samuel Hennell (Resident 1843–52) by threatening 'to throw himself into the arms of Persia' to regain his rulership of Bahrain, if the British would not help him.[204] Both Kemball and Hennell refused to help. In the end, the Shaikh's threat came to nothing as the Prince-Governor failed to deliver the 100 cavalry and 500 infantry the Shaikh had asked for.[205] In December 1843 Shaikh 'Abd Allāh tried a different approach, arguing that, as a signatory of the General Treaty of 1820, he was entitled to British naval protection from his foes. This was a common interpretation of the General Treaty by the Gulf rulers, first made in 1823 by Shaikh 'Abd Allāh himself and by Shaikh Sulṭān bin Ṣaqr al-Qāsimī of Sharjah (Ruler 1803–66).[206] Hennell rejected the interpretation,[207] as had all Residents prior to Britain's incorporation of the Coast of Oman and Bahrain into the trucial system in 1835 and 1861 respectively. In January 1844, the Shaikh argued that Hennell was to blame for his ousting because the British Government had lulled him into a false sense of security.[208] The Resident was, therefore, obligated to restore him to power. Hennell rejected the Shaikh's argument. In March 1844 the Shaikh again pleaded hard for the Resident's support and protection, but to no avail.[209] Shaikh 'Abd Allāh made his last bid for British support later that year. Trying the same tactic as before, he threatened to ally himself with the Amir of Najd and Hasa unless the Resident helped him retake Bahrain. Again, Hennell refused to help.[210]

At this point the Shaikh gave up on Hennell and took matters into his own hands. In October 1845 he made an attempt on Bahrain with the military assistance of the Wahhabi Governor of Qatif, but Shaikh Muḥammad foiled the operation almost before it began.[211] In June 1846, the Prince-Governor of Fars renewed his offer of military assistance to Shaikh 'Abd Allāh, but the Shaikh declined, not believing in it.[212] He made a second attempt on Bahrain in 1847, this time with the military assistance of Shaikh 'Īsā bin Ṭarīf Āl Bin 'Alī, who had helped oust him four years before, but Shaikh Muḥammad's military defeated the force near Fuwayriṭ in northern Qatar and killed Shaikh 'Īsā in battle.[213] In 1848 the Persian Consul-General in Baghdad assured Shaikh 'Abd Allāh of the support of the Persian Government should he again try to retake Bahrain. The Consul-General broke off his correspondence with the Shaikh at the insistence of the British Resident in Baghdad, however.[214] In 1849 Shaikh 'Abd Allāh set sail for Zanzibar in the hope of winning the support of his life-long enemy, Sayyid Sa'īd (Imam of Muscat and Zanzibar 1807–56). He died en route at Muscat, an old and bitter man.

This illustration of protection-seeking is drawn from just ten years in the life of one Gulf Arab ruler. Before the 1839 Egyptian occupation of Hasa, Shaikh 'Abd Allāh made at least ten requests for protection from various regional powers between 1796 and 1838, two of which were addressed to the British Resident. During 1843–44, he made repeated requests for British protection, as detailed above. Shaikh ‘Abd Allāh’s successors, Shaikh Muḥammad bin Khalifah (Ruler 1843–68), Shaikh ‘Alī bin Khalifah (Ruler 1868–69), Shaikh Muḥammad bin ‘Abd Allāh (Ruler 1869) and Shaikh ‘Īsā bin ‘Alī (Ruler 1869–1923), all made requests for either British, Persian, Ottoman, Wahhabi, or Muscati protection, or military alliances with less powerful rulers, whenever trouble threatened, often using the same tactics as Shaikh ‘Abd Allāh in attempting to play rival powers off against each other. This cyclical pattern of protection-seeking persisted until the British Government finally accepted responsibility for Bahrain’s defence in 1861 and diplomatic representation in 1880.

12. Britain and the Role of Protector

Before Britain accepted formal responsibility for the maritime protection of the Trucial States in 1835, the British Government had been extremely reluctant for a variety of reasons to assume the role of protector in the Gulf. The principal concerns were, first, that it might draw Britain into the unstable and unpredictable affairs of the mainland, forcing it to commit military forces there. Even the island shaikhdom of Bahrain had mainland dependencies. Shortly after the establishment of the Gulf Residency, Britain realized that the Pax Britannica would be more effectively maintained without land forces. The high death rate of the first Gulf garrison—444 soldiers and 10 officers killed in battles against just one interior Omani tribe during 1820–21 and the decimation of the garrison by disease during 1821–22—prompted Britain to withdraw its land forces from the Gulf in early 1823.[215] Thereafter, Britain limited its military activity to the range of its naval guns. It re-constituted its Gulf garrison only in wartime or when war threatened (1856–58, 1914–18, 1939–45 and 1961–71). Added to this was the problem that the imams of Muscat, the amirs of Najd and Hasa, the Persian prince-governors of Fars, and the Ottoman *vali*s of Baghdad all claimed Bahrain as a dependency and had attempted to subjugate it at one time or another. Successive Residents feared, rightly, that the protection of Bahrain would bring them into conflict with these regional powers.

The second principal concern was that permanent British protection might encourage despotism, as it had in some Indian princely states. The third, that the British Government would lose political leverage with the Gulf rulers if it switched from a conditional to an unconditional protection policy. The fourth, that permanent protection would shoulder Britain with the role of guarantor of the state. The British Government feared that such a role might considerably add to the Resident’s burdens by placing upon him ‘the onus and responsibility of being the arbiter in every dispute, and [the] settlement of endless claims’, to use the words of Major James Morrison (Resident 1835–37).[216]

Possible misunderstandings about what the Gulf rulers were asking of the Resident might have also contributed to the British Government's reluctance to assume a protective role in the Gulf. The British concept of protection relied on the protector's ability to defend his protégé physically and bring an attacker to justice. As a deterrent to attack, it relied on a would-be attacker's respect for the *firepower* of the protector. The Arabian concept relied more on a would-be attacker's respect for the *honour* of the protector. It also relied on the protector's secondary roles of mediator, arbiter and guarantor of settlements, to provide a peaceful channel for would-be attackers to settle their differences with the protégé, as discussed above. It seems that early Residents either misunderstood or rejected the duties of this role, in which Gulf rulers were trying to cast them. Many rulers were frustrated by the failure of successive Residents to live up to these expectations. For instance, early Residents were usually willing to mediate between rulers, but they refused to play the role of guarantor for the settlements reached, as illustrated by the history of the Āl Khalifah's tribute payments to the amirs of Najd and Hasa and the imams of Muscat. Settlement negotiations usually broke down as a result, as Lieutenant Arnold Kemball (Assistant Resident 1841–52, Resident 1852–55) observed in 1844:

> Experience has shown that the most solemn engagements between these chieftains … formed without the guarantee of the [British] Government, are no security whatever for the maintenance of peace … [They] deem the guarantee of the British to any sort of arrangement a sine qua non … Attempts have been made to induce the several chiefs to enter into a mutual agreement among themselves, without British guarantee … but these have ever been rendered nugatory by Arab pride and sense of honour.[217]

The greatest frustration, of course, came from early Residents' routine rejection of the rulers' requests for protection in the first place.

Before the first Maritime Truce in 1835, an experimental ban on maritime warfare during the pearling season, Residents feared that a larger naval presence and corresponding expenditure would be necessary if Britain were to assume responsibility for the maritime protection of the Gulf shaikhdoms. The acting Resident who proposed the truce to the rulers of the Coast of Oman, Lieutenant Samuel Hennell (1834–35), did so only because of the rulers' enthusiastic support for the idea.[218] So desirable was British protection in Eastern Arabia that, shortly after the signing of the General Treaty of 1820, the principal pearl merchants of Sharjah offered to pay *ẖūwah* to the Government of India at the rate of MTD 20 (Rs 40) per boat if the Gulf Squadron would permanently station a gunboat at the pearl banks to protect their pearling fleets.[219] British reports on the first Maritime Truces clearly indicate that its annual renewal was a product of the initiative and insistence of the majority of the rulers, and was not imposed upon them by the Resident. When the time came for the Truce's first renewal in April 1836, Lieutenant Kemball, observed that it was renewed 'with the undisguised satisfaction of the respective chiefs'.[220]

The idea to extend the Truce's coverage beyond the summer pearling season into a perpetual ban on all maritime warfare was first proposed by Shaikh Sulṭān bin Ṣaqr al-Qāsimī of Sharjah in September 1836, just sixteen months after the introduction of the first Maritime Truce. The Resident, Major James Morrison, rejected the Shaikh's proposal. The British Government, Morrison explained, lacked the resources to enforce a perpetual truce. Or so he believed.[221] The British were also convinced that, so long as the ban on maritime warfare permitted rulers to pursue feuds outside of the pearling season, they would be content 'to allow their feuds and animosities to remain in abeyance, under the idea that after a specified date it would always be in their power to indulge their deeply rooted feelings of animosity, should they feel disposed to do so.'[222] Were the ban to become perpetual, it could not provide for this. Lieutenant Samuel Hennell (Assistant Resident 1826–34, 1835–38) explained in 1830 that precluding the rulers

> from avenging insults, or taking satisfaction for wrongs, whether real or imaginary, would so embitter the sentiments of hatred entertained [by the rulers] towards each other, that a series of aggressions and retaliations would speedily arise, which would only tend to defeat the very object for which the peace had been negotiated.[223]

In 1838, when Captain Hennell, now Gulf Resident (1838–41, 1843–52), toured the Coast of Oman to renew the Maritime Truce for a third time, Shaikh Sulṭān bin Ṣaqr al-Qāsimī 'not only expressed his earnest desire for a renewal of the truce, but added that it would afford him sincere pleasure if it could be changed into the establishment of a permanent peace upon the seas.'[224] Hennell rejected the Shaikh's proposal, for the reasons just mentioned. Undeterred, the Shaikh urged the Resident to agree to an annual twelve-month truce instead. As the other rulers consented to the Shaikh's proposal, Hennell drew up a new truce accordingly, which the rulers readily signed.[225]

So successful were the annually-renewed Truces, that the Resident agreed to guarantee a ten-year Maritime Truce in 1843. The following year, Lieutenant Kemball observed that the rulers 'are now quite as much interested in its maintenance as ourselves; and of this they exhibited ample proof in their united readiness to renew it for so long a period as ten years, or even more, had such been desired or deemed expedient.'[226] J.B. Kelly explains that

> so changed had the shaikhs' outlook become by the time of the conclusion of the Ten Years' Truce that they often acted on their own initiative to punish infractions of the truce by their subjects, even before these had been brought to

> the notice of the Resident. Sometimes they even went further and acted to prevent the commission of piracy. The Shaikh of 'Ajman, for example, when a Qasimi vessel from Lingah ran aground in a storm off 'Ajman in 1845, hastened to the scene with his brothers, sword in hand, and swore to cut down the first man who tried to plunder the vessel.[227]

After the successful completion of the ten-year Truce in 1853, it was evident to the British that their fears and convictions had been seriously misplaced. That year, the Resident finally invited the rulers of the Coast of Oman to sign a Perpetual Maritime Truce, seventeen years after the Ruler of Sharjah first proposed the idea. All the rulers signed without hesitation.

The slow realization that earlier British fears were misplaced is reflected also in the British Government's gradual change in attitude towards the protection of Bahrain. Until 1838, it maintained a straightforward "no protection" policy for the reason mentioned above.[228] From 1839 to 1860, it observed an "unofficial protection only" policy, albeit on condition of the Resident's approval of the Ruler.[229] In 1861, after the Ruler of Bahrain became increasingly warlike, the British Government adopted a "permanent protection" policy and admitted Bahrain to the Perpetual Maritime Truce, making itself Bahrain's Protecting Power, as discussed above.[230] Finally, in 1880, it assumed responsibility for Bahrain's foreign affairs.[231] After 1861, it was able to maintain political leverage with the Ruler of Bahrain and avoid encouraging despotism, as experienced in the Indian princely states, by limiting its protection to the shaikhdom. It would not guarantee the Ruler's position within the shaikhdom. Time and time again, the Resident informed the Ruler that,

> it was highly desirable that the Chief of Bahrein should learn to rely on his own resources for the maintenance of his position, for as long as he could count on the constant presence of foreign support he would surely remain careless and pathetic and disinclined to exert himself in strengthening his position by good administration and a conciliatory policy towards his people.[232]

The only way the Ruler could secure British support for his rulership in moments of crisis was if the Resident wished it to continue. All the trucial rulers were in the same position. This motivated most of the rulers most of the time to maintain good relations with the Resident.

The strength of the British position in the Gulf in the nineteenth century was that it alone had the power to stop the cyclical pattern of protection-seeking, raiding and invasion amongst the rulers. Residents could use this position to their advantage as an indirect method of keeping in power those rulers who co-operated with them to maintain the Pax Britannica, and keeping out of power those who did not. For example, as related in the previous section, in 1842

Lieutenant-Colonel Henry Robertson (officiating Resident 1842–43) granted permission to two rulers wishing to help Shaikh Muḥammad bin Khalifah (Ruler 1843–68) oust Shaikh ʿAbd Allāh bin Aḥmad (Ruler 1796–1843) from his rulership of Bahrain. They succeeded the following year. A few months later, when the same two rulers sought the Resident's permission to help Shaikh ʿAbd Allāh regain his rulership, Lieutenant Arnold Kemball (acting Resident 1843) forbade them to interfere, depriving the Shaikh of allies.

After 1861, Residents employed more direct methods in Bahrain, intervening personally to remove rulers unwilling to co-operate with them and installing shaikhs who would uphold the Pax Britannica. This happened three times while Bahrain was under British protection. In 1868, Colonel Lewis Pelly helped the Āl Khalifah depose Shaikh Muḥammad bin Khalifah and recognized the Ruler's brother, Shaikh ʿAlī bin Khalifah, as the new Ruler. The following year, Shaikh ʿAlī was overthrown and killed by Shaikhs Muḥammad bin Khalifah and Muḥammad bin ʿAbd Allāh. Pelly imprisoned the Shaikhs and engineered the accession of the late Ruler's son, Shaikh ʿĪsā bin ʿAlī. Fifty-four years later, in 1923, Lieutenant-Colonel Stuart Knox forcibly retired Shaikh ʿĪsā from active rulership and handed the reins of government to his son, Shaikh Ḥamad bin ʿĪsā.

Conclusion

Was Britain's role as 'arbiter and guardian of the Gulf' one it assumed in response to appeals from the Gulf Arabs, as the 1908 Foreign Office memorandum quoted at the beginning of this study claims, or was British protection imposed as a form of domination, as some historians are now arguing?

This study has shown how the Gulf Arab rulers, faced by the endless problem of protection, defended their shaikhdoms during the nineteenth century by entering into culturally-sanctioned protector-protégé relationships. It has shown that the rulers tried to impose the role of protector on the Resident and the British Government from the very outset of the Gulf Residency and that, in time, the Resident came to accept the role of 'arbiter and guardian of the Gulf' and to behave, on the whole, as the rulers expected a protector to behave. This legitimized Britain's presence within the regional political system in terms of Eastern Arabian culture and meant that the Resident's authority in the Gulf was not based solely on treaties. From the rulers' perspective, the Resident was a Gulf ruler himself, except that he was the most powerful and influential ruler they had ever known. The Gulf rulers gave him the respectful titles of *Raʾīs al-ḫalīǧ* (Chief of the Gulf) and *Faḫāmat al-Raʾīs* (His Excellency the Chief).[233]

Although it cut off Bahrain from its dependencies in Qatar, the Pax Britannica in the Gulf benefited the shaikhdoms, including Bahrain, as much as it did the British. This explains why the Pax was so successful: it was largely self-enforcing. To assume, as many now do, that Britain imposed its protection on the Gulf shaikhdoms against the will of their rulers, is not only to ignore the Eastern Arabian tradition of protection-seeking and the successful use the rulers made of it, but also to completely disregard the historical record, set forth in this study, which shows that the treaties were initiated as much by the Gulf rulers as by the British, and that it was mainly the rulers who worked towards the establishment of the Perpetual Maritime Truce. British protection was not imposed on the Gulf shaikhdoms, but sought after and welcomed by the Gulf rulers.

The view of British protection as unsolicited and unwanted arose only when memories of the turbulent years before the Maritime Truce became distant, when the benefits of British protection became less apparent, and when Britain's exclusive presence (based on the Exclusive Agreements) was felt by some Gulf Arabs to be less beneficial to the shaikhdoms than to Britain.[234] Even so, the need for British protection remained. In 1968, when the British Government declared it could no longer afford the £12,000,000 per annum to keep its forces in the Gulf and would be withdrawing its military in 1971, the Ruler of Abu Dhabi, Shaikh Zāyid bin Sulṭān Āl Nahyān, offered to pay for the military presence himself. The Ruler of Dubai made a similar offer, adding that he believed all four oil-producing states under British protection—Abu Dhabi, Bahrain, Dubai and Qatar—would be willing to cover the cost. The British Government declined these offers, however, and withdrew its forces in December 1971.[235] One need only compare this with Britain's withdrawal from Egypt, Palestine, or Aden to appreciate the difference between Britain's involvement in the Gulf and its involvement in the rest of the Arab world.

Abbreviations

Asst.	Assistant
BJMES	*British Journal of Middle Eastern Studies*
For.	Foreign
Gov.	Governor
Govt.	Government
IO	India Office, London
JRAI	*The Journal of the Royal Anthropological Institute of Great Britain and Ireland*
JRGS	*Journal of the Royal Geographical Society*
Ks	Krans (principal unit of currency of Persia)
MEJ	*Middle East Journal*
MESA	Middle East Studies Association of North America
MTD	Maria Theresa Dollars
n.	footnote
OIOC	Oriental and India Office Collection, British Library, London
offg.	officiating

PA	Political Agent
Pol.	Political
PRPG	Political Resident in the Persian Gulf
Rs	Rupees
Sec.	Secretary
SNOPG	Senior Naval Officer in the Persian Gulf

Bibliography

1. Primary sources

Aitchison, Sir C.U. *A Collection of Treaties, Engagements and Sanads Relating to India and Neighbouring Countries*, Vol. XI: *The Treaties, &c., Relating to Aden and the South Western Coast of Arabia, the Arab Principalities in the Persian Gulf, Muscat (Oman), Baluchistan and the North-West Frontier Province*. Delhi: Manager of Publications, 1933.

Belgrave, Sir C. *Personal Column*. London: Hutchinson, 1960.

Bennett, T.J. 'The Past and Present Connection of England with the Persian Gulf', *Journal of the Society of Arts*, Vol. L, (13 June 1902), 634–52.

Disbrowe, Lt. H.F. 'Historical Sketch of the Uttoobee Tribe of Arabs (Bahrein), 1844–1853' (1853), *Selections from the Records of the Bombay Government*, No. XXIV, New Series. Bombay: Bombay Education Society Press, 1856, 407–25.

Durand, Capt. E.L. 'Notes on the Pearl Fisheries of the Persian Gulf', Govt. of India, *Report on the Administration of the Persian Gulf Political Residency for the Year 1877–78*. Calcutta: Foreign Dept. Press, 1878, Appendix A, 27–41.

Govt. of Bombay, Political Dept. *Selections from the Records of the Bombay Government*, No. XXIV, New Series. Compiled and edited by R.H. Thomas. Bombay: Bombay Education Society Press, 1856.

Govt. of India, Foreign Dept. *Report on the Administration of the Bushire Residency including that of the Muscat Political Agency for 1873–74.* Calcutta: Foreign Dept. Press, 1874.

——. *Reports on the Administration of the Persian Gulf Political Residency and Muscat Political Agency for the Years 1874–88*. Calcutta: Foreign Dept. Press, 1875–81; Superintendent of Govt. Printing, 1882–87.

——. *Administration Reports of the Persian Gulf Political Residency and Muscat Political Agency for the Years 1889–1908*. Calcutta: Superintendent of Govt. Printing, 1888–1909.

Hawley, Sir D. *Desert Wind and Tropic Storm: An Autobiography*. Wilby: Michael Russell, 2000.

Hennell, Lt. S. 'Historical Sketch of the Uttoobee Tribe of Arabs (Bahrein) from the Year 1817 to 1831' (1832), *Selections from the Records of the Bombay Government*, No. XXIV, New Series. Bombay: Bombay Education Society Press, 1856, 372–82.

H.M. Govt., Admiralty War Staff. *A Handbook of Arabia*, Vol. 1: *General*. London: Intelligence Div., Admiralty War Staff, 1916.

India Office. Correspondence relating to areas outside India for 1840. L/P&S/9/116, OIOC, London.

——. Correspondence for 1840. L/P&S/5/261, OIOC, London
——. Correspondence for 1851. L/P&S/5/471, OIOC, London
——. Native letters outward for 1856–72. R/15/1/180–82, OIOC, London.
——. Correspondence relating to areas outside India for 1861. L/P&S/9/162, OIOC, London.
——. Correspondence relating to areas outside India for 1869. L/P&S/9/15, OIOC, London.
——. Sketch of Abu Mahir Fort, Bahrain, 1868. W/L/P&S/5/15, OIOC, London.
——. Memorandum on Bahrain, 1875. R/15/1/192, OIOC, London.
——. Political and Secret Dept. subject files for 1905. L/P&S/10/81, OIOC, London.
——. 'Confidential memorandum respecting British interests in the Persian Gulf', Foreign Office, 12 Feb. 1908. L/P&S/18/B166, OIOC, London.
Kemball, Lt. A.B. 'Chronological Table of Events Connected with the Uttoobee Tribe of Arabs (Bahrein) from the Year 1716–1844' (1844), *Selections from the Records of the Bombay Government*, No. XXIV, New Series. Bombay: Bombay Education Society Press, 1856, 140–52.
——. 'Historical Sketch of the Uttoobee Tribe of Arabs (Bahrein) from the Year 1832 to 1844' (1844), *Selections from the Records of the Bombay Government*, No. XXIV, 382–407.
——. 'Observations on the Past Policy of the British Government towards the Arab Tribes of the Persian Gulf' (1844), *Selections from the Records of the Bombay Government*, No. XXIV, 61–74.
——. 'Memoranda on the Resources, Localities, and Relations of the Tribes Inhabiting the Arabian Shores of the Persian Gulf' (1845), *Selections from the Records of the Bombay Government*, No. XXIV, 91–119.
——. 'Statistical and Miscellaneous Information Connected with the Possessions, Revenues, Families, etc. … of the Ruler of Bahrain' (1854), *Selections from the Records of the Bombay Government*, No. XXIV, 285–97.
Lorimer, J.G. *Gazetteer of the Persian Gulf, 'Oman, and Central Arabia*, Vol. I: *Historical*. Calcutta: Superintendent of Govt. Printing, 1915.
——. *Gazetteer of the Persian Gulf, 'Oman, and Central Arabia*, Vol. II: *Geographical and Statistical*. Calcutta: Superintendent of Govt. Printing, 1908.
Miles, S.B. *The Countries and Tribes of the Persian Gulf*. London: Harrison & Sons, 1919.
Palgrave, W.G. *Personal Narrative of a Year's Journey through Central and Eastern Arabia (1862–63)*. 1st ed. London: Macmillan, 1865.
Pelly, Lt.-Col. L. *Report on a Journey to Riyadh in Central Arabia (1865)*. Bombay: Bombay Education Society Press, 1866.
Saldanha, J.A. *Précis of Bahrein Affairs, 1854–1904*. Calcutta: Superintendent of Govt. Printing, 1904.
——. *Précis of Katar Affairs, 1873–1904*. Calcutta: Superintendent of Govt. Printing, 1904.
——. *Précis of Commerce and Communications in the Persian Gulf, 1801–1905*. Calcutta: Superintendent of Govt. Printing, 1906.
——. *Précis of Correspondence Regarding the Affairs of the Persian Gulf, 1801–1853*. Calcutta: Superintendent of Govt. Printing, 1906.

——. *Précis of Correspondence Regarding the Trucial Chiefs, 1854–1905*. Calcutta: Superintendent of Govt. Printing, 1906.

Taylor, Capt. R. 'Extracts from Brief Notes containing Historical and Other Information connected with the Province of Oman; Muskat and the Adjoining Country; the Islands of Bahrain, Ormus, Kishm, and Karrack; and Other Ports in the Persian Gulf' (1818), *Selections from the Records of the Bombay Government*, No. XXIV, New Series. Bombay: Bombay Education Society Press, 1856, 1–40.

Warden, F. 'Historical Sketch of the Uttoobee Tribe of Arabs (Bahrein) from the Year 1716 to 1817' (1817), *Selections from the Records of the Bombay Government*, No. XXIV, New Series. Bombay: Bombay Education Society Press, 1856, 362–72.

Whitelock, Lt. H.H. 'An Account of Arabs who inhabit the Coast between Ras-el-Kheimah and Abothubee in the Gulf of Persia, generally called the Pirate Coast', *Transactions of the Bombay Geographical Society*, Vol. I. Bombay: American Mission Press, 1844.

Wilson, Maj. D. 'Memorandum Respecting the Pearl Fisheries in the Persian Gulf', *Journal of the Royal Geographical Society*, Vol. III (1833), 283–86.

2. Secondary sources

Abu Hakima, A.M. *History of Eastern Arabia, 1750–1800: The Rise and Development of Bahrain and Kuwait*. Beirut: Khayats, 1965.

——. 'The Development of the Gulf States', *The Arabian Peninsula: Society and Politics*. Edited by D. Hopwood. London: George Allen & Unwin, 1972, 31–53.

Alghanim, S. *The Reign of Mubarak Al-Sabah, Shaikh of Kuwait 1896–1915*. London: I.B. Tauris, 1998.

Anscombe, F.F. *The Ottoman Gulf: The Creation of Kuwait, Saudi Arabia and Qatar*. New York: Columbia Univ. Press, 1997.

Al-Baharna, H.M. *The Legal Status of the Arabian Gulf States: A Study of Their Treaty Relations and Their International Problems*. Manchester: Manchester Univ. Press, 1968.

——. 'The Consequences of Britain's Exclusive Treaties: A Gulf View', *The Arab Gulf and the West*. Edited by B.R. Pridham. London: Croom Helm, 1985.

Balfour-Paul, G. *The End of Empire in the Middle East: Britain's Relinquishment of Power in Her Last Three Arab Dependencies*. Cambridge: Cambridge Univ. Press, 1991.

Belgrave, Sir C. *The Pirate Coast*. London: G. Bell & Sons, 1966.

Busch, B.C. *Britain and the Persian Gulf, 1894–1914*. Berkeley: Univ. of California Press, 1967.

Choueiri, Y.M. *Modern Arab Historiography: Historical Discourse and the Nation-State*. London: Curzon, 2002.

Crystall, J. 'Authoritarianism and Its Adversaries in the Arab World', *World Politics*, Vol. 46 (Jan. 1994), 262–89.

——. *Oil and Politics in the Gulf, Rulers and Merchants in Kuwait and Qatar*. Revised ed. Cambridge: Cambridge Univ. Press, 1995.

Davies, C.E. 'Britain, Trade and Piracy: The British Expeditions against Ras al-Khaima of 1809–10 and 1819–20', *Global Interests in the Arab Gulf*. Edited by C.E. Davies. Exeter: Univ. of Exeter Press, 1992, 29–66.

——. *The Blood-Red Arab Flag: An Investigation into Qasimi Piracy, 1797–1820*. Exeter: Univ. of Exeter Press, 1997.

Dickson, H.R.P. *The Arab of the Desert: A Glimpse into Badawin Life in Kuwait and Sa'udi Arabia*. London: George Allen & Unwin, 1949.

Dresch, P. *Tribes, Government and History in Yemen*. Oxford: Oxford Univ. Press, 1989.

Farah, T. *Protection and Politics in Bahrain, 1869–1915*. Lebanon: American Univ. of Beirut, 1985.

Fattah, H. *The Politics of Regional Trade in Iraq, Arabia, and the Gulf, 1745–1900*. Albany: S.U.N.Y. Press, 1997.

Freitag, U. 'Writing Arab History: The Search for the Nation', *BJMES*, Vol. 21 (1994), 19–37.

Fuccaro, N. 'Understanding the Urban History of Bahrain', *Critique: Critical Middle Eastern Studies*, No. 17 (Fall 2000), 49–81.

Geller, E. and Waterbury, J., eds. *Patrons and Clients in Mediterranean Societies*. London: Gerald Duckworth & Co., 1977.

Ghareeb, E. and Al-Abed, I., eds. *Perspectives on the United Arab Emirates*. London: Trident Press, 1997.

Govt. of Bahrain, Directorate of Museums. *Al-baḥrayn: ḥaḍārah wa-ta'rīh* [*Bahrain: Culture and History*]. Bahrain: Ministry of Cabinet Affairs and Information, 1997.

Gulf Panorama. *Old Days*. Manamah: Oriental Press, 1986.

Harrison, P.W. *The Arab at Home*. New York: Thomas Y. Cromwell & Co., 1924.

Hawley, Sir D. *The Trucial States*. London: George Allen & Unwin, 1970.

Heard-Bey, F. *From Trucial States to United Arab Emirates*. 2nd ed. London: Longman, 1996.

——. 'The Tribal Society of the UAE and its Traditional Economy', *Perspectives on the United Arab Emirates*. Edited by E. Ghareeb and I. Al-Abed. London: Trident Press, 1997, 254–72.

Hopwood, D., ed. *The Arabian Peninsula: Society and Politics*. London: George Allen & Unwin, 1972.

Ismael, J.S. *Kuwait: Dependency and Class in a Rentier State*. Gainesville: Univ. of Florida Press, 1993.

Kelly, J.B. 'The Legal and Historical Basis of the British Position in the Persian Gulf', *St. Antony's Papers*, No. 4: *Middle Eastern Affairs*, Vol. I. London: Chatto & Windus, 1958, 119–40.

——. *Britain and the Persian Gulf, 1795–1880*. Berkeley: Univ. of Berkeley Press, 1967.

——. *Arabia, the Gulf and the West*. London: George Weidenfeld & Nicolson, 1980.

Al-Khalifa, H.I. *First Light: Modern Bahrain and Its Heritage*. London: Kegan Paul International, 1994.

Khuri, F.I. *Tribe and State in Bahrain: The Transformation of Social and Political Authority in an Arab State*. Chicago: Univ. of Chicago Press, 1980.

——. 'From Tribe to State in Bahrain', *Arab Society: Social Science Perspectives*. Edited by S.E. Ibrahim and N.S. Hopkins. Cairo: A.U.C. Press, 1985, 432–47.

——. *Tents and Pyramids: Games and Ideology in Arab Culture from Backgammon to Autocratic Rule*. London: Saqi Books, 1990.

Landen, R.G. 'The Arab Gulf in the Arab World 1800–1918', *Arab Affairs*, Vol. I (Summer 1986), 57–71.

Lawson, F.H. *Bahrain: The Modernization of Autocracy*. Boulder: Westview Press, 1989.

Lienhardt, P. 'The Authority of Shaykhs in the Gulf: An Essay in Nineteenth Century History', *Arabian Studies*, Vol. II. Edited by R.B. Sergeant and R.L. Bidwell. London: C. Hurst & Co., 1975.

——. *The Shaikhdoms of Eastern Arabia*. Edited by A. Al-Shahi. London: Palgrave, 2001.

Moyse-Bartlett, H. *The Pirates of Trucial Oman*. London: Macdonald, 1966.

Al-Muraikhi, K.M. *Glimpses of Bahrain from Its Past*. Bahrain: Ministry of Information, 1991.

——. *Events Enfolded in Time: A Journey into Bahrain's Past*. Bahrain: n.p., 1997.

Al-Naqeeb, K.H. *Society and State in the Gulf and Arabian Peninsula: A Different Perspective*. Translated by L. M. Kenny. Edited by I. Hayani. New York: Routledge, 1990.

Newbury, C. 'Patrons, Clients, and Empire: The Subordination of Indigenous Hierarchies in Asia and Africa', *Journal of World History*, Vol. II, No. 2 (Fall 2000), 227–63.

Niblock, T., ed. *Social and Economic Development in the Arab Gulf*. London: Croom Helm, 1980.

Onley, J.A. 'A Rose by Any Other Name: Bahrain and the Indian States under the Raj, 1880–1947', conference paper presented at MESA 1999, Washington DC.

——. 'Duty Without Dominion? British Influence and Control in Bahrain, 1820–1947', conference paper presented at MESA 2000, Orlando, Florida, 2000.

——. *The Infrastructure of Informal Empire: A Study of Britain's Native Agency in Bahrain, 1816–1900*. Oxford D.Phil. thesis, 2001.

Peterson, J.E. 'Tribes and Politics in Eastern Arabia', *Middle East Journal*, Vol. XXXI (Summer 1977), 297–312.

Pridham, B.R., ed. *The Arab Gulf and the West*. London: Croom Helm, 1985.

Al-Qasimi, S.M. *The Myth of Arab Piracy in the Gulf*. London: Routledge, 1986.

Al-Rasheed, M. *Politics in an Arabian Oasis: The Rashidis of Saudi Arabia*. London: I.B. Tauris, 1991.

——. 'The Rashidi Dynasty: Political Centralization among the Shammar of North Arabia', *New Arabian Studies*, Vol. II. Edited by R.L. Bidwell, J.R. Smart and G.R. Smith. Exeter: Univ. of Exeter Press, 1994, 140–53.

R[isso] Dubuisson, P. 'Qasimi Piracy and the General Treaty of Peace (1820)', *Arabian Studies*, Vol. IV. Edited by R. Sergeant and R. Bidwell. London: C. Hurst & Co., 1978, 47–57.

Risso, P. 'Cross-Cultural Perceptions of Piracy: Maritime Violence in the Western Indian Ocean and Persian Gulf Region during a Long Eighteenth Century', *Journal of World History*, Vol. 12 (Fall 2001), 293–319.

Rosenfeld, H. 'The Social Composition of the Military in the Process of State Formation in the Arabian Desert', Parts I & II, *The Journal of the Royal Anthropological Institute of Great Britain and Ireland*, Vol. 95 (1965), 75–86 and 174–94.

Roberts, D. 'The Consequences of the Exclusive Treaties: A British View', *The Arab Gulf and the West*. Edited by B.R. Pridham. London: Croom Helm, 1985.

Standish, J.F. 'British Maritime Policy in the Persian Gulf', *Middle Eastern Studies*, Vol. III, No. 4 (1967), 324–54.

——. *Persian and the Gulf: Retrospect and Prospect*. London: Curzon, 1998.

Taryam, A.O. *The Establishment of the United Arab Emirates, 1950–85*. London: Croom Helm, 1987.

Tuson, P. *The Records of the British Residency and Agencies in the Persian Gulf. IOR R/15*. London: India Office Records, 1979.

——. 'Introduction', *Records of Qatar*, Vol. 1: *1820–1853*. Slough: Archive Editions, 1991.

——. 'Introduction', *Records of Qatar*, Vol. 2: *1854–1879*. Slough: Archive Editions, 1991.

Vassiliev, A. *The History of Saudi Arabia*. London: Saqi Books, 1998.

Walls, A.G. *Arad Fort, Bahrain*. Manamah: Govt. Press, Ministry of Information, 1987.

Ward, P. *Bahrain: A Travel Guide*. Cambridge: Oleander Press, 1993.

Wheatcroft, A. *Bahrain in Original Photographs, 1880–1961*. London: Kegan Paul, 1988.

Wright, Sir D. *The English Amongst the Persians during the Qajar Period, 1787–1921*. London: Heinemann, 1977.

Zahlan, R.S. *The Creation of Qatar*. London: Croom Helm, 1979.

——. 'Hegemony, Dependence and Development in the Gulf', *Social and Economic Development in the Arab Gulf*. Edited by T. Niblock. London: Croom Helm, 1980.

Notes

1. Confidential FO memorandum respecting British interests in the Persian Gulf, 12 Feb. 1908, 5–6, L/P&S/18/B166, OIOC, London.
2. For more details of this episode in Gulf history, see C. Belgrave, *The Pirate Coast* (London: G. Bell & Sons, 1966); H. Moyse-Bartlett, *The Pirates of Trucial Oman* (London: Macdonald, 1966); S.M. Al-Qasimi, *The Myth of Arab Piracy in the Gulf* (London: Croom Helm, 1986); C.E. Davies, *The Blood-Red Arab Flag: An Investigation into Qasimi Piracy, 1797–1820* (Exeter: Univ. of Exeter Press, 1997); P. R[isso] Dubuisson, 'Qasimi Piracy and the General Treaty of Peace (1820)', *Arabian Studies*, vol. iv (1978), 47–57; and P. Risso, 'Cross-Cultural Perceptions of Piracy: Maritime Violence in the Western Indian Ocean and Persian Gulf Region during a Long Eighteenth Century', *Journal of World History*, vol. 12 (fall 2001), 293–319.
3. For a history of the Gulf Residency, see D. Wright, *The English Amongst the Persians during the Qajar Period, 1787–1921* (London: Heinemann, 1977), 62–93; P. Tuson, *The Records of the British Residency and Agencies in the Persian Gulf. IOR R/15* (London: India Office Records, 1979), 1–9; and G. Balfour-Paul, *The End of Empire in the Middle East: Britain's Relinquishment of Power in Her Last Three Arab Dependencies* (Cambridge: Cambridge Univ. Press, 1991), 96–136.
4. The title SNOPG was used only after 1869. Earlier variants were the 'Senior Indian Marine Officer in the Persian Gulf' (1822–30), the 'Senior Indian Naval Officer in

the Persian Gulf' (1830–63) and the 'Commodore at Bassadore' (1822–63). For the sake of simplicity, SNOPG is used for all four.

5. Sharjah and Ras al-Khaimah became separate Trucial States in 1869, although the British Govt. did not recognize this until 1921. Fujairah did not follow suit until 1901 and 1952 respectively.
6. For analysis of the treaties, see J.B. Kelly, 'The Legal and Historical Basis of the British Position in the Persian Gulf', *St. Antony's Papers*, no. 4: *Middle Eastern Affairs*, vol. i (London: Chatto & Windus, 1958), 119–40; D. Roberts, 'The Consequences of the Exclusive Treaties: A British View', *The Arab Gulf and the West*, edited by B.R. Pridham (London: Croom Helm, 1985), 1–14; H.M. Al-Baharna, 'The Consequences of Britain's Exclusive Treaties: A Gulf View', *The Arab Gulf and the West*, 15–37; and Al-Baharna, *The Legal Status of the Arabian Gulf States: A Study of Their Treaty Relations and Their International Problems* (Manchester: Manchester Univ. Press, 1968).
7. For details, see J. Onley, 'A Rose by Any Other Name: Bahrain and the Indian States under the Raj, 1880–1947' (conference paper presented at MESA 1999, Washington DC) and idem., *The Infrastructure of Informal Empire: A Study of Britain's Native Agency in Bahrain, 1816–1900* (Oxford D.Phil. thesis, 2001).
8. J.G. Lorimer, *Gazetteer of the Persian Gulf, 'Oman, and Central Arabia*, vol. i: Historical (Calcutta: Superintendent of Govt. Printing, 1915), vol. ii: *Geographical and Statistical* (Calcutta: Superintendent of Govt. Printing, 1908) and J.B. Kelly, *Britain and the Persian Gulf, 1795–1880* (Oxford: Oxford Univ. Press, 1968).
9. Kelly, *Britain and the Persian Gulf*, 837.
10. K.H. Al-Naqeeb, *Society and State in the Gulf Arab Peninsula: A Different Perspective* (London: Routledge, 1990), 27, 32, 45–52, 58–9, 62–3, 68, 71–5, 121; J.S. Ismael, *Kuwait: Dependency and Class in a Rentier States* (Gainsville: Univ. of Florida Press, 1993), 38–40, 43, 47–8, 51, 57; A.O. Taryam, *The Establishment of the United Arab Emirates, 1950–85* (London: Croom Helm, 1987); and S.M. Al-Qasimi, *The Myth of Arab Piracy in the Gulf* (London: Routledge, 1986). For an analysis of Arab historical revisionism, see U. Freitag, 'Writing Arab History: The Search for the Nation', *BJMES*, vol. 21 (1994), 19–37 and Y.M. Choueiri, *Modern Arab Historiography: Historical Discourse and the Nation-State* (London: Curzon, 2002).
11. Al-Qasimi, *The Myth*, xiv.
12. Ibid., xiii.
13. Ibid., xv.
14. R.G. Landen, 'The Arab Gulf in the Arab World 1800–1918', *Arab Affairs*, vol. i (summer 1986), 59, 64.
15. Pelly (PRPG) to Gonne (Sec., Bombay For. Dept.), 19 June 1869, L/P&S/9/15, OIOC, London.
16. For more details, see H. Fattah, *The Politics of Regional Trade in Iraq, Arabia, and the Gulf, 1745–1900* (Albany: S.U.N.Y. Press, 1997), 63–90; F. Heard-Bey, *From Trucial States to United Arab Emirates*, 2nd ed. (London: Longman, 1996), 164–97; idem., 'The Tribal Society of the UAE and its Traditional Economy', *Perspectives on the United Arab Emirates*, edited by E. Ghareeb and I. Al-Abed

(London: Trident Press, 1997), 254–72; and P. Lienhardt, *The Shaikhdoms of Eastern Arabia*, edited by A. Al-Shahi (London: Palgrave, 2001), 24–32, 114–64.

17. Doha and Bid' were separate towns in the nineteenth century. During his visit to them in early 1863, William Palgrave noted that Doha was about half the size of Bid'. W.G. Palgrave, *Personal Narrative of a Year's Journey through Central and Eastern Arabia* (London: Macmillan, 1865), 236–7.
18. Trade reports on the Gulf ports in the nineteenth century can be found in the Govt. of India's annual *Reports on the Administration of the Persian Gulf Political Residency and Muscat Political Agency for the Years 1874–1900* (Calcutta: For. Dept. Press, 1875–81; Superintendent of Govt. Printing, 1882–1900) and Saldanha's *Précis of Commerce and Communications in the Persian Gulf, 1801–1905* (Calcutta: Superintendent of Govt. Printing, 1906). For an assessment of Bahrain's economy, see Lorimer, *Gazetteer*, vol. ii, 233–53 and A.M. Abu Hakima, *History of Eastern Arabia, 1750–1800: The Rise and Development of Bahrain and Kuwait* (Beirut: Khayats, 1965), 165–80.
19. Govt. of India, *Report on the Administration of the Bushire Residency, 1873–74* (Calcutta: For. Dept. Press, 1874), 10, 15.
20. Saldanha, *Précis of Commerce*, 170, 173, 176, 179, 182, 184.
21. Or MTD 1,466,515. British trade reports on Muscat were always listed in Maria Theresa Dollars.
22. Or MTD 751,400.
23. The table identifies the Trucial States as the 'Arab Coast'.
24. Saldanha, *Précis of Commerce*, 170, 176, 182.
25. See, for example, Maj. D. Wilson, 'Memorandum Respecting the Pearl Fisheries in the Persian Gulf', *JRGS*, vol. iii (1833), 283–6; Capt. E.L. Durand, 'Notes on the Pearl Fisheries of the Persian Gulf', Govt. of India, *Report on the Administration of the Persian Gulf Political Agency for the Year 1877–78* (Calcutta: For. Dept. Press, 1878), appendix a, 27–41; and Kelly, *Britain and the Persian Gulf*, 29–30.
26. Govt. of India, *Report on the Administration of the Bushire Residency for 1873–74*, 15 and Lorimer, *Gazetteer*, vol. ii, 246.
27. Lorimer, *Gazetteer*, vol. ii, 238, 243 and R.S. Zahlan, 'Hegemony, Dependence and Development in the Gulf', *Social and Economic Development in the Arab Gulf*, edited by T. Niblock (London: Croom Helm, 1980), 63.
28. S.B. Miles, *The Countries and Tribes of the Persian Gulf* (London: Harrison & Sons, 1919), 291; Fattah, *The Politics of Regional Trade*, 5–6, 31, 36–8, 47–9, 60, 126; F.I. Khuri, *Tribe and State in Bahrain: The Transformation of Social and Political Authority in an Arab State* (Chicago: Univ. of Chicago Press, 1980), 19–20; M. Al-Rasheed, *Politics in an Arabian Oasis: The Rashidis of Saudi Arabia* (London: I.B. Tauris, 1990), 111–17; Al-Naqeeb, *Society and State in the Gulf Arab Peninsula*, 11, 13–16; Davies, *The Blood-Red Arab Flag*, 263; and Abu Hakima, *History of Eastern Arabia*, 170 (n. 1).
29. The British referred to the Ruler of Muscat as the 'Imam of Muscat' (often spelt 'Imaum') until the mid-nineteenth century and as the 'Sultan of Muscat' thereafter. The Ruler himself used the title of Imam until 1786, after which he used the title of Sayyid (Lord). The British Government first referred to the Ruler as the 'Sultan

of Muscat' in the Anglo-Muscati Treaty of 1839. For more details, see Kelly, *Britain and the Persian Gulf*, 11–12.

30. Fattah, *The Politics of Regional Trade*, 48–51, 54 and Al-Rasheed, *Politics in an Arabian Oasis*, 95–132.
31. Davies, *The Blood-Red Arab Flag*, 263–4 and Heard-Bey, *From Trucial States to United Arab Emirates*, 228–9. Patricia Risso prefers to describe *ġazū* as 'piracy'. P. R[isso] Dubuisson, 'Qasimi Piracy and the General Treaty of Peace (1820)', 47.
32. H. Rosenfeld, 'The Social Composition of the Military in the Process of State Formation in the Arabian Desert', part ii, *JRAI*, vol. 95 (1965), 184 and H.R.P. Dickson, *The Arab of the Desert: A Glimpse into Badawin Life in Kuwait and Sa'udi Arabia* (London: George Allen & Unwin, 1949), 440–1, 443–4.
33. P. Lienhardt, 'The Authority of Shaykhs in the Gulf: An Essay in Nineteenth Century History', *Arabian Studies*, vol. ii (1975), 64–5; idem., *Shaikhdoms of Eastern Arabia*, 19–20, 222–3; and Crystal, *Oil and Politics in the Gulf, Rulers and Merchants in Kuwait and Qatar*, rev. ed. (Cambridge: Cambridge Univ. Press, 1995), 4, 21, 24–5.
34. Abu Hakima, *History of Eastern Arabia*, 35, 181 and Lienhardt, *Shaikhdoms of Eastern Arabia*, 21, 186, 200–1.
35. Lt. A.B. Kemball, 'Memoranda on the Resources, Localities and Relations of the Tribes Inhabiting the Arabian Shores of the Persian Gulf' (1845), *Selections from the Records of the Bombay Government*, no. xxiv, new series (Bombay: Bombay Education Society Press, 1856), 94.
36. Ibid. and Khuri, *Tribe and State in Bahrain*, 66–7, 97.
37. C.U. Aitchison, *A Collection of Treaties, Engagements and Sanads Relating to India and Neighbouring Countries*, vol. xi: *The Treaties, &c., Relating to Aden and the South Western Coast of Arabia, the Arab Principalities in the Persian Gulf, Muscat (Oman), Baluchistan and the North-West Frontier Province* (Delhi: Manager of Publications, 1933), 193 and R.S. Zahlan, *The Creation of Qatar* (London: Croom Helm, 1979), 42–3.
38. Al-Rasheed, *Politics in an Arabian Oasis*, 114.
39. Rosenfeld, 'The Social Composition of the Military', part i, 79.
40. Lienhardt, *The Shaikhdoms of Eastern Arabia*, 15.
41. For a discussion of the military in nineteenth century Arabia, see Rosenfeld, 'The Social Composition of the Military', parts i and ii, 75–86, 174–94; Al-Rasheed, *Politics in an Arabian Oasis*, 133–58; and Crystal, *Oil and Politics in the Gulf*, 60.
42. Lorimer, *Gazetteer*, vol. ii, 252.
43. Ibid., 1010–14 and H.M. Govt., *A Handbook of Arabia* (London: Intelligence Div., 1916), 84–5, 608.
44. Capt. G.B. Brucks, 'Memoir Descriptive of the Navigation of the Gulf of Persia', part 1 (1829), *Selections from the Records of the Bombay Government*, no. xxiv, 566.
45. Rosenfeld, 'Social Composition of the Military', part ii, 178.
46. There has been extensive work on alliance-seeking in Arabia. See Al-Rasheed, *Politics in an Arabian Oasis*; F.F. Anscombe, *The Ottoman Gulf: The Creation of Kuwait, Saudi Arabia, and Qatar* (New York: Columbia Univ. Press, 1997); Alghanim, *The Reign of Mubarak Al-Sabah: Shaikh of Kuwait, 1896–1915*

(London: I.B. Taurus, 1998) and F.I. Khuri, *Tents and Pyramids: Games and Ideology in Arab Culture from Backgammon to Autocratic Rule* (London: Saqi Books, 1990), 114–17.

47. For a discussion of the subsidy system, see Al-Rasheed, *Politics in an Arabian Oasis*, 81–2, 116.
48. Lorimer, *Gazetteer*, vol. ii, 252.
49. Landen, 'The Arab Gulf in the Arab World 1800–1918', 59 and Al-Rasheed,'The Rashidi Dynasty: Political Centralization among the Shammar of North Arabia', *New Arabian Studies*, vol. ii (1994), 152 (n. 20).
50. For a discussion of the first two conditions, see Lienhardt, *The Shaikhdoms of Eastern Arabia*, 184–6, 212–14.
51. H.R.P. Dickson, *The Arab of the Desert: A Glimpse into Badawin Life in Kuwait and Sa'udi Arabia* (London: George Allen & Unwin, 1949), 52–53, 118, 120–21.
52. P.W. Harrison, *The Arab at Home* (New York: Thomas Y. Cromwell & Co., 1924), 126. Also see 139–45.
53. Dickson, *The Arab of the Desert*, 52.
54. Ibid., 53 and Lienhardt, 'The Authority of Shaykhs in the Gulf', 68.
55. Dickson, *The Arab of the Desert*, 53.
56. Ibid., 441.
57. Dickson, *The Arab of the Desert*, 53.
58. For more details, see Lienhardt, *The Shaikhdoms of Eastern Arabia*, 197–9, 206.
59. Al-Rasheed, *Politics in an Arabian Oasis*, 93.
60. Harrison, *The Arab at Home*, 150.
61. Dickson, *The Arab of the Desert*, 53.
62. Al-Rasheed, *Politics in an Arabian Oasis*, 115 and Lienhardt, *The Shaikhdoms of Eastern Arabia*, 31, 229.
63. Dickson, *The Arab of the Desert*, 118.
64. P. Dresch, Tribes, *Government and History in Yemen* (Oxford: Oxford Univ. Press, 1989), 59–61, 63–4, 122–3, 373.
65. Al-Rasheed, *Politics in an Arabian Oasis*, 115.
66. Dickson, *The Arab of the Desert*, 53.
67. Al-Rasheed, *Politics in an Arabian Oasis*, 116.
68. Ibid., 115–16; Lienhardt, *The Shaikhdoms of Eastern Arabia*, 118, 188, 200; C. Belgrave, *Personal Column* (London: Hutchinson, 1960), 37; and T. Farah, *Protection and Politics in Bahrain, 1869–1915* (Lebanon: American Univ. of Beirut, 1985), 14.
69. Al-Rasheed, *Politics in an Arabian Oasis*, 81–82 and Al-Rasheed, 'The Rashidi Dynasty', 146.
70. Kemball, 'Memoranda on … the Tribes …' (1845), 94.
71. This is the earliest estimate available. Capt. F.B. Prideaux (PA, Bahrain) to Maj. P.Z. Cox (PRPG), 24 June 1905, L/P&S/10/81, register no. 1508/1905, OIOC, London. This is reproduced in Lorimer, *Gazetteer*, vol. ii, 251.
72. Ross to Sec., Indian For. Dept., 3 Nov. 1877, Saldanha, *Précis of Bahrein Affairs, 1854–1904* (Calcutta: Superintendent of Govt. Printing, 1904), 50.
73. Saldanha, *Précis of Bahrein Affairs*, 49.
74. Lienhardt, *The Shaikhdoms of Eastern Arabia*, 209–10; Khuri, *Tribe and State in*

Bahrain, 51–2; idem., 'From Tribe to State in Bahrain', *Arab Society: Social Science Perspectives*, edited by S.E. Ibrahim and N.S. Hopkins (Cairo: A.U.C. Press, 1985), 435.
75. Idem., 'The Authority of Shaykhs in the Gulf', 69 and Khuri, *Tribe and State in Bahrain*, 435.
76. Lienhardt, 'The Authority of Shaykhs in the Gulf', 69.
77. Ibid., 68. Lienhardt was summarizing the ideas of 'Abd al-'Aziz Al-Rashid in *Ta'rīẖ al-kuwayt* [History of Kuwait] (Cairo, 1926).
78. Lienhardt, *The Shaikhdoms of Eastern Arabia*, 19–21.
79. Idem., 'The Authority of Shaykhs in the Gulf', 63–5, 72–3 and idem., *The Shaikhdoms of Eastern Arabia*, 19–23.
80. Rosenfeld, 'Social Composition of the Military', part i, 78–9 and Landen, 'The Arab Gulf in the Arab World 1800–1918', 59.
81. Rosenfeld, 'Social Composition of the Military', part i, 76.
82. Harrison, *The Arab at Home*, 125.
83. For examples of customary tribute payments, see Dickson, *The Arab of the Desert*, 443–44 and Al-Rasheed, *Politics in an Arabian Oasis*, 113–14.
84. For more information on *zakāt*, see Dickson, *The Arab of the Desert*, 440–1 and Heard-Bey, *From Trucial States to United Arab Emirates*, 161.
85. Khuri, *Tribe and State in Bahrain*, 20.
86. Al-Rasheed, *Politics in an Arabian Oasis*, 115. Al-Rasheed discusses *ẖūwah* at length on 111–17.
87. Harrison, *The Arab at Home*, 156.
88. Rosenfeld, 'Social Composition of the Military', part i, 79.
89. Al-Rasheed, *Politics in an Arabian Oasis*, 116–17.
90. Rosenfeld, 'Social Composition of the Military', part i, 85 (n. 3).
91. Ibid., 79.
92. Unless otherwise indicated, the following account is based on Govt. of Bombay, *Selections from the Records of the Bombay Government*, no. xxiv (1856), 91–119, 140–52, 361–425; Saldanha, *Précis of Bahrein Affairs* (1904), 1–36, 152; Lorimer, *Gazetteer*, vol. i, 169–277, 841–8, 851–9, 879–80; Miles, *The Countries and Tribes of the Persian Gulf*, 291–7, 318, 322, 329; and Kelly, *Britain and the Persian Gulf*, 103–4, 121–2, 126, 221–2, 229–30, 303–5.
93. These are the dependent tribes the Resident identified in 1869 (reprinted in Aitchison's *Treaties*), with the exception of the 'Ağmān, Āl Bin 'Alī, Kibīsah, Manāna'ah and Sādah, whom the British had identified in previous years. This list is based on a compilation from: Aitchison, *Treaties*, vol. xi, 193; Brucks, 'Memoir Descriptive', part 1 (1829), 559–63; Kemball, 'Memoranda on … the Tribes …' (1845), 104–8; Kemball, 'Historical Sketch of the Uttoobee Tribe of Arabs (Bahrein) from the Year 1832 to 1844' (1844), *Selections from the Records of the Bombay Government*, no. xxiv, 390; Lorimer, *Gazetteer*, vol. i, 840 and vol. ii, 754, 1530–5; and Zahlan, *The Creation of Qatar*, 18–19, 33–4, 36–7, 39, 41–3.
94. **?** indicates the known location of a tribe at the time of Lorimer's investigations during 1904–07. This may or may not have been the tribe's location at the time of Āl Khalifah's overlordship of eastern and northern Qatar (c.1766–1871). See Lorimer's footnote comments on this: Gazetteer, vol. ii, 1505 (n. *).

95. There is some confusion over the precise dates of the two Muscati attacks on, and occupation of, Bahrain between 1799 and 1801. See Kelly, *Britain and the Persian Gulf*, 104 (n. 1).
96. Davies, *The Blood-Red Arab Flag*, 327.
97. Alexei Vassiliev incorrectly identifies the force as British. Vassiliev, *The History of Saudi Arabia* (London: Saqi Books, 1998), 108. In marked contrast to the sources above, Charles Davies argues that it was the *wakīl*'s brother, Fahd bin Sulaymān bin 'Ufayṣān, who was captured. Davies, *The Blood-Red Arab Flag*, 327.
98. Davies, 327.
99. Kemball, 'Historical Sketch … 1832 to 1844' (1844), 414.
100. Ibid., 415.
101. Lorimer misprints $4,000 as 84,000. *Gazetteer*, vol. i, 880. For the correct amount, see Lt. H.F. Disbrowe, 'Historical Sketch of the Uttoobee Tribe of Arabs (Bahrein), 1844–1853' (1853), *Selections from the Records of the Bombay Government*, no. xxiv, 416.
102. Kelly, *Britain and the Persian Gulf*, 384–5.
103. Comdr. Porter (SNOPG) to Hennell, 21 July 1851, L/P&S/5/471, 6, OIOC, London.
104. Hennell to Malet, 9 Aug. 1851, L/P&S/5/471, 28–9, OIOC, London.
105. Disbrowe, 'Historical Sketch … 1844 to 1853' (1853), 423 and Kelly, *Britain and the Persian Gulf*, 399–402.
106. Disbrowe, 'Historical Sketch … 1844 to 1853' (1853), 424.
107. Kelly, *Britain and the Persian Gulf*, 501–10.
108. Ibid., 512–14, 523, 528.
109. Ibid., 514.
110. Ibid., 515–16, 518.
111. Ibid., 514, 524.
112. Jasim to Jones, 23 May 1861, L/P&S/9/162, OIOC, London.
113. Jones to Muḥammad bin Khalifah, 18 May 1861, L/P&S/9/162, OIOC, London.
114. 'Purport of two conversations held between Capt. Jones and Ali ben Khaleefa', 21 & 23 May 1861, L/P&S/9/162, OIOC, London.
115. Jones to Comdr. Drought, 26 May 1861, L/P&S/9/162, OIOC, London.
116. Jones to Muḥammad bin Khalifah, 28 May 1861, L/P&S/9/162, OIOC, London.
117. Marginal note, ibid.
118. Jones to Chief Sec., Bombay Govt., 1 June 1861, L/P&S/9/162, OIOC, London.
119. Ibid. and Kelly, *Britain and the Persian Gulf*, 525–7.
120. Muḥammad bin Khalifah to Jones, 31 May 1861 and Jones to Chief Sec., Bombay Govt., 1 June 1861, L/P&S/9/162, OIOC, London.
121. Kelly, *Britain and the Persian Gulf*, 525–7.
122. Henvey (offg. Under-Sec., Indian For. Dept.) to Ross (PRPG), 10 Dec. 1874, qtd. in Kelly, *Britain and the Persian Gulf*, 761.
123. Pelly to Muḥammad bin Khalifah, 2 Sept. 1868, enclosed in Gonne (Sec., Bombay Pol. Dept.) to Seton-Karr (Sec., Indian For. Dept.), 9 Oct. 1868, L/P&S/5/261, OIOC, London.
124. Pelly to Gonne, 25 Sept. 1868, L/P&S/5/261, 2, OIOC, London.
125. Ibid., 3.

126. Ibid. and Agreement of 6 Sept. 1868 (signed 9 Sept.), Aitchinson, *Treaties*, vol. xi, 193, 236–7. Kelly asserts, incorrectly, that it was Pelly who deposed the Ruler. *Britain and the Persian Gulf*, 674.
127. Pelly to Gonne (Sec., Bombay Pol. Dept.), 25 Sept. 1868, L/P&S/5/261, 4, OIOC, London.
128. Ibid.
129. Pelly to Sec., Bombay Pol. Dept., 12 Apr. 1869, L/P&S/9/15, 127–8, OIOC, London; Lorimer, *Gazetteer*, vol. i, 895; and Kelly, *Britain and the Persian Gulf*, 675, 732. For more details of the events of 1867–68, see Saldanha, *Précis of Bahrein Affairs*, 13–18; Kelly, *Britain and the Persian Gulf*, 672–6; and Zahlan, *The Creation of Qatar*, 41–2, 44–5 (n. 9–13).
130. Kelly, *Britain and the Persian Gulf*, 730, 738; Zahlan, *The Creation of Qatar*, 46; P. Tuson, 'Introduction', *Records of Qatar*, vol. 2: *1854–1879* (Slough: Archive Editions, 1991), xi; and F.F. Anscombe, *The Ottoman Gulf*, 32–3, 190 (n. 74).
131. Saldanha, *Précis of Bahrein Affairs*, 35.
132. Talal Farah has done an extensive analysis of this British policy towards Zubarah and the Na'īm. Farah, *Protection and Politics in Bahrain*, 37–68. Also see Saldanha, *Précis of Bahrein Affairs*, 13–18, 35–37; idem., *Précis of Katar Affairs, 1873–1904* (Calcutta: Superintendent of Govt. Printing, 1904), 1–10; Lorimer, *Gazetteer*, vol. i, 906; Kelly, *Britain and the Persian Gulf*, 761–2, 789–91, 795, 798, 842–51; and Zahlan, *The Creation of Qatar*, 47–50.
133. Kelly, *Britain and the Persian Gulf*, 761.
134. Belgrave, *Personal Column*, 152–9 and Zahlan, *The Creation of Qatar*, 85–90.
135. P. Dresch, *Tribes, Government and History in Yemen* (Oxford: Oxford Univ. Press, 1989).
136. Dickson, *The Arab of the Desert*, 133–5, 349–50, 440–1, 443–4.
137. Dresch, *Tribes*, 258.
138. Dresch refers to the protégé as *al-ǧār*, but *al-daẖīl* was more common in Eastern Arabia.
139. Dresch, *Tribes*, 59. *waǧh* literally means 'face' and *fī waǧhihi* means 'in his face'.
140. Ibid., 59–60.
141. Ibid., 60–1.
142. Dickson, *The Arab of the Desert*, 133–4 and H. Wehr, *A Dictionary of Modern Written Arabic*, 3rd ed. (Ithaca, N.Y.: Spoken Language Services, 1976), 273.
143. Dickson, *The Arab of the Desert*, 133–4.
144. Dresch, *Tribes*, 59, 62, 64.
145. Dickson, *The Arab of the Desert*, 135.
146. Dresch, *Tribes*, 60–1.
147. Lienhardt, 'The Authority of Shaykhs in the Gulf', 73.
148. Dresch, *Tribes*, 64.
149. Dickson, *The Arab of the Desert*, 440–1, 443–4.
150. Dickson, *The Arab of the Desert*, 125.
151. Harrison, *The Arab at Home*, 126.
152. Heard-Bey, *From Trucial States to United Arab Emirates*, 101–2.
153. I am indebted to Frauke Heard-Bey of the Centre for Documentation and Research, Abu Dhabi for this information.

154. Heard-Bey, *From Trucial States to United Arab Emirates*, 81.
155. Ibid., 81–2.
156. Abu Hakima, *History of Eastern Arabia*, 65–76, 88–9, 108–17, 181; History of 'Utub tribe, enclosed in Jasim to Ross (PRPG), 11 Sept. 1873, R/15/1/192, OIOC, London; Khuri, *Tribe and State in Bahrain*, 24; and H.I. Al-Khalifa, *First Light: Modern Bahrain and Its Heritage* (London: Kegan Paul International, 1994), 37, 41–3.
157. Abu Hakima, *History of Eastern Arabia*, 117; Khuri, *Tribe and State in Bahrain*, 25; P. Ward, *Bahrain: A Travel Guide* (Cambridge: Oleander Press, 1993), 9; Al-Khalifa, *First Light*, 54 and correspondence with 'Ali Akbar Bushiri, 8 Sept. 2001, Bahrain.
158. For a history and description of Dīwān Fort, see Belgrave, *Personal Column*, 34. For images, see Belgrave, 33; Gulf Panorama, *Old Days* (Manamah: Oriental Press, 1986), 43; K.M. Al-Muraikhi, *Events Enfolded in Time: A Journey into Bahrain's Past* (Bahrain: n.p., 1997), 130, 189; and A. Wheatcroft, *Bahrain in Original Photographs, 1880–1961* (London: Kegan Paul, 1988), 67.
159. Al-Khalifa, *First Light*, 54 and correspondence with 'Ali Akbar Bushiri, 8 Sept. 2001, Bahrain.
160. Abu Hakima, *History of Eastern Arabia*, 117; Khuri, *Tribe and State in Bahrain*, 25; Ward, *Bahrain*, 9; and correspondence with 'Ali Akbar Bushiri, 8 Sept. 2001, Bahrain.
161. Abu Hakima, *History of Eastern Arabia*, 117; Kelly, *Britain and the Persian Gulf*, 28–9; Khuri, *Tribe and State in Bahrain*, 26; F.H. Lawson, *Bahrain: The Modernization of Autocracy* (Boulder: Westview Press, 1989), 30; and correspondence with 'Ali Akbar Bushiri, 8 Sept. 2001, Bahrain.
162. Ahmad Abu Hakima is the only historian who believes Salmān ruled alone before the 1810s. *History of Eastern Arabia*, 197.
163. Khuri, *Tribe and State in Bahrain*, 26; Lawson, *Bahrain*, 30; and correspondence with 'Ali Akbar Bushiri, 8 Sept. 2001, Bahrain.
164. For history and detailed study of 'Arād Fort, see A.G. Walls, *Arad Fort, Bahrain* (Bahrain: Ministry of Info., 1987).
165. Lorimer, *Gazetteer*, vol. i, 850 and Belgrave, *The Pirate Coast*, 75.
166. Ibid. and Ward, *Bahrain*, 195. Abu Hakima and Kelly say Salmān moved to Rifā' in 1796, while Khuri says 1800.
167. Lorimer, *Gazetteer*, vol. i, 844, 850.
168. For an analysis of Abū Māhir Fort's strategic positioning, see Walls, *Arad Fort*, 35, 41–3 and Brucks, 'Memoir Descriptive', part 1 (1829), 568. For a history see K.M. Al-Muraikhi, *Glimpses of Bahrain from Its Past* (Bahrain: Ministry of Information, 1997), 262. For images, see Lewis (PRPG) to Bombay Govt., 25 Sept. 1868, appendix 4, W/L/P&S/5/15, OIOC and Ward, *Bahrain*, 114.
169. For histories and images of Qaṣr Khalifah, Qaṣr Rifā' and Bayt 'Īsā, see Govt. of Bahrain, *Al-baḥrayn: haḍārah wa-ta'rīḫ* (Bahrain: Ministry of Cabinet Affairs and Info., 1997), 238–9, 303 and Ward, *Bahrain*, 92–7, 196.
170. Brucks, 'Memoir Descriptive', part 1 (1829), 568.
171. Khuri, *Tribe and State in Bahrain*, 43–4.
172. Ibid., 43, 51–2.

173. Brucks, 'Memoir Descriptive', part 1 (1829), 566 and Lorimer, *Gazetteer*, vol. i: 238.
174. The *Hawalah* are Sunni Arabs from southern Persia who link themselves genealogically to one of the tribes of Arabia. Many could be described as 'Persianized Arabs' in the nineteenth century. Lorimer, *Gazetteer*, vol. i: 754–55 and Khuri, *Tribe and State in Bahrain*, 2, 4.
175. For a detailed census from 1905, see Lorimer, *Gazetteer*, vol. ii, 237–41.
176. Lorimer, *Gazetteer*, vol. ii, 248; Khuri, *Tribe and State in Bahrain*, 44–53; and Farah, *Protection and Politics in Bahrain*, 10, 45.
177. Lorimer, *Gazetteer*, vol. i, 850.
178. See the Gulf Residency's few surviving files of Arabic correspondence. These cover the years 1856–72 and can be found in R/15/1/180–182, OIOC. Also see Lienhardt, *Shaikhdoms of Eastern Arabia*, 185 and H.A. Qafisheh, *NTC's Gulf Arabic–English Dictionary* (Chicago: NTC Publishing Group, 1997), 17, 153.
179. Qafisheh, *Gulf Arabic–English Dictionary*, 17.
180. Lorimer, *Gazetteer*, vol. i, 842–946.
181. The Āl Ṣabāḥ were ancient allies of the Āl Khalifah. These dates indicate those times when the Āl Ṣabāḥ came, or were asked to come, to the military assistance of the Āl Khalifah.
182. The Āl Ǧalāhimah were also ancient allies, but fell out with the Āl Khalifah in 1783. These dates indicate those times when the Āl Ǧalāhimah came to the military assistance of the Āl Khalifah.
183. Lorimer, *Gazetteer*, vol. i, 842–946.
184. My thanks to Yoav Alon of St. Antony's College, Oxford for this insight.
185. J.E. Peterson, 'Tribes and Politics in Eastern Arabia', *MEJ*, vol. xxi (1977), 302.
186. Lienhardt, *Shaikhdoms of Eastern Arabia*, 15.
187. Lorimer, *Gazetteer*, vol. i, 863–5.
188. Ibid., 865.
189. Ibid., 866.
190. Ibid.
191. Ibid., 866–7.
192. Dr T. MacKenzie (acting Asst. PRPG) to Secret Committee, Court of Directors, London, 18 Sept. 1840, L/P&S/9/116, 223, OIOC, London.
193. Lorimer, *Gazetteer*, vol. i, 867.
194. Ibid., 868.
195. The Āl Ǧalāhimah were a former ally of the Āl Khalifah and the Āl Bin 'Alī a former dependant. They broke with Āl Khalifah in 1783 and 1835 respectively. Shaikh Bašīr was the son of Shaikh Raḥmah, the Ruler of the Āl Ǧalāhimah who waged war against the Āl Khalifah from 1783 until his death in 1826.
196. Lorimer, *Gazetteer*, vol. i, 868.
197. Kemball, 'Historical Sketch … 1832 to 1844' (1844), 396.
198. Lorimer, *Gazetteer*, vol. i, 869.
199. Kemball, 'Historical Sketch … 1832 to 1844' (1844), 397, 397–8 (n. *).
200. Lorimer, *Gazetteer*, vol. i, 870.
201. Ibid., 872–3.
202. Kemball, 'Historical Sketch … 1832 to 1844' (1844), 405–6.

203. Ibid., 402 and Lorimer, *Gazetteer*, vol. i, 873.
204. Lorimer, *Gazetteer*, vol. i, 873.
205. Ibid., 874.
206. Kelly, *Britain and the Persian Gulf*, 202.
207. Lorimer, *Gazetteer*, vol. i, 874.
208. For details of his argument, see Lt. Kemball's own account of the incident in 'Historical Sketch … 1832 to 1844' (1844), 397–8 (n. *).
209. Lorimer, *Gazetteer*, vol. i, 874.
210. Ibid., 876.
211. Ibid., 877, 879–80.
212. Ibid., 877.
213. Ibid., 878.
214. Ibid., 878–9.
215. Kelly, *Britain and the Persian Gulf*, 167–192.
216. Paraphrase of Morrison (PRPG) to Sulṭān al-Qāsimī, Sept. 1836, qtd. in Kemball, 'Observations on the Past Policy of the British Government towards the Arab Tribes of the Persian Gulf' (1844), *Selections from the Records of the Bombay Government*, no. xxiv, 69.
217. Kemball, 'Observations on the Past Policy' (1844), 62–3, 68, 73.
218. Ibid., 68.
219. Ibid., 68 (n. *).
220. Ibid., 69.
221. Ibid.
222. Hennell (Asst. PRPG) to Sec., Bombay Pol. Dept., 19 Apr. 1830, qtd. in Kemball, 70 (n. *).
223. Ibid.
224. Kemball, 'Observations on the Past Policy' (1844), 69–70.
225. Ibid., 70.
226. Ibid., 74.
227. Kelly, *Britain and the Persian Gulf*, 369.
228. For details of this policy and the motives behind it, see Kemball, 'Observations on the Past Policy' (1844), 69 (n. *).
229. Kemball, 'Historical Sketch … 1832 to 1844' (1844), 288–89 and Disbrowe, 'Historical Sketch … from 1844 to 1853' (1853), 417, 420.
230. Saldanha, *Précis of Bahrein Affairs*, 10–11.
231. Ibid., 67–8.
232. Paraphrase of a report by Col. Ross (PRPG), July 1874, Saldanha, *Précis of Bahrein Affairs*, 41.
233. D. Hawley, *Desert Wind and Tropic Storm: An Autobiography* (Wilby: Michael Russell, 2000), 44.
234. My thanks to Frauke Heard-Bey of the Centre for Documentation and Research, Abu Dhabi for this insight.
235. J.B. Kelly, *Arabia, the Gulf and the West* (London: George Weidenfeld & Nicolson, 1980), 49–50.

Indecisive Reactions to the Portuguese by Mamluk and Ottoman Turk

An annotated translation of extracts from al-Nahrawālī *al-Barq al-Yamānī**

Clive Smith

Al-Nahrawālī was well placed to write of these and later Turkish campaigns in the Yemen. Brought to Mecca at an early age by his father from Gujerat, he had studied under the Yemeni historian Ibn al-Dayba‘, and had a cousin in legal service in the Yemen. He had furthered his education in Cairo and, with fluent Turkish, he had visited Istanbul twice. His Gujerati family and connections would have added to the broad perspective these experiences would have given him.

As *muftī*, *qāḍī*, teacher and *ḥadīth* scholar, he had clearly cultivated good relations with the sharifs of Mecca and with senior Ottoman officials; and, by the time this history was complete in 981/1573, he had become the most sought-after guide for Ottoman visitors, many of whom came with fresh experience of the Yemen, most notably, of course, the minister, Sinān Pasha, who had asked him to write an account of his successful campaign there in 977–79/1569–71, to which these and other early chapters are introductory.

Al-Nahrawālī's account of the brutal campaigns that follow is relieved by his father's and his own personal reminiscence in Egypt and Mecca. The latter extract of his work is especially valuable as one of the few surviving early

* In translating these chapters I am deeply indebted to two Arab scholars, Professor Osman Sid Ahmed Ismail al-Billi of Sudan and Mr Mohamed Nasir al-Mahruqi of Oman. I am also indebted to Winifred Rennie for translating extracts from one of Corsali's letters in Ramusio's *Navigationi et Viaggi* (see n. 10 and passim below).

accounts, little distorted by the prejudice in favour of Ottoman Turk and Meccan sharif which is obvious in the later part of his work and which, to a great extent, must have been dictated by the circumstances under which he lived and wrote.

These two extracts introduce the Portuguese menace to the Muslim world in the Indian Ocean and the Red Sea and charter efforts by the Mamluks and the Ottomans to resist the Portuguese presence, which were continually frustrated by campaigns to seize the Yemen, often for opportunistic motives on the part of the successive leaders concerned.

In the first extract the author covers the five years beginning 917/1511–12, as the veteran leader of the unsuccessful earlier Mamluk expedition, Ḥusayn al-Kurdī, returns from India and is appointed governor of Jeddah after beginning reconstruction work to the Jeddah walls. The extract finishes with the conquest of Cairo by the Ottomans in Muḥarram 923/January 1517 as the Mamluks are leading a concerted campaign against the Tahirid state in the Yemen which has already led to the seizure of Zabīd but has failed to wrest Aden from the last determined Tahirid ruler.

Although the author has been widely criticized for misrepresenting the sequence of events, it is possible to argue that his account is based on historical truth: indeed once one accepts that he was in no way attempting to describe Ḥusayn al-Kurdī's first expedition in 913–15/1507–9, the continuing thread of his link with Muẓaffar Shah's sultanate of Gujerat becomes clear, through the probable request for help before he returned to Jeddah (n. 6 below); the call on the sultan in Cairo with Muẓaffar's envoy (n. 6); the message for Muẓaffar sent from Aden, whatever the exact circumstances (n. 29); and, of course, the later visit to Diu (n. 14).

The second extract covers the years 930–36/1524–30 and highlights Salmān Rayyis' activities after the Ottomans had established control of Jeddah. We see him with the new governor of Jeddah, Ḥusayn al-Turkī, in another campaign in the Yemen: we see him in charge of a new Ottoman fleet, again in the Yemen, but in circumstances where policy at first seems clearer until hubris leads him to seize control in Zabīd and then to be murdered off the Yemeni coast at the hands of his co-commander, Ḫayr al-Dīn when it is left to his nephew, Muṣṭafā Bayram, to avenge his uncle and sail to India to offer his services to the Gujerati state.

Salmān Rayyis had originally been sent by the Ottoman sultan with a party of *levend*[1] to help the Mamluk expedition against the Portuguese. After the fall of Cairo, he had been clever in establishing relations with the Ottoman government at the highest level which appears to have backed his judgement that it was necessary to subdue the Yemen before proceeding against the Portuguese. However, his calamitous exploitation of the situation there was to abort any such action by the fleet over which he had been put in charge.

The author's account of the brutal campaigns is relieved by his father's and his own personal reminiscence in Egypt and Mecca. The latter extract from his work is especially valuable as one of the few surviving contemporary accounts, little distorted by his prejudice in favour of Ottoman Turk and Meccan sharif!

[18] Part 1

Chapter 2

Concerning the transfer of power in Yemen from the Banū Ṭāhir to Commander Ḥusayn, the Circassian

Among the rare calamities that took place at the beginning of the tenth century was the entry to the land of India of the cursed Portuguese, one of the nations of the detested Franks. A group of them had taken to sea from the Straits of Sabtah, set out for the Atlantic [lit. the Sea of Darkness] and passed a spot near to Jibāl al-Qumr [the Mountains of the Whites], that is 'white' which is the substance of the river Nile. They had reached the east and passed by a place near the coast, in a strait [the Cape of Good Hope] one side of which was a mountain and the other the Atlantic Ocean, where there were many waves which their ships could not ride and were shattered. And none of them was saved; and they continued like that for a time, perishing in that place, without any of the group reaching Indian waters; until one of their grabs reached India.[2]

They had continued their efforts to gain an understanding of this ocean until a skilful sailor called Aḥmad Ibn Mājid[3] showed them. [19] The Portuguese captain called Almilandī [i.e. Almirante] had befriended him and used to drink with him; and he [the pilot], in his cups, let him know the way and said to him, 'Don't approach the coast from here but advance deep into the ocean and then turn [to the coast of India]. The waves won't take you.' When they did this many of their ships were spared. So they grew in number in the Indian Ocean and they built in Goa in the Deccan a stronghold called Kūtā.[4] They took Hurmūz where they became powerful and supplies began to build up from Portugal. Then they began to waylay Muslims for prisoners and plunder and to take each ship by force until the damage they did to Muslims increased and the trouble they caused travellers spread.[5]

So Sultan Muẓaffar Šāh,[6] son of Maḥmūd Šāh, son of Muḥammad Šāh, son of Ahmad Šāh, sultan of Gujerat at that time, wrote to Sultan al-Ašraf Qanṣawh al-Ǧawrī[7] seeking help from him against the Franks and asking for armament, weapons and guns to defend the Muslims against injury by the Franks. Indeed the Indians at that time had no knowledge of guns, cannon and muskets. Among those who wrote for help from Sultan al-Ǧawrī against the Franks was Sultan 'Āmir b. 'Abd al-Wahhāb[8] because of the large amount of damage suffered by

Plate 1. Reception in Cairo by Qanṣawh al Ḡawri, the Mamluk sultan, of a Venetian embassy led by Domenico Trevisano. 1512. Painting of the Venetian School. The Louvre, Paris. The visit is probably that described by Ibn Iyās for Monday, 10 May 1512, when he states that the envoy was a large and venerable figure, with a white beard and dressed in a robe of yellow silk threaded with gold. He was escorted by a suite of seven and brought with him as gifts 100 loads containing valuable cloth and crystal. On this occasion the subject at issue would appear not to have been trade but the reopening of the Church of the Resurrection in Jerusalem which had been closed on the sultan's orders. Ibn Iyās, *Badā'i'*, iv, 259. (Photo: AKA London, Eric Lessing)

Plate 2. One of a series of tiled panels or *azulezos* in the hall of the Braganza Institute in Panaji, Goa, depicting the Portuguese colonization of Goa. The panel depicts the vision of Adamastor at the Cape of Storms to be renamed the Cape of Good Hope. See the penultimate sentence of paragraph one of the text. (Photo: C.K.S.)

Muslims from the Franks in Yemeni waters and their ports, and because of the recurrent harm they caused and the inability of the Muslim troops in Yemeni waters[9] to resist them due to their lack of knowledge of sea warfare and the use of cannon and such like.

So Sultan al-Ġawrī prepared one of his senior lieutenants, Ḥusayn al-Kurdī, to be accompanied by a large number of *levend* led by Salmān Rayyis,[10] and allocated to them a vast fleet and about fifty grabs with large cannon and *ḍarbzanāt*.[11]

He appointed him [Ḥusayn al-Kurdī] governor of Jeddah and his importance grew. He was brave, courageous and brutal, a great tyrant but a clever politician. As soon as he arrived, in 917/1511–12,[12] he built a wall round Jeddah into which the merchants carried earth and stone. He destroyed and appropriated those Muslim houses he wished and included them in the construction. He put one of the merchants in the middle of the building so that they would build over him. He [the merchant] had to spend a great deal of money to save himself after some had intervened on his behalf. Indeed he constructed the wall to protect the port from the depredation of the bedouins; for during those days followers of Muḥammad were at odds. At that time the late Sharif Barakāt[13] was not entirely secure, nor did he have the power to keep the bedouins at bay until he grew strong and God bestowed on him the power to rule and govern and gave authority to him and his followers.

[20] When Commander Ḥusayn had attended to the construction of Jeddah's wall, he set off with his grabs for India, entered Diu and met with Sultan Muẓaffar Šāh by whom he was given a great deal of assistance. However, the Franks had gone up to Goa and Commander Ḥusayn was not able to continue in India. So he returned without doing anything and arrived at the port of Kamarān, where he had with him armament, weapons and many of the *levend*, including Salmān Rayyis who was brave and brutal, with a knowledge of warfare, especially concerning guns and muskets.[14]

Commander Ḥusayn sent off to Sultan al-'Āmir asking for provisions and assistance from him, referring to the letters he [the sultan] had written before to Sultan al-Ġawrī requesting help from him.[15] So, when Commander Ḥusayn's messenger reached 'Āmir with a large gift,[16] 'Āmir wanted to extend to him the help and other things for which he had asked but his minister prevented him from such action, saying, 'If you were to give him something, it would become his practice to ask for it each year.' A counsel of meanness is persuasive. Miserliness and parsimony are planted in nature. His [the minister's][17] view prevailed. How often do mean words destroy homes and lead to ruin and disaster! So Sultan 'Āmir sent an unfitting reply to Commander Ḥusayn. He sent nothing to him and prohibited provisioning from Kamarān. And as a result ill will grew between them.

Ḥusayn al-Kurdī was bent on damaging Sultan ʿĀmir and destroying his house and settlements. So he resolved to take the Yemen; and the troops and *levend* around him supported him in such action and he set about the task in earnest.[18]

Among those encouraging him were the hillsmen of the Zaydī sect;[19] for they were hard and sorely pressed by ʿĀmir b. ʿAbd al-Wahhāb because of their destruction at his hands and his continual slaughter of their leaders. So they saw it as an opportunity and went down to him, asking him for 200 *levend* whose pay and expenses they would meet and whom they would equip with horses.[20]

[21] The lord of Ǧīzān came to him, at the time being Sayyid Sharif ʿIzz al-Dīn b. Aḥmad b. Durayb,[21] with his close connection with ʿĀmir bin ʿAbd al-Wahhāb and the continual services he had rendered him. He gave him no special respect; nor did he respect kinship or covenant.

The lord of al-Luḥayyah, Faqīh Abū Bakr b. Maqbūl, also came to Commander Ḥusayn and stated, 'We will open the road for you from the port of al-Luḥayyah.' And he welcomed Commander Ḥusayn and promised that his guide would be on the roads and gave him provisions and supplies. He [the lord of al-Luḥayyah] donned his robe of honour and walked in front of him.

The people of the Yemen had no knowledge of muskets and cannon with the result that the Mamluks, in their first battle with ʿĀmir's forces, discharged cannon at a great throng of ʿĀmir's soldiers thousands of whom died. It terrified them and they were frightened and panic-stricken, and retreated. They took one of the stone balls with them to Zabīd, and they stared at it and showed it to people. They were amazed by it and made a great fuss of it.[22]

Numerous battles broke out between the Mamluks and ʿĀmir b. ʿAbd al-Wahhāb in all of which he was worsted until Commander Ḥusayn took Zabīd and entered it with a large number of Mamluks, *levend*, Moroccans, Egyptians and Syrians, together with Commander Salmān al-Rūmī and his Zaydī partisans and people of Ǧizān. This was after a great battle; and his entry into Zabīd was on Friday morning, 19 Ǧumādā I, 922/20 June 1516. His troops then took to plunder and assault, causing Muslims great distress.

And ʿĀmir and his brother ʿAbd al-Malik and his son ʿAbd al-Wahhāb[23] escaped, each of them having lost several horses beneath him, and experienced great hardship. They fought but fate was of no help to them; and they all fled to Taʿizz. Among his commanders at the time were ʿAlī b. Muḥammad al-Naẓārī[24] and Ḥusām al-Dīn ʿĪsā al-Ḥağarī and others.

After they had fled and Commander Ḥusayn had occupied Zabīd, he oppressed its population after it had been plundered, and he put in charge an assistant called Tawğan who then registered the houses of people in Zabīd, [22] together with the names of their occupants and seized a great deal of

Plate 3. Inside of the al-Ašā'ir mosque in Zabīd, with historic minbar and water vessels. See n. 23. (Photo: C.K.S.)

their property. He [Commander Ḥusayn] stayed in Zabīd for twenty-seven days, oppressing them and collecting their property until he had impoverished them.[25]

He then left for the coast on Thursday, 17 Ǧumādā II/17 July where he stayed for ten days and then, with Salmān Rayyis, travelled to Aden in the grabs to capture it, while they appointed Badr al-Dīn al-Ḥağabī to collect the tithe on the palm trees of Zabīd who was tyrannical and oppressive, seizing their property and making them suffer terribly.

One of Commander Ḥusayn's mamluks, Commander Barsbāy, took over in Zabīd; and Sharif 'Izz al-Dīn, lord of Ǧīzān, helped him.

He regulated the country, organized the remaining troops in Zabīd and stayed until 12 Ša'bān, 922/31 August 1516. Then he pitched his camp outside Zabīd by the Šabāriq Gate,[26] bringing out his escort with the large and small cannon, and stayed there for five days collecting the troops.

He then travelled to the town of Ḥays[27] where he pitched his tents. He then went, together with his party, to Mawza' where the lord of Mawza', Commander 'Abdallāh b. Salāmah, reached agreement with him over the money to be handed to him to stop him plundering the town and causing trouble to anybody. So he entered the town and had taken over the money when he broke the agreement and plundered the house of the afore-mentioned commander; and inside were the deposits belonging to people of the town.

He then returned to Zabīd which he entered on Sunday 8 Ramaḍān, 922/5 October 1516.

[23] Chapter 3

Concerning what happened to Commander al-Ḥusayn and the end of the Circassian state

As for as Commander Ḥusayn, he travelled with Salmān Rayyis in a fleet of twenty grabs and two galleons to the port of Aden where at the time was Commander Mirǧān al-ʿĀmirī;[28] and they arrived on 13 Raǧab 922/12 August 1516.

Aden was populous, frequented by ships from Indian ports and with substantial traders and vast wealth. But Commander Ḥusayn ran into the end of the Indian monsoon when the ships had already left and they saw their ships already under sail. Salmān went to them by grab and seized a ship from them belonging to ʿĀmir b. ʿAbd al-Wahhāb. Then Salmān occupied it and placed in it a pilot and a *karrānī* [clerk] at his behest and dispatched it to Gujerat. He sent with it letters for Sultan Muẓaffar Šāh[29] indicating that Commander Ḥusayn had taken the Yemen and established his authority there, and that, afterwards, he would return to India to seize the cursed Portuguese.

Commander Ḥusayn's troops gathered under Ṣabir's fortress[30] and strafed it with artillery, hitting most of its houses, but they were not able to take it; nor to take Aden. Aden's population came out and a mighty battle took place in which Salmān received three wounds. [24] Then other engagements took place and they fought each other with alternate success. From Taʿizz arrived ʿĀmir b. ʿAbd al-Wahhāb's brother, together with his troops, who entered Aden; then the Egyptian troops despaired of taking Aden, so they seized what sailing craft they found around the fortress and embarked on their ships.

They departed on Saturday 24 Raǧab 922/23 August 1516[31] and travelled to populous Jeddah with the property and plunder they had taken from Aden's population. He [Ḥusayn al-Kurdī] continued as governor in Jeddah without any constraint on him; nor any opposition to his actions. No day did he cease his hanging, staking or ganching,[32] or various forms of political chicanery. And every time he descended to his place by the gallows or the ganching apparatus, he committed God knows what outrage and got himself involved on the slightest pretext. During this period the Circassian state met its end.

His Majesty the Sultan, lord of the Arabs and non-Arabs, Sultan Selīm H̱ān,[33] son of Bāyezīd H̱ān, Almighty God protect him with mercy and compassion, entered Egypt on the first of Holy Muḥarram 923/24 January 1517 after the Circassians had been defeated at Marǧ Dābiq and Sultan al-Ḡawrī had been lost beneath the horses' hooves. Their remaining forces in Egypt had collected under Tūmān Bey but were overwhelmed at al-Raydāniyyah outside Cairo. Tūmān Bey fled and was then caught and Sultan Selīm ordered him to be hanged on the Zuwaylah gate.[34] With him ended the Circassian state and thus started the imperial conquest and the beginning of Ottoman rule over the Arabs, may Almighty God let it last for ever.

Our lord, the late holy Sayyid Barakāt, Almighty God save him, sent his son, our lord and master, Sharif Abū Numayy,[35] God give him victory, to do obeisance to the sultan. At the time he was thirteen years old. He was welcomed by His Majesty the Sultan with honour and kindness. He [the sultan] regarded the appearance of a sharif of Mecca as propitious and was delighted by his arrival at his august feet. [25] He gave orders that he write with sultanic authority in the customary way and the sharifs of Mecca are blessed with such authority until now, and he wrote in his presence a sultanic death warrant for Ḥusayn al-Kurdī, the governor of Jeddah.

Our lord, Sayyid Sharif Abū Numayy returned to Mecca happy with the help he had been given; and the city was decorated for his arrival. People were delighted at the end of Circassian rule because of the extent of their oppression, their infringement of the holy law, their failure to recognize Quranic rules on inheritance, their seizure of inherited wealth and their deprivation of boys, let alone girls and blood relations. For that Almighty God took them.

My father, Almighty God have mercy upon him, has spoken to me about one of Almighty God's saints whose prayer was answered, when he saw in Egypt a Circassian take some goods from a merchant without paying for them. The merchant did not stand for it and said to him. 'Almighty God's holy law is between us.' Then he struck him with his *dabbūs* (staff) until he made his head bleed and fractured it. The saint said, 'I have invoked Almighty God against that Circassian.'

'I have witnessed such things before that case,' (my father said), 'especially in matters of inheritance; for they did not leave property to anybody. Gradually they ended up in taking over the entire property of a dead person, depriving the natural sons of the inheritance, let alone anybody else.' 'I slept in, having done my ablutions, reflecting on their concerns and praying to Almighty God to bring their rule to an end and for a government that treats gently Muslims under them. And I saw in my sleep an angel come down from heaven, with a brush in his hand with which he was sweeping away the Circassians and casting them into the waters of the Nile.

Then I learnt that their state had come to an end and not a year had passed before I saw the tents of Sultan Selīm H̱ān by the side of the Nile and his troops leading Circassian prisoners. Then he gave orders for them to be decapitated until their heads resembled large hills while they threw their bodies into the River Nile so that they would not pollute the air and cause infection. They followed this by throwing the heads into the river as well, rolling them along. In this there is a lesson to be learnt, an event to be remembered.[36] It is said that the late Sultan Selīm H̱an, God water his time with mercy and favour, had dispatched to al-Ḡawrī [26] a copy of the Holy Quran, omitting the verse dealing with inheritance, intimating that he had abolished the law of inheritance in his kingdom.[37] This situation only hardened during the sultanate of al-Ḡawrī, intensifying during his final days when his rule collapsed. It was the reason for the end of his rule and sultans in Islam should beware the fact. It is veritable death; and let them devote their energies to supporting the Holy Law of Muḥammad, most excellent prayer and peace be upon Him; for he who supports the holy law, extends justice to the weak as well as the strong, prohibits wrong doing, keeps the hand of the oppressor from the oppressed and works in accordance with God's Book and the *sunnah* of His Prophet. His rule will last for ever and he will be counted among kings. For where justice obtains, rule will endure, and where oppression arises, destruction and defeat will obtain. Rule endures with infidelity but not with tyranny.

And after Sayyid Sharif Abū Numayy had arrived with Sayyid ʻArār b. ʻIǧl b. ʻArār al-Numawī, in Holy Mecca on their return from kissing the feet of the august Sultan Selīm, with the august sultanic credentials, carrying the sultan's robe of honour for our lord Sharif Barakāt, the mercy of Almighty God be upon him, the sultan's diploma was read out at al-Ḥutaym[38] concerning our lord Sayyid Barakāt's authority over the Holy Places, the area of the Hejaz and the port of populous Jeddah, delegating to him all aspects of its government, powers of dismissal and the like, on behalf of the Sublime Porte.

Then the Grand Sharif donned the robe of honour and paraded in it through the Holy Mosque. The president prayed for him at Zamzam and he walked to Dār al-Saʻādah (his official residence), followed by the *faqīh*s. The people congratulated him upon the new administration and the felicitous robe of honour, and henceforth sermons were delivered from the *minbar* in the name of His Majesty the Sultan Selīm H̱ān. People were content and injustice was at an end.

Then Sayyid ʻArār took up his seat in the Ḥanafī *maqām*[39] and asked Commander Ḥusayn to heed the sultanic decree. So he came full of regret and submission, sorrowful and submissive after that pride and arrogance, such that one who saw him enter the Holy Mosque told me that there was none to bring to him his slippers. 'I felt compassion for him,' he said, 'and I brought him mine,' and he put them on, and when he reached Sayyid ʻArār, he [the latter] did not stand up but said to him 'The sultan's order has come, Almighty God give him victory, to get you ready for Egypt.' And he replied, 'I hear and obey.' [27] Then he assigned some slaves to him with orders to take him down to Jeddah and put him on a dhow, and, after they had reached between the two signs[40] with him, they drowned him there in the sea where the fish ate him. The sharks ripped away at his skin while his servants and relatives made their escape and scattered in all directions.[41] 'And they find all that they did confronting them, and thy Lord wrongeth no one.'[42] No trace of the Circassian Mamluks was left in Mecca. Those who survived fled to the Yemen and joined Commander Barsbāy in Zabīd where they collected. They began a furore of fighting, oppressing and overpowering people, and collecting property. They grew more powerful with the Zaydī tribes and the lord of Ǧīzān, and collected in a throng to fight Sultan 'Āmir b. 'Abd al-Wahhāb[43] and his family. God will bring the kingship to whom He wishes; for God is all-powerful.

[37] Chapter 8

(In this second extract action moves to late 930/early 1524 when a group of *levend* had just seized control in Zabīd and Ta'izz, and a state of chaos and oppression obtained in the area. The Ottoman governor of Jeddah, Ḥusayn the Turk, had conducted a short and unsuccessful campaign in the Yemen. Salmān Rayyis had gone to Cairo to meet the new Ottoman governor there, Aḥmad Pasha, who had come out in rebellion. The *levend* governor of Zabīd was Iskandar Bey al-Qurmānī who had Friday prayers said in the joint names of the Ottoman sultan and himself.)

Salmān Rayyis' withdrawal in fear and his arrival at Mecca: his journey, with Commander Ḥusayn the Turk for the second time, from Jeddah to the Yemen

[38, 2 from b.] And Salmān Rayyis was in Egypt at the beginning of the insurrection, and when he heard of it, he withdrew to Mecca and recommended to Commander Ḥusayn the Turk, Governor of Jeddah, that he return to the Yemen and occupy [39] it. There was plenty of armament in Jeddah.[44] So the two of them joined forces, made preparations and travelled to the Yemen. That was Commander Ḥusayn the Turk's second visit to the Yemen, [this time] with Salmān Rayyis.

The Franks lay hidden in the hills of Kamarān,[45] snatching Muslims on the coast and taking what plunder they could. But when Salmān Rayyis arrived, he defended them from harm, killing some of them [the Franks] and taking others prisoner. He cleaned them off the coast and sent a message to Iskandar Bey al-Qurmānī asking him to submit. However, the troops refused to do so. He was minded to take sides with Salmān and Commander Ḥusayn in secret but his troops made that impossible so he appeared to go along with their wishes but he sent a message in secret to Commander Salmān and to Commander Ḥusayn indicating his agreement.

And Salmān sent messages to the Yāfi‘ tribe and the Mahrah[46] asking for help from them against the Mamluks who were in Zabīd; and they came to him. He engaged them and they became his soldiers. Then he sent a message to Sayyid ‘Izz al-Dīn, lord of Ǧīzān, seeking his help also; for he had been very friendly with him before during the time of Ḥusayn al-Kurdī,[47] and he came to him with his horses and his men and weapons. The Mamluks in Zabīd came out to fight Salmān who set out to meet them, leaving the grabs, galleys and equipment they contained in the care of Commander Ḥusayn the Turk, together with a section of the army.

Then Salmān joined forces with the Yāfi‘ and Mahrah who had come by sea and with Sayyid ‘Izz al-Dīn by land from [via] the village of al-Marāwi‘ah.[48] Commander Iskandar al-Qurmānī came out to do battle with Salmān together with all the Mamluks in Zabīd and a large battle was fought between them in which Iskandar al-Qurmānī and those with him were worsted. They [the latter] entered Zabīd and closed its gates while Salmān surrounded Zabīd wishing to set its gates on fire and get at them inside. Then they sought a truce from him which he granted them, and he entered Zabīd but left outside the commander of Ǧīzān, ‘Izz al-Dīn b. Durayb. He seized Iskandar al-Qurmānī and banished him. Then disagreement broke out between Salmān and Commander ‘Izz al-Dīn, lord of Ǧīzān, and a mighty battle between them ensued in which over 200 of Salmān's Turkish troops were slain; and Sayyid ‘Izz al-Dīn, lord of Ǧīzān, was killed in the engagement.

[40] Salmān occupied Zabīd, oppressing its population and pursuing the trouble makers who at first connived against him, and appealing to Commander Ḥusayn who came and treated the town's population with courtesy; for he inclined to fair play and justice. So people crowded round him and his reputation swelled. And Salmān was afraid for himself and fled to the sea. Commander Ḥusayn took possession of the town from the month of Raǧab 930/May/June 1524 and the town calmed down and the trouble makers dispersed.

Then in 931/1524–5 the bedouin came out in revolt and became unruly. They disrupted the roads and committed hostile acts. The damage they did became general and their ill-doing increased. He [Commander Ḥusayn] emerged personally to fight them and pursued them to their encampments, seizing their horses and men. The population calmed down and men felt safe. And he returned in triumph and victory, praised and thanked for the way he had acted.

The lord of Ta‘izz, Commander al-Ašrafī, had sent a message to Commander Ḥusayn asking him for some funds to meet the wages of those troops he had with him. But he turned him down, so he [Commander al-Ašrafī] increased the taxes on the local people and turned to seizing their property. Then, when the news reached Commander Ḥusayn, he was not pleased about his action, went and did battle with him, and slew him. He also killed his bunch of trouble makers and established his authority in the countryside. The population thanked him for what he had done and with that entered the rule of the sublime sultan.

It so happened that when Aḥmad Pasha was killed in Egypt, the Grand Vizier, Ibrāhīm Pasha, came to Cairo to sort out what had gone wrong with matters in Egypt, and look into the sultanate's finances and the affairs of the populace. Among those who approached him from the Yemen was Salmān Rayyis who informed him as to affairs in the Yemen in that the state was bereft of a head; for Commander Ḥusayn had occupied it but that brought no advantage since he was incapable of looking after it. He was full of disparagement for Ḥusayn Bey, as he had excluded him from authority in the Yemen which had prompted his removal from the country. He asked for troops to take with him to the Yemen and also to seize the Franks who were in India.[49]

He [the Grand Vizier] promised such action but sent a sultanic decree to Commander Ḥusayn for his continued rule over the country, winning him over so as to deceive him till [41] he could arrange support for Salmān. So the said decree reached him and his power waxed and his position and status increased. He was able to get a grip over the country and control it. He established his authority there and put an end to its disturbed state. He liked the ulema, believed firmly in the pious and the saints, and followed the Islamic law. He won over sections of the strong and the weak, so that the people of the Yemen held him in affection and, during his time, the fires of revolt died down.

[42] Chapter 9

Concerning the death of Ḥusayn Bey, the governorship of Muṣṭafā Bey, the arrival of Salmān Rayyis in the Yemen from Egypt with a vast army, and the various movements of revolt that took place there

God in his majesty and divine might, ordained and inescapable, in his rule that operates over all men and nations, fated the death of Commander Ḥusayn in 932/1525–6, after a long illness and a period of growing and protracted ill-health. So when he felt the approach of departure, and that he was going to the Glorious Lord, he made bequests and offered good works and alms, and established in his place Commander Muṣṭafā the Turk, establishing Ḫwāǧā Maḥmūd, his *hwāǧā*, as minister with him and ordering Commander Muṣṭafā to seek Maḥmūd's advice in all matters. And the two of them calmed the agitation in the country, kept at bay those calling for trouble and continued doing so until the arrival of Salmān from Egypt.

Information concerning Salmān included the fact that, when he withdrew from the Yemen, he approached the Grand Vizier, Ibrāhīm Pasha, in Egypt and arranged for him to send an army with him with which to avert damage by the Franks, and at the same time seize the Yemen and gain property and treasure for the sublime sultanate. And Ibrāhīm Pasha obliged him and assigned to him four thousand of the Turkish *levend* whom he equipped with him in ships for Jeddah in which to travel from there to India and to the Yemen. And the army comprised all sorts of cobblers, artisans, brigands, ignorant young men etc.; and to each ten of them there was a chief called a *bolokbāshī*, [43] and to each fifty of them was a chief with a standard under whom they served. Over them all there was one of the sultan's *sanjaks* whose name was Ḫayr al-Dīn Ḥamzah. He

Plate 4. Kurdish cavalryman. From a woodcut thought to be from a seventeenth-century German printed book. (Royal Armouries, Leeds)

was not without good qualities. He [the Grand Vizier] made Salmān captain[50] over them all.

And they reached Jeddah in the month of Ramaḍān 932/June/July 1526, and that was at the beginning of the rule of His Excellency the Grand Sharif, Almighty God perpetuate his glory and good fortune and assist his state and regency. When Salmān arrived in Jeddah the *levend* did a lot of damage there and began to meddle with the bedouin and rob the markets. The supply of provisions for Mecca was cut when a dire scarcity obtained, and rampant inflation, so that it became a matter of history for the people of Mecca who called it the year of Salmān.

That did a lot of damage to people and prices were raised. Provisions disappeared from the markets. A bowl of wheat reached five *muḥallaqs* and a *raṭl* of fat, twelve *muḥallaqs*.[51] But it did not last for long; nor was it protracted. Then joy came through Almighty God at the time of the pilgrimage, and prices fell, thanks and blessings to God.

Salmān's troops scattered, a group of whom reached Mecca where they occupied people's houses by force and expelled their occupants. They gathered in Mecca and caused a lot of damage there. They got the better of the populace and the bedouins but the bedouins overcame them at Bīr Šamīs. They were emerging from Ḥiddah, when the bedouins charged them from a gully at Bīr Šamīs. They attacked them, killing and crucifying them until they had slaughtered a great number, and the road to Jeddah was putrid with their corpses. The road to Jeddah became fearful and the Grand Sharif abandoned its care, for Salmān and his crowd to abuse the officers of the Grand Sharif and his supporters in Mecca and Jeddah.

The bedouins took advantage of the situation and began to waylay the *levend* on the road and to put them to death till among those they had killed were two highly regarded and important traders, one of whom was Ḫwājā Shaykh 'Alī al-Kaylanī and the other Ḫwājā Muḥammad Šāh Qiwām al-Lārī. They were among the most charitable of people who kept an eye on the poor and people mourned for them. The Grand Sharif then gave orders for them not to be molested and to keep the bedouins from interfering with them and others. However, the Jeddah road stank with the corpses of the dead; so the most holy and ever watchful on God's account, Shaykh Muḥammad b. 'Irāq, God bless his soul [44] and cast light on his tomb, dispatched a group of his supporters and *faqīrs* to bury the corpses on the Jeddah road. So they carried out his order and none other than he dared to do so, Almighty God have mercy upon him, because of the dispute over the road and the strength of the alarm.

Once there was a large number of *levend* in Mecca who raised their standards in the Holy Sanctuary, in lines from the Gate of al-Salām to the Gate of 'Alī, and attacked the houses of the great. The people were absolutely fed up with this, so they complained about what they found to Shaykh Muḥammad b. ʻIrāq who took up his seat in the Holy Sanctuary and summoned Commander Ḫayr al-Dīn and some of the officers and *levend* chiefs.

I[52] was standing in front of the shaykh, Almighty God be merciful to him, and I saw he had reddened in the cheek: every hair stood up on his body and his jugular vein was swollen. He scolded the group and reviled them. He charged them and I saw Commander Ḫayr al-Dīn kissing the shaykh's feet and apologizing to him; and I saw everybody bowing over and kissing his feet while they apologized to him for their folly. He ordered them to stop the damage they were doing to people and to produce the wrongdoers among them and to get out of people's houses. They said 'The pilgrimage draws close, and our intention is to perform the pilgrimage and to go and attack the Franks; so where are we to live?' He said to them, 'Go to Minā where there are empty houses in which you can live until the pilgrimage time. Don't harm anyone and don't use any force on Muslims.'

(The author tells how the shaykh's orders were obeyed and then goes on to describe Salmān's seizure of the entire Jeddah revenue of 9,000 gold dinars, half of which was due to the sultanate and half to the Grand Sharif. The Sharif had to swear fealty to the sultan: Jeddah was full of rumour and alarm over his reaction and the Ottoman leaders had to adjudicate over demands by members of his family. The Grand Sharif was appointed superintendent of Mecca which he entered in triumph. However, alarmed by Salmān's presence with his *levends*, he avoided the annual pilgrimage.)

[47, 9] In the forenoon of Thursday, 5 Ḏū al-Ḥijjah 932/12 September 1526, Salmān Rayyis arrived at Mecca with all his troops. He entered from al-Ḥuğūn along with his entire army of *levend*, rank after rank in front of him, all of them on foot, carrying their muskets on their shoulders. I saw the beginning of his army at al-Maʻlāh at the place where afterwards was constructed the building for the mother of the sultans, al-Ḫāsikiyyah, Almighty God have mercy upon her, and the last of them at al-Ḥuğūn. I saw Salmān and Ḫayr al-Dīn riding their horses, and, apart from them, none of the troops was riding. It was a terrifying entrance and continued till the Gate of al-Ṣafā. Then Commander Ḫayr al-Dīn entered his house, descending at al-ʻAyniyyah connecting with the Gate of al-Ağyad which used to be the al-Muğāhidiyyah school built by King al-Muğāhid of the Bānū Ġassān, Kings of the Yemen. In former times lessons were given in it; then it changed hands and Aḥmad al-ʻAynī took the school where he instituted a reading of the Holy Quran and charity work. Later the official magistrates of Holy Mecca occupied it. It then fell into ruin and remains as such till God foredains someone to rebuild it.[53]

After Commanders Salmān and Ḫayr al-Dīn had arrived at the latter's house, Commander Ḫayr al-Dīn emerged from his quarters and made the rounds from the small market in front of the Ibrāhīm Gate till he arrived at al-Suwayqah where he entered the house prepared for him, that is the house belonging to H̱wājā [48] al-Ṭāhir which is now part of the *awqāf* of the four schools of Sultan Sulaymān in Mecca. Then, on 8 D̲ū al-Ḥijjah/15 September, the pilgrims and populace went to ʻArafāt, in a state of ritual purification for carrying out the pilgrimage.[54]

That year His Highness the Grand Sharif was absent as was much of the population of Mecca for fear of the outbreak of sedition. The Holy Waqfah fell on Monday and the population did not witness excitement or violence, thank God.

[49] Chapter 10

Concerning the arrival in the Yemen of Commanders Salmān and H̱ayr al-Dīn

After completing the pilgrimage, Salmān and H̱ayr al-Dīn returned to Jeddah and embarked with the troops in grabs[55] for the Yemen, persevering in taking revenge on Commander Ḥusayn for what he had done to him [Salmān] before, for his expulsion from the state of the Yemen and for his attempt to rule without him. That journey of his was not propitious; for he and Commander H̱ayr al-Dīn, with most of their army, were slain because of their violence in Almighty God's Holy Sanctuary: their presumptuous behaviour with our lord, the Grand Sharif, Guardian of Almighty God's town: their verbal abuse of him; their seizure of his share of the Jeddah revenue; and his forbearance with them for all they had done until Almighty God took revenge on them for him.

Herein is the consequence for oppressors and the outcome for those who endure. In that lies a warning for him who takes notice and a lesson for him on whom Almighty God bestows sight and hearing.

After his arrival in the Yemen, Commander Salmān was informed of the death of Ḥusayn Bey and the ensuing succession of Muṣṭafā Bey. He mobilized the *levend* forces he had with him and headed for Zabīd but when Muṣṭafā Bey realized the situation he went out to him with those with him and sent to him a *ğāwīsh* asking what he intended from such a battle, and what his intention was in drawing swords and shedding the blood of troops on both sides. Once the *ğāwīsh* had reached Salmān Bey and handed his message, he said in reply that 'His Majesty the Sultan Sulaymān, God make his rule endure, has bestowed upon Commander H̱ayr al-Dīn the state of Yemen and ordered [50] you to go to the Sublime Porte. Submit and hand over the town to Commander H̱ayr al-Dīn and hand yourself over to us so that we can prepare you for the Sublime Porte.'

So when the *ǧāwīsh* returned to Muṣṭafā Bey with his reply, he realized that it had fallen to the hand of Commander Salmān to kill him, and he devised a trick in the matter. He began to win over the *levend* who accompanied Commander Salmān with gifts and presents. They forsook Salmān and formed a band for Commander Muṣṭafā. There is a proverb: dirhams are as balm; cash loosens agreements.

Then Muṣṭafā Bey's position grew and his army multiplied; and with that he grew puffed up and feckless. So Commander Salmān determined to meet him and decided to do battle with him and fight him. There remained with Commander Salmān a band of brave *levend* and a group that withstood the heat of the contest; and the two bodies met at al-Ṣalīf[56] where Salmān stood firm to face the challenge.

It was not long before Muṣṭafā took to flight and was on the very brink of disaster. He continued in flight as far as Aden and Kamarān. Muṣṭafā's troops returned to Salmān, apologizing to him for their desertion and indiscipline. So he accepted their apology and forgave them their betrayal. He entered Zabīd with them, where he was generally hard on the population, causing public and private damage and taking between one and three thousand dinars from every trader and business man he encountered. This he conferred upon the *levend* and, in so doing, raised their spirits.

He went to Ta'izz, appointing in Zabīd Commander Yūnis. He travelled with the *levend* who took and plundered Ta'izz, killing its commander. Then they took Ibb and Ḏū Ǧiblah, robbing them of a great deal of wealth.

Ibn Ḥamzah who had a great deal of money was in Zaydiyyah; so they fought him, and he fled from them. He was determined not to meet them but fled and left all the money he had which Salmān and the *levend* with him then seized. And Ibn Ḥamzah continued his flight until he reached the Commander of Bayt al-Faqīh, 'Alī Bey al-Qurmānī, with whom he agreed to go to Zabīd and take it from Commander Yūnis, Salmān's deputy in the town. They had no sooner reached Zabīd, occupied it and begun to oppress its people than Salmān and the *levend* and bedouins with him, arrived outside the town, [51] and fought an extremely fierce battle with them at the western gate from which they fled to the eastern gate.

He [Salmān] pursued them and broke them. Then they entered the town of Zabīd and closed its gates, so he set siege to them and sent to the Yāfi' and Mahrah who came to him bringing large guns from al-Ṣalīf. He went to the palm grove above the river and fired at them with cannon, gun and musket. He took Zabīd by force and sent in the *levend* and other forces. But a bullet had hit him in the leg that day and prevented him from entering the town, so he stayed in his camp in the grove and stopped them from interfering with the town's people who began to bring to him the troops who had deserted him and allied themselves with others who had prompted the revolt and trouble. Then some he slew: others he blinded till he had put out the eyes of a great number who continued for a time in Mecca till the days and nights had consumed them and left them like others who were powerful, resembling dried up water skins, every commander who had been in charge of hundreds and important figures whom time had debased and returned to the ranks of the weak.[57]

Thus is the way of unjust time and the oppressive and false epoch dragged on, apportioning the same fate to all at the beginning and the end. All who escaped from the hand of Salmān, and did not fall among his senior *levend* and Turkomans, joined Muṣṭafā Bey around Aden, with their spirits lifted and assuaged but treacherous time was playing false with such peace of mind; and this is the way of time with its sons on all occasions.

[52] Concerning the murder of Muṣṭafā Bey and Salmān's seizure of authority in the Yemen[58]

Seeing Muṣṭafā Bey's recovery and his union with some of the army, Salmān made for him with his forces and went to do battle with him; and the latter made for him, together with Ibn Ḥamzah and his soldiers. They met at al-Turaybah[59] at the end of 933/October 1527 and there was a number of clashes between them, the majority won by Salmān. So Muṣṭafā fled from him; and he [Salmān] pursued him till he overtook him and cut off his head. Ibn Ḥamzah fell into his hands and he [Salmān] defeated most of Muṣṭafā's army save a very few who had escaped at the beginning of the engagement; and that was at the beginning of Holy Muḥarram, 934/27 October 1527.

And he blinded Ibn Ḥamzah, slaying many of those in captivity and blinding the rest. He inflicted on them appalling suffering but thought that the situation was right for him and that the epoch had crowned him with its generosity and granted him its good favour; and that it had granted his wishes and welcomed his hopes.

> But oh how far away is al-'Aqiq[60] and its people,
> and how far is the beloved in al-'Aqiq for whom we yearn!

[53] Chapter 11

Concerning the murder of Salmān and the rule of his sister's son, Muṣṭafā bin Bayram

Commander Ḫayr al-Dīn saw that Salmān had seized power, and that his own status had fallen with his independence; for in the first place, one of them had not been accustomed to give orders without the other, and, in fact, Commander Ḫayr al-Dīn was the person to whom one referred while Salmān was in charge at sea when, and only then, were naval matters referred to him. He was then minded to kill Salmān, in all treachery. He began to observe him all the time and wait for the opportunity for his purpose.

He set a band of *levend* against Salmān who bore down on him and cut off his head with a sword at a place called the isle of al-Muḥāmilah.[61] They then went enthusiastically to Commander Ḫayr al-Dīn. That was at the end of 934/September 1528.

Muṣṭafā Bey Ibn Bayram, Salmān's nephew, then took charge of matters. He was a bold killer, with a knowledge of war, especially the taking of castles by artillery and the conquest of impregnable fortresses. Muṣṭafā Bey then collected all Salmān's former supporters, his attendants and his mamluks among the bravest being Ḫwājā Ṣafar[62] who was with the grabs that had been under Salmān's control. He made Ḫwājā Ṣafar minister and made preparations to take revenge on Ḫayr al-Dīn.

So Ḫayr al-Dīn Bey got ready for battle, sending on his part Sinān al-Qubṭān, Karīm al-Ḥalabī and Bālī Ḥalabī with some troops to Zabīd to seize Salmān's supporters who were there. They reached Zabīd and occupied it at the beginning of Ša'bān 935/mid-April 1529, and took prisoner Salmān's followers who were there. They stayed there for 13 days while Muṣṭafā Bayram [54] and his uncle's troops travelled towards them, asking Ḫwājā Ṣafar to bring the cannon and *ḍarbzanāt*, together with the *levend* and Arab troops who were with him or at his base. He [Muṣṭafā] then entered Zabīd secretly and killed Sinān al-Qubṭān and Ḫayr al-Dīn's followers who were there. Then he released his men and set out to do battle with Ḫayr al-Dīn.

Concerning the murder of Commander Ḫayr al-Dīn and Muṣṭafā bin Bayram's resolve on India and departure from the state of Yemen

As Muṣṭafā Ibn Bayram went to take revenge on Commander Ḫayr al-Dīn for his uncle, Salmān, the commander [Ḫayr al-Dīn] realized the fact but he was cowardly, spiritless and bewildered. He had in his prison a group of administrative officers, agents and men entrusted with state funds. He released them from his prison and gave orders for the slaughter of the administrative officers and agents; and they killed them on the spot.

And it has been said, 'The killer is sure to be killed, even if after a time.' No sooner had battle lines been drawn up and the lightning of the swords flashed than Ḫayr al-Dīn took fright. Trembling and quaking gripped him. No sooner had he watched the flashing of the swords than all manner of evil rained upon him and punishment struck him from the archer's hand. The dove of death flew at him from the quiver of calamity and vulture arrows with their feathered wings tore across the sky towards him.

Broken, he took to flight and turned his back; and Muṣṭafā Ibn Bayram pursued him and killed him with his own hands. His weapons of war and equipment were of no use to him; then Muṣṭafā took control of the whole country, its mountains and its plains. However, once Muṣṭafā had observed the insolence of the *levend* in slaughtering the commanders and putting them to death one after the other, he was not comfortable in the Yemen; nor did he have any confidence in living there because of the frequency of revolt. So he assembled his cherished weapons, cannon and guns as well as his dear family and his uncle's supporters, and left the Yemen territories where he established one of his companions, Sayyid ʻAlī al-Rūmī, as governor of the entire country and his deputy there with whom he yoked in authority one of Commander Salmān's mamluks [55] called Aḥmad Bey.

He then set out for Kamarān indicating that he wished to construct there a fortress with which to ward off damage by the Franks. He brought masons and tools and set about the construction of a strong castle. When the time came for the ships to sail to India, during the return monsoon, he embarked in his ships, taking with him the weapons of war and large cannon and loading them with his choice possessions.

He, with his special group and Commander Salmān's party, then set out for India where, with Ḫwājā Ṣafar, he called upon Sultan Bahādur Šāh,[63] lord of Gujerat. That was in 936/1529–30. Sultan Bahādur entertained him with tremendous generosity and was delighted by his arrival there. He was extremely kind to him and showered gifts upon him. He fulfilled and confirmed his expectations in him, giving the title and name, in accordance with the sultans of India, of Rūmī Ḫān. On Ḫwājā Ṣafar he bestowed the name of Ḫudāwand Ḫān. To Rūmī Ḫān he gave the port of Diu and to Ḫudāwand Ḫān the port of Ṣurat. Their reputation grew large in India, with salary and a vast residence. Their lives and exploits in those regions were on the lips of trader and traveller.[64]

The outcome was that, after he [Muṣṭafā Ibn Bayram] had gained favour with Sultan Bahādur Šāh and the lord of Delhi, Sultan Humāyūn Šāh,[65] had come to do battle with him, he fled from Bahādur Šāh to Humāyūn Šāh and gained even greater favour with him but certain khans envied him his position and gave him poison. He passed away to God Almighty in 945/1538–9.

Bibliography

Albuquerque, Alfonso. 1875–84. *Commentaries of Alfonso Alberquerque*. Translated with notes by Walter de Gray Birch. London: Hakluyt Society nos 53, 55, 62 & 69. 4 vols.

Ayalon, D. 1956. *Gunpowder and Firearms in the Mamluk Kingdom*. London.

Bacqué-Grammont, J.-L. & Kroell, Anne. 1988. *Mamlouks, Ottomans et Portugais en Mer Rouge*. Cairo.

Barbosa. Duarte. 1918. *The Book of Duarte Barbosa*. Translated by M. Longworth Dames. London: Hakluyt Society 2nd Series no. 44.

Beckingham, C.F. 1983. Some early travellers in Arabia. Article XI. In *Between Islam and Christianity*. London.

Burckhardt, J.L. 1829. *Travels in Arabia*. London

Corsali, A. 1554. Lettera della Navigatione del Mar Rosso. In Ramusio, G.B., *Della Navigationi et Viaggi raccolta*. Venice.

Danvers, F.C. 1894. *The Portuguese in India*. London.

Denison Ross, E. 1921. The Portuguese in India and Arabia between 1507 and 1517. *JRAS* 1–28.

Encyclopaedia of Islam. 2nd edit. [*EI2*]

The Glorious Koran. 1930. Translated by Marmaduke Pickthall. London.

al-Ḫazraǧī, 'Alī b. al-Ḥasan. 1906–18. *El-Khazreji's History of the Resúliyy Dynasty of Yemen*. Edited and translated by Muḥammad 'Asal and J.W. Redhouse. London. 5 vols.

Hinz, Walther. 1970. *Islamische Masse und Gewichte*. Leiden & Cologne.

Ibn al-Dayba', 'Abd al-Raḥmān. 1977. *Qurrat al-'uyūn fī aḫbār al-Yaman al-maymūn*. Edited by Muḥammad al-Akwa'. Cairo. 2 vols.

Ibn Iyās, Muḥammad b. Aḥmad. 1931. *Badā'i' al-zuhūr wa-waqā'i' al-duhūr*. Edited by P. Kahle et al. Istanbul.

Inalcik, Halil. 1999. *An Economic and Social History of the Ottoman Empire*. Cambridge.

Knolles, R. 1603. *General History of the Turks*. London.

Lesure, M. 1976. Un document ottoman de 1525 sur l'Inde portugaise et les pays de la Mer Rouge. *Mare Luso-Indicum* 3: 137–60.

Luqmān. Ḥamzah. 1972. *al-Ǧuzur al-Yamaniyyah*. Beirut.

Mundy, Peter. 1907. *The Travels of Peter Mundy 1608–1667*. Edited by Lt Col. Sir Richard Carnac Tempe. Cambridge: Hakluyt Society 2nd Series no. 17.

al-Nahrawālī, Muḥammad b. Aḥmad. 1965. *al-Barq al-Yamānī fī al-fatḥ al-'Uṯmānī*. Edited by Ḥamad al-Ǧasir. Riyadh.

Randels, W.G.L. 1956. South East Africa as shown on selected printed maps of the sixteenth century. *Imago Mundi* 13: 69–88.

Rutter, E. 1928. *The Holy Cities of Arabia*. London.

Sālim, Sayyid Muṣṭafā. 1974. *al-Fatḥ al-'Uṯmānī al-awwal li-l-Yaman*. Cairo.

Schuman, L.O. 1960. *Political History of the Yemen at the Beginning of the 16th Century*. Groningen.

Serjeant, R.B. 1974. *The Portuguese off the South Arabian Coast*. Beirut.

Smith, G. Rex. 1997. The Ṭāhirid sultans of the Yemen etc. Article XV. In *Studies in the Medieval History of the Yemen and South Arabia*. Aldershot.

Stone, Francine (ed.) 1985. *Studies on the Tihāmah*. London.

Stookey, R.W. 1978. *Yemen*. Bolder.

Tibbets, G.R. 1971. *Arab Navigation in the Indian Ocean before the Coming of the Portuguese*. London.

al-Ulughānī, 'Abdallāh Muḥammad. 1910. *An Arabic History of Gujarat*. Edited by E. Denison Ross.

Varisco, Daniel Martin. 1994. *Medieval Agriculture and Islamic Science*. Seattle & London.

Wüstenfeld, F. 1861. *Geschichte der Stadt Mekka*. Leipzig.
Yaḥyā b. al-Ḥusayn. 1968. *Ġāyat al-amānī fī aḫbār al-quṭr al-Yamānī*. Edited by Sa'īd 'Āšūr. Cairo. 2 vols.
al-Zayla'ī, Aḥmad 'Umar. 1992. *Political Conditions and Foreign Relations of the Jāzān Region*. Riyadh.

Notes

1. These were privateers who joined the Ottoman navy with their ships when their services were needed. Inalcik, *Economic and Social History*, 1, xviii. In Yemen they clearly acted as irregular mercenaries, often far from the sea.
2. The author's description of the passage from the Atlantic to the India Ocean carries some resonances of that by the famous Arab navigator, Aḥmad Ibn Mājid, who lived in the second half of the fifteenth and early sixteenth centuries. *EI2*, 3, 858. His reference to the Mountains of the Whites, however, appears based on more traditional Ptolemaic cartography which the discoveries of the early sixteenth century were rapidly modifying, although at first the Mountains of the Whites were projected even further southwards! In this connection it is interesting to note that Duarte Pacheco in his *Esmeraldo in situ orbis* (c. 1508), mistakenly taking Ptolemy for his authority, identified the Mountains of the Whites with the 'the rocky mountains of the Cape of Good Hope'. Randels, 'South East Africa', 69–88. Sabtah refers to Ceuta, the Mediterranean entrance to the Straits of Gibraltar, taken by the Portuguese in 1415. Tibbets, *Arab navigation*, 209. The author assumed that the Portuguese had set out from a Mediterranean port.
3. The paragraph devoted to Aḥmad Ibn Mājid and the Portuguese in the Article in *EI2*, 3, 858–9, gives pride of place to this identification of the pilot by Nahrawālī. It is odd that an Arab navigator of such experience should have allowed himself to give away such a secret in such circumstances. For an argument that the pilot was in fact a Gujerati Moor, or that the author wished to pin blame on the famous navigator through spite, see Tibbets, *Arab navigation*, 9–11.
4. The name often given to a bastion or fort, especially with a Portuguese connection, such as those at Hurmūz, Socotra and Kūt al-Ğalālī in Oman. cf. the diminutive Kuwait, the Kūt in Hufūf and Ceuta in North Africa.
5. Socotra had been seized by the Portuguese as early as 1507 and Goa in 1510, and in Hurmūz a fort was rather insecurely constructed in 1508 by the great Albuquerque who became governor of the Portuguese settlements in 1509 and whose plans to seize Aden and enter the Red Sea and threaten the Holy Places caused consternation in the area, prompting the Tahirid king of the Yemen to appeal to the Mamluk sultan for help as we shall see.

   The early Portuguese success in diverting round the Cape the lucrative trade in eastern spices from the Red Sea to Alexandria, and then Venice, had a devastating effect on the economies of the countries concerned. To illustrate the point, in 903–4/1498 the Venetians had not the funds to buy all the spices available in Alexandria whereas in 907–8/1502 the ships could not find enough spices to load; and again, the Venetian fleet of 8–13 ships which had been coming to Alexandria twice a year (apart from other trading vessels) and returning laden with spices, was reduced, after the discovery of the Cape route, to three ships, only to be seen in Egyptian ports once every two years. Sālim, *al-Fatḥ al-'Uṯmānī*, 45–6 and 55–6.

6. Scholars have assumed that Nahrawālī was mistaken in stating that Muẓaffar, rather than his father Maḥmūd, had sought help from the Mamluk sultan, one going as far as claiming that he had the whole story mixed up. Stookey, *Yemen*, 297, Ch. 6, no. 1: Denison Ross, 'The Portuguese in India and Arabia', 546 and 552–3 (although he conceded the remote possibility); and Schuman, *Political History*, 62.

   The problem appears to lie in the fact that the author makes no mention of the expedition leader Ḥusayn al-Kurdī's previous expedition to India (913–4/1507–9, ending with his defeat at Diu); and no effort to read that campaign into his account can be successful. In fairness to Nahrawālī, however, it should be remembered that his history is essentially an account of the Mamluk and Ottoman invasions of the Yemen and had earlier been given such a title. *EI2*, 7: 911–2. Ḥusayn al-Kurdī, during his earlier passage to India, had been instructed not even to enter Aden, let alone to attack the country.

   Muẓaffar (917–32/1511–1526) succeeded his father in Ramaḍān, 917/Nov. 1511 when we can assume that Ḥusayn al-Kurdī was still in Gujerat since Albuquerque states that al-Kurdī was so devastated by the Portuguese reconquest of Goa in Ša'bān 916/November 1510 that he decided to make arrangements to leave India. Albuquerque, *Commentaries*, iii, 19. He was reluctant to return without doing something substantial for the Mamluk sultan and therefore asked the Gujerati king, the governor of Diu, and various nobles for 'a great sum of money' for the strengthening of the wall at Jeddah which, when collected, he then used for the purchase of spices and other wares which were placed in three ships and conveyed to Jeddah. *Duarte Barbosa*, I, 46–50. The whole exercise would have kept him in India for some time and made it impossible for him to leave immediately by the early spring monsoon. A passage the following spring (Ḏū al-Q.-Ḏū al-Ḥ. 917/Jan.–Feb. 1512) would have allowed him to begin the reconstruction work in Jeddah before he called on the sultan in Cairo, for the first time in over seven years, in Ramaḍān, 918/Nov. 1512, when, significantly, he was accompanied by an envoy from the recently acceded Muẓaffar. In Ğumādā/August of that year, he had sent a representative to the sultan, presumably to give advance news of the situation. Ibn Iyās, iv, 269. Such a schedule would be consistent with al-Nahrawālī's present account, and also accords with the record of Ḥusayn al-Kurdī's reception by the Mamluk sultan of which we have a pertinent record. Ibn Iyās, *Baḍā'i' al-zuhūr*, iv, 286–7.

7. Penultimate Mamluk sultan in Egypt from 906–22/1501–1516 who was sixty when he acceded.
8. The last of the Tahirid kings. Ruled 894–923/1489–1517. He had appealed to Qānṣawh al-Ğawrī on learning of the imminent threat to Aden by Albuquerque in Muḥarram 919/March 1513. Denison Ross, 'The Portuguese in India', 557, following Ibn al-Dayba' and Ulughānī, *An Arabic History*, I, 218–9.
9. Lit. the sea of Yemen, the term sometimes used for the southern part of the Red Sea. Varisco, *Medieval Agriculture*, 222.
10. It appears that he was dispatched with 1,000 *levend* by the Ottoman sultan to help the Mamluk sultan in his expedition against the Portuguese. The historian rather

dryly adds that the Ottoman sultan had no idea that Qānṣawh al-Ḡawrī and Ḥusayn al-Kurdī intended to seize the Yemen! Ibn al-Dayba‘, *Qurrat*, 226. Largely from the Italian and Portuguese sources we understand that, by origin a Turk from Mitylene, he had built up experience and wealth as a sea captain in Mediterranean waters and had much impressed the Mamluk sultan when constructing ships in Suez after which he was appointed captain of the fleet whereas Ḥusayn al-Kurdī was given charge of the expedition, an arrangement which demanded a great deal of cooperation but appeared, at any rate in the early years, to have worked well. (Ibn Iyās, *Baḍā'i'*, iv, 365–6, 466: Corsali 'Lettera della Navigatione', i, 205 d. He was to play a major role in campaigns in Yemen with both Mamluk and Ottoman.

11. Guns of small calibre, such as the falconet. Ayalon, *Gunpowder*, 127. They probably weighed 85–100 pounds and fired lead balls of 14–17 ounces. Lesure, 'Un document ottoman', 152, n. 20. Varying estimates of the numbers of men, ships and arms involved are tabled in J-L Bacqué-Grammont and Kroell, *Mamlouks*, between 6 and 7.
12. He can only have just begun the wall's reconstruction when he reported to the sultan in Cairo in Ramaḍān 918/Nov. 1512. We hear of him actively supervising its rebuilding in Jeddah when, on enquiring from a visiting merchant from India about the Portuguese fleet, he was told of Albuquerque's construction of a fort at Calicut. Permission was not granted for the construction of such a fort until December 1513. *Barbosa*, II, 86 no. 2: Danvers, *The Portuguese*, I, 281–4. This date would be consistent with that of 920/1514–15 for the continuing Jeddah wall reconstruction given in Serjeant, *Portuguese*, 160–2. Serjeant observes that the description tallies closely with the illustration facing p. 48 depicting Lopo Soares de Albergaria's expedition before Jeddah in 1517.
13. Barakāt II. Grand Sharif of Mecca 903–31/1497–1525.
14. This potentially exciting paragraph has been rather discredited as indicated in n. 6 above but, given Ḥusayn al-Kurdī's previous contact with Muẓaffar, we should at least consider its implications; and it is worth remarking that the author elaborates in more detail Ḥusayn al-Kurdī's tyrannical behaviour in Jeddah as well as this visit to Gujerat in his history of Mecca. Wüstenfeld, *Geschichte*, 245–8. There he repeats mid–921/autumn 1515 mid-late 921/end 1516, or at least 'about (*fī ḥudūd*)' 921, as the year for the visit. A possible scenario could have Ḥusayn al-Kurdī sailing to Gujerat by the south-west monsoon in the autumn of 1515 and returning at the end of the year by the first winds of the north-east monsoon to join Salmān Rayyis, who had been made captain of the new fleet, in Kamarān. The sailing time need not have been long; and we know that in 1513 in August Albuquerque sailed from Aden to Diu in 12 days. Ḥusayn al-Kurdī would have gone with his own grabs as he was not formally appointed to the expedition until Muḥarram 922/Feb. 1516. We know that Albuquerque returned from Hurmūz to die in Goa in November and that his successor, Lopo Soares, arrived in Goa with a new fleet in September. Ibn Iyās, v, 3, and Danvers, *The Portuguese in India*, I, 323 and 333–4. In these circumstances the Portuguese would indeed have been preoccupied at Goa and not be near Gujerat! But this is only a possible scenario.

    The fleet had arrived in Kamarān on 7 Ḏū al-Q./13 December 1515. Schuman, *Political History*, no. 127.

15. See n. 8 above.
16. These gifts could be prodigious. A previous gift from Egypt to the Tahirid king took the form of a crystal lamp, about the height of a man, two crystal boxes and some large swords; Serjeant, *Portuguese*, 41, no. 4.
17. Commander ʻAlī b. Muḥammad al-Baʻdānī.
18. In an analysis of Egyptian motives for action in the Yemen, Schuman comes down against the idea of a concerted plan by the Mamluks to seize the country. His *Political History*, 70–1. It is unlikely, however, that Ḥusayn al-Kurdī and Salmān Rayyis, who may have been closer to the thinking of Qānṣawh al-Ǧawrī, would have been so diverted, had they not thought that such action would suit the Mamluk sultan. On the other hand, they would have realized his danger from the Ottomans and may have viewed the Yemen as a vehicle for their own adventures. They must also have had strong reason to secure their rear in further engagements with the Portuguese. But one is left pondering their reason for their further delay in confronting the Portuguese about whose increasing naval power they cannot have been in doubt.
19. Their leader at the time was the Imam al-Mutawakkil ʻalā Allāh Šaraf al-Dīn Yaḥyā (877–965/1473–1555). Although he announced his claim to the imamate in 912/1506, it was not until 941/1535 that he imposed his full authority.
20. According to the Zaydi historian, Yaḥyā Ibn Ḥusayn, the Imam Šaraf al-Dīn had asked for Ḥusayn al-Kurdī's help against ʻĀmir b. ʻAbd al-Wahhāb before Ḥusayn had written to seek assistance from the Tahirid king. Only when the latter refused to help, did Ḥusayn agree to help the imam and then send 200 men with muskets as requested. Yaḥyā Ibn Ḥusayn, *Ǧāyat*, II, 644–5.
21. At that time he was commander of the forces of his brother who was lord of Ǧīzān and who, during the previous year, had pledged his support to the Mamluk sultan against ʻĀmir, even naming his son Qānṣawh after him. ʻIzz al-Dīn seized the emirate from his brother in 1519. Zaylaʻī, *Political Conditions*, 201–2 and 206.
22. This must refer to the incident near Hodeida in mid Dhū al-Ḥijjah 921/January 1516, when the expedition fired on the inhabitants after they had refused to supply them with provisions. Schuman, *Political History*, n. 129. The first battle where muskets, or perhaps primitive hand guns, were used took place four months later in Ǧumādā I/May at al-Mazḥaf in Wādī Mawr. Ibn al-Daybaʻ, *Qurrat*, II, 224 and Zaylaʻī, *Political Conditions*, 202. The famous account of the new weapon is given in Ibn al-Daybaʻ, II, 224 and translated into English by Smith, 'The Ṭāhirid Sultans of the Yemen', 154. In fact, of course, artillery had been used by the Tahirids during the siege of Aden by Albuquerque in 1513. For this and its earlier presence in Yemen see Schuman, *Political History*, 13 and n. 92.
23. A forceful character who had ordered the people of Hodeida not to supply the Egyptian forces and had played a leading role in the fighting at al-Mazḥaf. The previous year he had attended the three day mourning prayers for a senior member of the al-Naẓārī family in the old al-Ašāʻir mosque in Zabīd. He was badly wounded in the fighting at Zabīd and died soon after in Taʻizz. Ibn al-Daybaʻ, *Qurrat*, II, 221, 226–8.
24. His father had acquired the celebrated castle of Ḥabb east of Ibb from Ḥusayn al-Kurdī during the break up of the Tahirid state. It was to pass to Commander ʻAlī's

nephew whose father-in-law had extensive shipping and trading connections with India. *Barq*, 129–131.

25. The Tahirid historian, Ibn al-Dayba' was clearly outraged by the devastation inflicted upon Zabīd and gives a graphic account of the plunder, torture, abuse and extortion suffered by its inhabitants and the arson and destruction the town underwent. Ḥusayn al-Kurdī seems to have had little control over his troops and eventually escaped to the coast, allegedly to obtain for them the money he had promised! *Qurrat*, II, 228.

    Into this scene of carnage it is bizarre to insert the reported release by Commander Ḥusayn of a Portuguese captain, Gregorio de Quadra, and his crew who had been imprisoned in Zabīd after being arrested off Zayla' in 1509 and taken to the Tahirid king, 'Āmir b. 'Abd al-Wahhāb! The party feigned Islam and succeeded in escaping to Basra and Hurmūz after visiting the Prophet's grave in Medina with the Grand Sharif of Mecca. Beckingham, *Between Islam and Christianity*, 169–172.
26. The eastern gate.
27. Village S.S.E. of Zabīd, long known for its pottery. According to one source, he intended to help with the siege of Aden but, on hearing that Ḥusayn al-Kurdī had arrived at Mocha, he went there to join him before his visit to Mawza'.
28. Governor of Aden and apparently one of the Tahirid sultan's slaves, perhaps from Ethiopia. He appeared very wily in his efforts to preserve the independence of the port from Mamluk and Portuguese influence. He repelled Albuquerque in 919/1513, and Ḥusayn al-Kurdī in 922/1516; and was ambivalent with the Portuguese expedition led by Lopo Soares in 923/1517, offering the keys to Aden on their way to the Red Sea, and then on the way back (when his defences were restored) withdrawing his offer! Serjeant, *Portuguese*, 50, n. 5 and Danvers, *Portuguese*, 265–7, 334–5.
29. A variant of the incident states that Salmān chased and captured a large Malaccan ship containing a valuable cargo which he dispatched to Diu with a message for its return with provisions etc. and the promise of his own speedy presence to overthrow the Franks. Whatever the truth it indicates continuing contact with the Gujerati sultan. Corsali, *Navigationi*, I, 205 a. Corsali incidentally gives an extremely detailed account of Aden's position, fortifications and former trade. Ibid, I, 200, b and c.
30. The citadel of al-Qāhirah.
31. The text gives 11 Rağab which must be incorrect in view of the date of arrival, 13 Rağab, which is agreed by others. 24 Rağab would be consistent with the Saturday after the action. Schuman, *Political History*, n. 150 and 153. For an argument delaying the attack on Aden by a month see Bacqué-Grammont and Kroell, *Mamlouks*, 11–12.
32. The Turkish practice of staking apparently involved the driving of a pointed pole through the body from the anus to its exit between the head and shoulders. Victims could survive for many hours. In ganching the victim is trussed like a chicken and hoisted up on a gallows and then suddenly dropped on to one of a number of large pointed iron hooks attached to a bar below. The victim could survive for up to a day depending on which part of the body was impaled by the hook. *Peter Munby*, 55–56, with sobering illustration facing 55.
33. Ottoman sultan, known as Selīm the Grim, 918–26/1512–20.

34. The gate in Cairo where criminals were often hanged and their remains exhibited.
35. Muḥammad Abū Numayy. Succeeded his father, Barakāt, as grand sharif in 931/1525 and died in 974/1566.
36. The Mamluk abuse in Cairo witnessed by his father (Shaykh 'Alā' al-Dīn Aḥmad Muḥammad b. Qāḍī Ḫān 871/1466–7—949/1542–3) took place when Nahrawālī was about four years old. We do not know when he was brought to Mecca by his father but we are told that he obtained his early education from him. *EI2*, 7: 911–12. Ḥamad al-Ǧāsir illustrates how he was in Mecca by Ramaḍān, 932/June 1526 when the Ottoman commander, Ḫayr al-Dīn, was upbraided for the misbehaviour of his troops. *Barq*, 18.
37. cf. Sūrah IV, 7–12.
38. The name given to the semi-circular wall to the north of the Ka'bah in front of the Ḥanafī pavilion.
39. The pavilion where the imam of the Ḥanafī sect takes his station and guides the congregation in prayer. Burckhardt, *Travels*, 142. The author's history of Mecca was one of Burckhardt's principal sources.
40. The exact meaning of *al-'alamayn* is elusive. There are echoes of Sūrah XLII, 32, with ships plying the ocean but it may just refer to markers for the passage to the sea. Jeddah harbour was girt with sharp pointed ridges of rock-like little islands. Albuquerque, *Commentaries*, IV, 35. It may simply be the name of a place.
41. Corsali states that, when he had fled to Mecca after a difference with Salmān Rayyis, the Meccan sharifs had in fear dispatched him to Salmān Rayyis who had him drowned as he supposedly sailed to meet the Ottoman sultan in Cairo. Corsali, *Navigationi*, I, 205, a. Even Knolles mentions such a difference leading to the drowning and claims that whereas Ḥusayn al-Kurdī favoured the last Mamluk sultan, Salmān Rayyis was ready to attach his colours to the Ottomans. Knolles, *General History*, 553. There are signs of developing disagreement during the attack on Aden. Schuman, *Political History*, n. 153. Salmān himself, in a letter to Sultan Selīm explaining his own inability immediately to come to Cairo, disclaimed any role in the drowning and upraided Barakāt for his highhandedness and oppression. Bacqué-Grammont and Kroell, *Mamlouks*, 35. These last authors, in a lengthy analysis of the situation, express the view that al-Nahrawālī's account is the most acceptable. Ibid, 14–19.
42. Sūrah XVIII, 50. *The Glorious Koran*, translated by Marmaduke Pickthall. (London 1930).
43. The sultan was to be killed near Ṣan'ā' by the Mamluk forces on 23 Rabī' II 923/15 May 1517.
44. Considerable armament had been left by Ḥusayn al-Kurdī. Salmān Rayyis, in the first part of a report to the grand vizier in Cairo dated June 2 1525, gives details of 18 ships and a vast amount of weaponry, including 57 *ḍarbzanāt* (See n. 11 above). Lesure, Document, III, 152–3. What authority Salmān had received from Cairo in late 930/early 1524 is conjectural but we can see how he later gained the confidence of the sultan's grand vizier.
45. We know that the Portuguese commander, Eitor da Silveira, was in Red Sea waters that winter with an expedition and we are told that Albuquerque's successor's policy of allowing all Portuguese to trade had increased the amount of their activity

in the area. Serjeant, *Portuguese*, 18 and 172, n. L. and Danvers, *Portuguese*, 369–70.

46. Mahrah mercenaries were used by the Tahirids and in India. Serjeant, *Portuguese*, 71, n. 7.
47. See [21] above and n. 21.
48. An interesting village, now straddling the main road between Bāğil and Hodeida and within the Wādī Sihām system. Nearby was the medieval town of al-Kadrā' and present al-Quṭay', where, at least until recently, spectacular, if irregular, horse races were held. For other information see F. Stone, *Tihāmah*, passim.
49. Ibrāhīm Pasha, c. 898–9–942/1493–1536, had been appointed grand vizier in 929/1523, much to the chagrin of Aḥmad Pasha. He had married the sultan's sister in 930/1524, and so was at the height of his power when he was dispatched to Cairo. *EI2*, 3: 998–9. Salmān Rayyis' report to him (see n. 44 above) could well have been written in the context of such a meeting. He does not disparage Ḥusayn in the report but writes of the Yemen being without a head (while he is still in charge of Zabīd): he claims that the armament in Jeddah was adequate to conquer all the Portuguese forts in Hurmūz and India and goes on to describe the lands on both sides of the Red Sea. He states that the Yemen is richer than Egypt, estimates the number of *sanjaks* into which it could be divided and draws particular attention to the importance of the export of madder to India (Gujerat). Lesure, Document, 154–160.
50. The author makes clear their respective authority in (53) below, a precedent for which was established in the previous expedition with Ḥusayn al-Kurdī but, on this occasion, Salmān's co-commander was to take over in Zabīd as governor of the Ottoman state in the Yemen.
51. The *muḥallaq* was a circular coin of similar value to the *buqshah*. Serjeant, *Portuguese*, 143. The *raṭl* in Egypt is equivalent to 449.28 grams. Hinz, *Masse*, 28–9.
52. The author would have been about 15 years old. See n. 36 above.
53. According to Yaḥyā Ibn Ḥusayn, there were 4,000 troops. Ġāyat, ii, 667. Most of the gates mentioned in the text are clearly marked on the plan in Rutter, *Holy Cities*, I, facing 252. The map also shows Bāb al-Quṭbī, the single arched gate named after the author, who lived in an adjoining lane and opened this small gate into the Ḥaram. Burckhardt, *Travels*, 153. al-Ḥuğūn, on the way to Jeddah, is about 1200 metres west of al-Ma'lāh. Banū Ġassān is the patronymic of the Rasūlid dynasty which ruled from 626–845/1228–1441 and al-Muğāhid 'Alī b. Dā'ūd had the school constructed in 740/1339–40, with a *waqf* funded from his estates in Zabīd. He ruled from 721–64/1322–1363 and, in 731/1330, his court in Ta'izz was visited by the traveller, Ibn Baṭṭūṭah. 'Alī al-Ḫazrajī, *History*, iii, 2, 55 and iii, 3, n. 1199.
54. The author was awarded the first Ḥanafī professorship at Sulaymān's newly completed college for the four orthodox rites in Ğumādā I 975/November 1567. *EI2*, 7, 911. al-Suwayqah, or the little market, was at the east of the Ḥaram and was traditionally the area where rich Indian merchants exposed their goods for sale. Burckhardt, *Travels*, 118.
55. They had twenty galleys. Lesure, Document, 141.
56. Port opposite Kamarān island.

57. One gets the impression that the author, as a young man, remembered seeing them in Mecca!
58. Salmān had long entertained such an ambition but he cannot have thought that the Ottoman sultan would condone this behaviour.
59. A village 4 km east of Zabīd of historical interest. The last Tahirid king had returned to fight a fierce but unsuccessful two day battle there with the Egyptians, in Šawwāl 922/early November 1516, after his loss of Zabīd. Ibn Dayba‘, *Qurrat*, II, 230. There is a small but interesting three domed mosque with Rasulid features.
60. A *wādī* near Medina.
61. Ulug̲hānī states that Salmān was killed by H̱ayr al-Dīn while he was playing chess. He claims the island to be near Buq‘ah, a port or anchorage S.W. of Zabīd. *History*, I, 319. Both Salmān and Ḥusayn al-Kurdī often used al-Buq‘ah, the latter also using al-Mutaynah, not far to the north. Al-Muḥāmilah may, however, be identical with Rās Muǧāmilah, an island in Ghulāfiqah bay opposite two named fishing villages. Ḥamzah Luqmān, *al-Ǧuzur al-Yamaniyyah, 16.* I have not been able to find any corroboration for the author's account of the circumstances leading to H̱ayr al-Dīn's blinding by Salmān. See [52] above.
62. An Italian renegade who, despite favourable treatment by the Portuguese, was to prove loyal to the Gujerati sultanate and died in 953/1546 in a later attempt to relieve Diu. Serjeant, *Portuguese*, 106.
63. Sultan of Gujerat 923–43/1526–37. He ceded the island of Diu to the Portuguese in 942/1535.
64. Their timely arrival in 937/1531 helped the governor of Diu to defeat a full-scale attack by the Portuguese viceroy. *EI2*, 2: 322. Muṣṭafā gave Bahādur a cannon called Laylā which his uncle, Salmān Rayyis, had cast for the Ottoman sultan, Sulaymān, and cast another for him which, in the best tradition of the Arabian love story, he called Maǧnūn! For further information, consistent with what this author states, see Ulug̲hānī, *History*, index s.v.
65. 913–63/1508–56. Second Mughal ruler. From Agra he confronted Gujerat's expanding power in early 941/1535 and Bahādur fled to Diu. *EI2*, 1, 575–6.

Three Tales from Arabia—Story-telling in Ibn al-Muǧāwir's 7th/13th Century Guide

G. Rex Smith

The following paper is an attempt to highlight one last facet of Ibn al-Muǧāwir's *Tārīḫ al-Mustabṣir* (*TM*) before final publication of a complete annotated translation of the work for the Hakluyt Society.

The author of the *TM* was Abū Bakr b. Muḥammad b. Mas'ūd b. 'Alī b. Aḥmad Ibn al-Muǧāwir (*IM*) who must have been travelling in the Arabian Peninsula in the early decades of the seventh/thirteenth century. His two *nisbah* s, al-Baġdādī and al-Nīsābūrī, as well as the internal evidence of the text, indicate that he was from the east of the Islamic world, probably from Ḫurāsān (Smith 1991). The basic format of the text is a route description, using parasangs (*farsaḫ*, *farāsiḫ*) (Smith 1985: 82–3 and 1993) probably the distance covered on foot in one hour, but it is much more besides. Clearly our author was interested in doing business in the west and south of Arabia, so such matters as prices, taxes, customs dues, markets, currency etc. were important to him, but equally so were the people who lived in these areas, their habits, customs, clothes, food and agriculture, their antiquities, their towns, their buildings and their history. He was particularly fond of sorcery and the bizarre (Smith 1988: 113–5 and 1995). He did not hesitate at all to deviate from his route presentation to provide any information he may have acquired on any of these or allied subjects. Very roughly, his itinerary (or itineraries) was (were) south from the Holy Cities into Tihāmat al-Yaman, the Red Sea coastal plain, Aden and right along the southern coast of Arabia—though mentioning also the important inland towns like Ṣan'ā', even Ṣa'dah and Naǧrān in the north—round the corner at Ra's al-Ḥadd into the Gulf. His last port of call was Bahrain and presumably he returned to the east by land via Iraq. The text of the *TM* was edited by Oscar Löfgren and published by Brill in Leiden in two volumes with continuous pagination in 1951–4. I have followed this text throughout work on this paper.

IM's Sources

Undoubtedly much of what is reported in the TM was personally observed by IM. He frequently uses the introduction '*qāla Ibn al-Muğāwir*' and on one occasion '*qāla Abū Bakr*', the one clue to his given name in the whole of the text (p. 212). He also makes good use of informants and about seventy are named. Only occasionally does he include a vague source of information: 'A certain Christian said …' (p. 33); 'A Jewish silversmith in Aden informed me …' (p. 32). Infrequently he makes no mention of his source, but this may simply point to personal observation. He does cite named literary works, both prose and poetry. One notices particularly in places, when reading the *TM*, the atmosphere of the all-male gathering, where men are wont to tell their tales, more and more elaborated and exaggerated, tales of the wondrous and the bizarre, tales of magic and of sex, tales of far-off lands and of strange people. It is such story-telling which is the subject of this paper and three examples are studied below in some detail.

The Stories

A translation of each story is given, free of brackets etc. and other distractions, though including words added for clarity, and in an English as appropriate as can be produced for the atmosphere of the original and for the genre as a whole. This is followed by a commentary on the text.

Story 1

This story appears under the heading 'The Building of the Wall of Aden', p. 127, line 9, to p. 128, line 6, of the printed text. IM here has an informant, one 'Abdallāh b. Muḥammad b. Yaḥyā.

Translation (* indicates mention in the Commentary below)

A ship coming from the west to Aden anchored at night. The *nāẖūḏah** disembarked from the ship and had a walk around Aden. All at once he came upon a lofty house, with lit candles and burning aloes wood.* He knocked at the door and a servant came down and opened up for him, saying to him, 'Is there anything I can do for you?' The merchant replied, 'Yes', so the servant gave him permission to enter and the owner of the house invited him up. Up he went and each greeted the other without being aware of who the other was. The conversation flowed and eventually the *nāḫūḏah* said, ‘I have come tonight from the west and am wanting, if you, sir, will be so kind, to hide some of my precious commodities with you.’ The owner of the house asked him why. He replied, ‘Out of fear of the Dā‘ī*.’ The owner of the house said, ‘Come, be not afraid of tyrants! Transport all you have to such-and-such a house.’ The merchant left the house and the mariners began to put the goods from the ship into chests and transport them to the house indicated by the owner of the house until they had cleared out two thirds of the contents of the ship. In the morning the *nāḫūḏah* discovered that his host of the previous evening was none other than the Dā‘ī himself! He said to himself, ‘There was I afraid of the rain, and I fell under the drain-pipe!’ He became perplexed and felt ashamed. The Dā‘ī summoned him and said, ‘I was your host last night, but today I am the Dā‘ī, ruler of Aden. Don’t worry! Relax! The custom fee of your ship is my gift to you along with the house to which you came. Here are a thousand dinars which you can spend while you are in our town. It would be wrong for me to take anything from you, either by way of a gift or in the process of buying and selling.’ The *nāḫūḏah* asked, ‘Why are you doing this?’ The Dā‘ī replied, ‘Because you came into our house yesterday at midnight.’*

COMMENTARY

I have transliterated the word *nāḫūḏah* as it appears in its Arabized form in the original. It is the Persian *nā-ḫūḏa* and can be interpreted ‘ship’s captain’, ‘master’. It is important to remember, however, that it frequently, as here, means ‘owner-captain’, ‘supercargo’, i.e. someone engaged in trade as well as commanding the ship (Landberg 1920–42, iii: 2729–30; Yule & Burnell 1969 (nacoda, nacoder); Löfgren 1936–50: 58–9; Steingass 1930: 1368).

Dr James Mandaville informs me that *‘ūd*, although called aloes or eagle wood in English, has nothing to do with the true aloes (Arabic *ṣabir*). *‘ūd* is in fact a type of heartwood, *Aquilaria agallocha* Roxb.

This story dates from the time of the Ismā‘īlī dynasty in Aden, the Zuray‘ids, 473–569/1080–1173, whose rulers all had the title *dā‘ī*.

The last remark of the dā‘ī I interpret to refer to the fact that the *nāḫūḏah* was his guest the previous night and the law of hospitality obliged him to treat the *nāḫūḏah* in this way.

Story 2

This story appears under the heading ‘Destruction of the Dam of al-Ma’zimayn’ (text p. 195, line 5 to p. 196, line 18). Al-Ma’zimayn are the two narrows of Wādī Aḏanah where the dam of Mārib was built (Hamdānī 1968: 80 and 1983: 219; *EI* 2, ‘Mārib’).

Translation

The people of Šaddād and ʻĀd* blocked the passage between two mountains with stones and lead, taking it up in height until the wall of rock came up to the top of the mountains. So the flood waters began quickly to come up against it and the water collect until it had become like a sea dammed up. From it they would water their lands and their flocks. It is said that they watered right up almost as far as Syria* cultivated plots where grapes, date-palms and other agricultural produce grew, and settlements connected one to another. The whole region remained inhabited until God destroyed it.

The reason for this—according to al-Rāzī*—was that a caravan from Syria departed and suddenly a rat jumped from the ground and rode on the back of one of the camels in the caravan. The rat moved around from camel to camel, crossing over from one place to another until the town of Mārib was reached. The rat leapt from the camel into the dam and began its work. Now it is said that al-Nuʻmān b. al-Mun̲dir* went out one day hunting. He was pursuing his quarry when he found the rat with its canine teeth made of iron, digging away at the dam. When he returned to his father, al-Mun̲dir, he told him the story of the rat and gave him a description of its canine teeth, that they were made of iron, as it dug away at the dam. Al-Mun̲dir said, 'What we find in books, my son, is true, namely that the Mārib dam will be destroyed by a rat whose canine teeth were made of iron. When we enter the monastery and churches on Sunday, I want you to come up to me while all the people are assembled there and pick a quarrel with me on some matter. Be rude to me and when you think things have gone on long enough, come up and slap me with the palm of your hand across my cheek.' 'How can I do this?', asked al-Nuʻmān. 'Do as you are told, my son', replied al-Mun̲dir, 'I have a plan and there will be some benefit in this for you.' So the boy did as his father had commanded him. When he slapped the old man, the latter became angry (now from that time onwards he was called al-Malṭūm [he who is slapped]), got up among all the people and said, 'O leading Arabs! I can't stay with you any longer!' They all asked him why. He replied, 'How could a young lad cause me such pain and in front of you break the respect and honour which he had from me?' He then immediately cried out that the dam was for sale. So the Arab tribes assembled and came together at the sale of the dam. They asked for how much it was being sold. 'Cover', he said, 'this sword of mine to the hilt', and he planted the point of the sword in the ground. The Arabs began to bring gold, silver and ornaments, continuing to pour out their gold until his sword was covered in it up to the hilt. The old man took the wealth, went up to the mountain and dwelt facing the dam (and the mountain is called Ḥifā[?]*), he and his family all waiting for the destruction of the dam.

When the rat was able to destroy the dam, by piercing it, it reduced it to ruins and the flood struck. Salāmah b. Muḥammad b. Ḥaǧǧāǧ told me the following. When it pushed aside the dam, the water carried away among other things a thousand beardless youths on a thousand piebald horses, apart from the greys, the sorrels, the blacks and the chestnuts. As the poet recited:

> The dam of al-Ma'zimayn was utterly destroyed; time passed,
> [the water] being carried all over the place!

COMMENTARY

For Šaddād, the son of 'Ād, see Ibn Ḫaldūn nd:11; *EI* 2, 'Iram Ḏhāt al-'Imād'. The people of 'Ād were the rebellious folk to whom Hūd was sent to turn them from their idolatry. See Qur'ān 7: 65 ff.

Syria may be what is meant here and one should put it down to hyperbole. However, *šām*, as always in the Arabian Peninsula, may simply mean rather vaguely 'north'.

One would expect IM's informant here, al-Rāzī, to be Aḥmad b. 'Abdallāh b. Muḥammad al-Rāzī who died in 460/1068 and who was the author of the famous *Tārīḫ Madīnat Ṣan'ā'*. Although al-Rāzī mentions the dam several times in his work, the story of the rat does not appear.

Al-Nu'mān is presumably the son of the famous al-Munḏir IV and was the last of the Lakhmid kings of al-Ḥīrah in southern Iraq in the sixth century AD. The Lakhmids conquered far and wide within the Arabian Peninsula, although they have never elsewhere to my knowledge been directly associated in this way with Mārib. Their participation in the actual event of the destruction of the dam, which incidentally is now thought to have taken place in the sixth century AD, does of course add spice to the story (*EI* 2, 'al-Ḥīra', 'Lakhmids' and 'Mārib'). The Lakhmids became Christians, hence reference to monasteries and churches in the story (Šahīd 1971: 266–72).

Ḥ fā is not vocalized in the text and the MSS and indeed the *fā'* is only certain from the diagram of Mārib (text p. 198). I wonder if it is Ḥifā, which Yāqūt (*Mu'jam*, ii, 274) says is a place and a mountain, although he does not say where. Also, none of the Yemeni geographers appears to mention it.

Story 3

Under the heading 'The Genealogy of the Ǧāšū*', the story (p. 290, line 6, to 291, line 9) begins without mention of an informant, implying the story comes from IM himself, although the intervention under his name (lines 8–12) may well imply that it is a story he has heard from others which requires, so he thinks, clarification from him.

Translation

A certain king was attacked by pleurisy* and the omens indicated to him that, if he had intercourse every night with a virgin Nubian slave girl, his unfortunate illness would disappear. IM comments, 'In all creation there is nothing as hot as the vagina of a Nubian slave girl. With the heat the pleurisy gradually dissolves, descending along with the sperm into the Nubian slave girl. When the woman gets up, she shakes the sperm, now free of the ill effects of the disease, from her vagina. No harm comes to the slave girl. But others say it does do her harm.' When the king heard this, he sent one of his viziers to the Sudan, commanding him to buy one hundred virgin Nubian slave girls. When the vizier was ready, he cut off his penis, put it into a box and handed it over to the king. He journeyed until he reached the Sudan, where he bought the virgin slave girls and took them to the king. When the latter came to one, he found her with sexual experience—and thus the second, the third, the tenth, right up to the hundredth! He found them all in the same condition. When the vizier had entered into the presence of the king's courtiers, the king said to those present, 'There has been some poking (*ğāshak*)!' That is, 'He has been penetrating them,' That is, 'He has deflowered them!' The king added, 'There was indeed no doubt'. That is, 'Certainty has emerged out of doubt in the matter.' So when the vizier realized what the king was saying, he called for the box, opened the lid and there was the penis inside. 'What made you do that?, enquired the king. 'I was afraid of exactly what has happened.' Then the king called all the slave girls and asked them about their condition. They replied, 'We stopped at such-and-such an island and swam in a spring of sweet water. We knew nothing of what happened to us, but each one of us was accompanied by a jinni who deflowered her.' The king said, 'Return them to their island.' So they dwelt in the island of Qays* where they built houses. They multiplied and the inhabitants became many. They were called Ğāšak because of the utterance made by the king. The expression remained with them. They became known as Ğāšū.

Commentary

The word *birsām* might also be used of a tumour (Lane 1863–93, I: 187), but the commoner meaning is that given and this would, in any case, seem to fit the context of the story better. It is made up of the two Persian words, *barr*, 'breast' and *sām*, 'swelling' (Steingass 1930:166 and 643).

The true etymology of the word may be nothing more than the colloquial Persian word *čāšū* (Löfgren 1936–50 ii: 25). The Arabic *ğāšak* (*ğā' al-šakk*) of the text can also of course mean 'there was some doubt', hence the two glosses. 'There was indeed no doubt' begins the punning which is almost impossible to render into English and could either mean 'There was indeed no doubt' or

'There has not been any penetration'. In order to make anything of this in English, one has to assume that the meaning of *ǧāšak* has been taken to refer to 'doubt'; viz. 'there was some doubt.' 'there was indeed no doubt.'

The island of Qays—Kīsh in Persian—is in the Gulf, only about twenty miles from the coast of Iran, almost due north of Abu Dhabi.

The above then are three examples of the story-telling which is quoted from time to time in IM's *TM*, in vivid contrast to his route lists, his long, difficult, technical passages and his social, anthropological and economic excursuses. The supercargo, trying to hide his precious cargo in Aden to avoid the payment of customs dues, asks the owner of a large house there to help, only to discover, red-faced, that the man is the local ruler whose dues he is trying to evade! The wily Mund̲ir, knowing of the impending undermining and collapse of the Mārib dam, contrives to sell it, using his son, al-Nuʿmān, as accomplice, and then sits back to view the disaster! The wise vizier who foresees trouble when he is despatched by his king to buy Nubian virgins, but who has to pay dearly to remain in his post!

The tales are effectively told and reflect the milieu of the all-male social gathering to which allusion has been made above. Each one of them—and others in the *TM* too not dealt with here—might well have earned a place in the *1001 Nights*. One can only guess at the meal Burton would have made of them!

Bibliography

al-Hamdānī, al-Ḥasan b. Aḥmad. 1968. *Ṣifat Ǧazīrat al-ʿArab*. Edited by David Heinrich Müller. Leiden.

——. 1983. *Ṣifat Ǧazīrat al-ʿArab*. Edited by Muḥammad b. ʿAlī al-Akwaʿ. Ṣanʿāʾ.

Landberg, Le Comte de. 1924–42. *Glossaire dat̲înois*. Leiden.

Lane, Edward William. 1863–93. *An Arabic–English Lexicon*. London & Edinburgh.

Löfgren, Oscar. 1936–50. *Arabische Texte zur Kenntnis der Stadt Aden im Mittelalter*. Uppsala.

Shahīd, I. 1971. *The Martyrs of Najrān—New Documents*. Brussels.

Smith, G. Rex. 1985. 'Ibn al-Mujāwir on Dhofar and Socotra'. *PSAS* 15: 79–92.

——. 1988. 'Ibn al-Mujāwir's 7th/13th century Arabia—the wondrous and the humorous'. In Irvine, A.K., Serjeant, R.B. & Smith, G. Rex (eds), *A Miscellany of Middle Eastern Articles—in Memoriam Thomas Muir Johnstone 1924–83*. Harlow.

——. 1991. 'Ibn al-Mujāwir's 7th/13th century guide to Arabia—the eastern connection'. *Occasional Papers of the School of Abbasid Studies* 3: 71–89.

——. 1993. 'Some "anthropological" passages from Ibn al-Mujāwir's guide to Arabia and their proposed interpretation'. In Gingrich, Andre et al. (eds), *Studies in Oriental Culture and History—Festschrift for Walter Dostal*. Frankfurt.

——. 1995. 'Magic, jinn and the supernatural in mediev1al Yemen: examples from Ibn al-Muǧāwir's 7th/13th century guide'. *Quaderni di Studi Arabi* 13: 1–18.

Steingass, F. 1930. *A Comprehensive Persian–English Dictionary*. London.

Yule, H. & Burnell, A.C. 1969. *Hobson-Jobson—a Glossary of Anglo–Indian Words etc.* London.

The Ma'āzibah and the Zarānīq of Tihāmah

Francine Lida Stone

In the year 759/1357–8 the Rasulid historian, Ḥasan al-Ḫazraǧī, chronicled the following about a tribe known as the Ma'āzibah. Sir J.W. Redhouse translated it:

> And on the 28th of Dhú'l-Qa'da the Ma'áziba attacked Feshál at dawn. … Feshál then became waste, and all government was abrogated in the whole of the vale of Rima'. … The Sultan then went forth with an imposing column in quest of the Ma'áziba tribesmen … but they moved away from their villages, and the Sultan did not succeed in getting at any of them; so he burnt their villages and returned [to Zabīd]. … The Ma'áziba, with the other depredators, then came [back] down to their villages. When they had settled themselves they sojourned for a while, and then assembled to attack Kedrá', in the month of Ṣafer. … They laid it waste and set fire to it, so that all government was done away with in the vale of Sihám. Devastations and depredations became continual, the roads were barred to all traffic, and the inhabitants of Zebíd could not communicate with the people of Mehjem, nor those of Mehjem with the men of Zebíd. … On the 7th of Sha'bán in this said year … the Ma'áziba and other depredators attacked the date plantations of the vale of Zebíd, and plundered their inhabitants, so that all government was banished thence. … On the 25th of Shewwál the depredating gangs of the Ma'áziba, of the archers [al-Rumāh], and of Qaḥrá', assembled and attacked Jeththa. … After this the [same] Arabian tribesmen came together, all of them in the month of Dhú'l-Ḥijja and sent to the inhabitants of Surdud, stirring them up to an attack on Mehjem. Thus ruin lorded it over the whole of the western seaboard countries, nothing remaining except Zebíd and Ḥaraḍ.[1]

In 1915 G. Wyman Bury wrote this about the Zarānīq (which he spells Dheranik) tribe:

> Some years ago a previous Kaimakam was shot dead at the door of his residence in Beit al-Fakih, by the followers of a Dheranik chief whom he had ordered his gendarmes to arrest. The chief and his followers escaped in the confusion, and since then the Dheranik have been out of hand. They muster 10,000 men, and their paramount chief—Mohamed Yehya Fâshik—has his headquarters at Huseiniya, a village nine miles north of Zabîd. … It [Zabîd] is outside Dheranik limits, but the tribes of the district are also lawless and predatory. In 1913, it was proposed to march a battalion from Zabîd to Hodeida via Beit al-Fakih, but the Dheranik chief refused to let them through except at the prohibitive rate of £T. 1 a head. They went round through the Reimah hills eventually.[2]

The Maʿāzibah of the medieval period are characterized in official chronicles as unruly, rebellious, fearless and cunning rogues. They obstructed the roads, attacked the date groves, thieved, ambushed, murdered and incited rebellion. Between the middle of the 7th/13th century and the middle of the 10th/16th century there was hardly a year without some record of their misdeeds against the government of the day. Equally the Zarānīq of the early 14th/20th century have been described as a 'powerful and war-like tribe' who have 'always been hostile to the Turks, and are strong enough to close the road to Turkish convoys or small bodies of Turkish troops' according to the *Gazetteer of Arabia* (1917) which describes Tihāmah as being 'in the hands of the Turks, except in the territories of certain rebellious tribes, of which the Zarāniq [sic], occupying a belt from the coast to the hills south of Hodeidah, are the most important.'[3] Later in 1923–4 and 1928–9 it was their ferocious resistance to the forces of Imām Yaḥyā, led by his son Aḥmad, that earned them the retroactive epithet 'Sons of the Revolution' after independence was achieved in 1962.[4]

The question is, are the historical Maʿāzibah and the modern Zarānīq fundamentally the same? The answer is yes. They are closely related subsections of the ʿAkk tribe, descendants of ʿAkk b. ʿAdnān. They coexisted in the medieval period at which time the Maʿāzibah were the dominant group, both older and more wide-spread. However the Zarānīq eclipsed and eventually absorbed them. The Maʿāzibah name disappeared, and knowledge of the link between the two fell into obscurity. It is the purpose of this paper to revive the understanding of that link which has escaped Western scholars attention if not that of Yemeni writers who appreciate the relationship but have not examined it closely.[5] The fact is that the Maʿāzibah, the most notorious tribe on medieval Tihāmah, and the modern Tihāmah tribe with the greatest name recognition in Yemen, the daring Zarānīq, are the same people, living in the same place and, yes, behaving with much the same incorrigible grit.

Before fleshing out the story, the bare-boned connection between the two clans must be established. The evidence appears in a long genealogical section of a book about the spiritual leaders of Tihāmah, their tribes and their histories.

The author is a man named Waṭyūṭ. He was a native Tihāmī who lived in the 8th–9th/14th–15th century. His untitled *History* (*Tārīḫ*) exists in manuscript form in the Library of the Great Mosque, Ṣan'ā'.[6] To the extent that facts which Waṭyūṭ narrates—men's lives, historical events, geography or social structure—are known from other, well-accepted sources we can adjudge Waṭyūṭ to be reliable, if refreshingly unsophisticated and a touch garbled at times. Where his information is unique, as much of it is—including these thirty, dense pages of genealogies—only further study will confer upon them the ultimate stamp of approval. For now, the main value is in publishing here the portion which deals with the Ma'āzibah/Zarānīq lineage. It does not exist elsewhere in this detail. Waṭyūṭ himself did not assume that his humble word would suffice. He prefaced his version of the family tree with one which had been written down by a well respected member of the 'Uğayl family, and he also gave the name of the middle man, equally well-known, who had passed the document on to him.[7]

The schematized tree which appears in Figure 1 is a conflation of the 'Uğayl version and that of Waṭyūṭ, found on pages 122, 125, 150–152 and 154–5 of his manuscript. For the purpose of this paper the wide-ranging narrative is distilled down to the main line of descent from 'Akk b. 'Adnān through Ḏu'āl b. Šabwah to the Ma'āzibah and the Zarānīq. Introducing it is the genealogy of 'Akk b. 'Adnān taken from *Ṭurfat al-aṣḥāb* by al-Malik al-Ašraf 'Umar b. Yūsuf, the learned Rasulid sultan (d. 629/1296–7). Although 'Umar b. Yūsuf skips over Ḏu'āl, the comparison with Waṭyūṭ's tree is useful. There are also inserts giving alternative lineages according to al-Murtaḍā al-Zabīdī (d. 1205/1790), compiler of the *Tāğ al-'arūs*.[8]

It should be noted that possibilities for variant spellings of these names abound. All the texts consulted, both contemporary and modern, contain discrepancies and corruptions. Significant variations are added in parentheses, the source given in brackets and abbreviated thus: WAṬ (Waṭyūṭ), HAĞ (al-Ḥağarī) and TĀĞ (*Tāğ al-'arūs*). Unfortunately the format of Figure 1 does not allow for an apparatus criticus detailing all the various options. In general the names have been left unvocalized as they are found in Waṭyūṭ. Even though it would be tempting to apply the *mafā'ilah* form to all cases of the tribal plural (Maṯāwibah, Mašākirah, etc.), this might introduce errors. For instance Mujāmilah and Muğālisah are both clearly heard to day. The names taken from *Ṭurfat al-aṣḥāb* appear according to the vocalizations in the Zetterstéen edition, although there are several unhappy choices in this writer's view. Definitive spellings must await further study.

Looking at the family tree in Figure 1, one sees that the great progenitor of the Ma'āzibah and Zarānīq and many others was Ḏu'āl b. Šabwah. Ḏu'āl is an eponym. It is also a toponym. The personal name and the place name Ḏu'āl have only one application in Yemen, and that is in association with central Tihāmah in the region between Wādī Rimaʻ and Wādī Sihām from the mountains to the sea. The thumb-nail sketch provided in *Tāǧ al-ʻarūs* sums up the matter. It says that Ḏu'āl is a tribe in Yemen for which the area half a day distant from Zabīd is known and they are sons of Ḏu'āl b. Šabwah … from whom come the *fuqahā'* of the B. ʻUǧayl as well as subsections which include the B. Ḏu'āl of Fašāl, the B. Ṣuraydiḥ and the B. ʻAwā'iǧ, a tribe of Laḥj.[9] As far as this writer can ascertain, the name Ḏu'āl occurs in no other lineage and in no other locality. Furthermore it no longer exists as a place name today on Tihāmah. Like the name al-Maʻāzibah, the place name Ḏu'āl apparently vanished sometime after the first Turkish invasion.

Waṭyūṭ's genealogy is not the only place in the sources where the medieval Zarānīq are mentioned, nor is it the only text in which the kinship between them and the Maʻāzibah shows up. However, the other known contemporary references to the Zarānīq occur in the context of discussions about their close relationship to other family groups famous for their spiritual attainments and religious learning. It may well be that there are other documents from the period which allude to the Zarānīq in secular contexts. But it so happens that the documents which survive concern themselves in large measure with profiles of religious leaders and their families. The Zarānīq are associated with these families in the following instances: the *Tāǧ al-ʻarūs* highlights the fact that the Zarāniqah [sic] produced the learned notables (*fuqahā'*) of the B. ʻUǧayl and the B. ʻUlays.[10] Waṭyūṭ says that the B. ʻĪsā, sufi mystics in Ḏu'āl, were from among the Zarānīq;[11] while another comment in Waṭyūṭ points out that a clan of Zarānīq called the B. Ḡānim were known for their particular religious persuasion.[12] Elsewhere Waṭyūṭ quotes a revered *faqīh* of the ʻUǧayl clan as saying that of all the Maʻāzibah clans (*buyūt*) the clan (*bayt*) closest to their own is known for this same brand of sufism, and they are Zarānīq.[13] This remark helps underscore the fact, evident from Figure 1, that the B. ʻUǧayl were a Zarānīq family which coexisted with other kin groups all of whom were Maʻāzibah.[14] We shall return to these curious mentions of sufism among the Zarānīq when the question of Maʻāzibah links with the highlands is explored.

While the earliest datable references to the Zarānīq all come from Waṭyūṭ in the 8th–9th/14th–15th centuries, textual references to the Maʻāzibah begin to appear in the 7th/13th century in Ibn al-Muǧāwir's travel guide-cum-history entitled *Tārīḫ al-mustabṣir* and in Ibn Ḥātim's *Simṭ*, a chronicle of the Ayyubid and early Rasulid dynasties. From both sources one can infer that the Maʻāzibah were an established feature on the coastal plain, not newcomers or outsiders for that matter. One would expect to find mention of them earlier still, in the 3rd–4th/9th–10th century geographer, al-Hamdānī. But any such reference eludes this writer.[15]

The traveller Ibn al-Muǧāwir mentions al-Maʻāzibah only once in passing

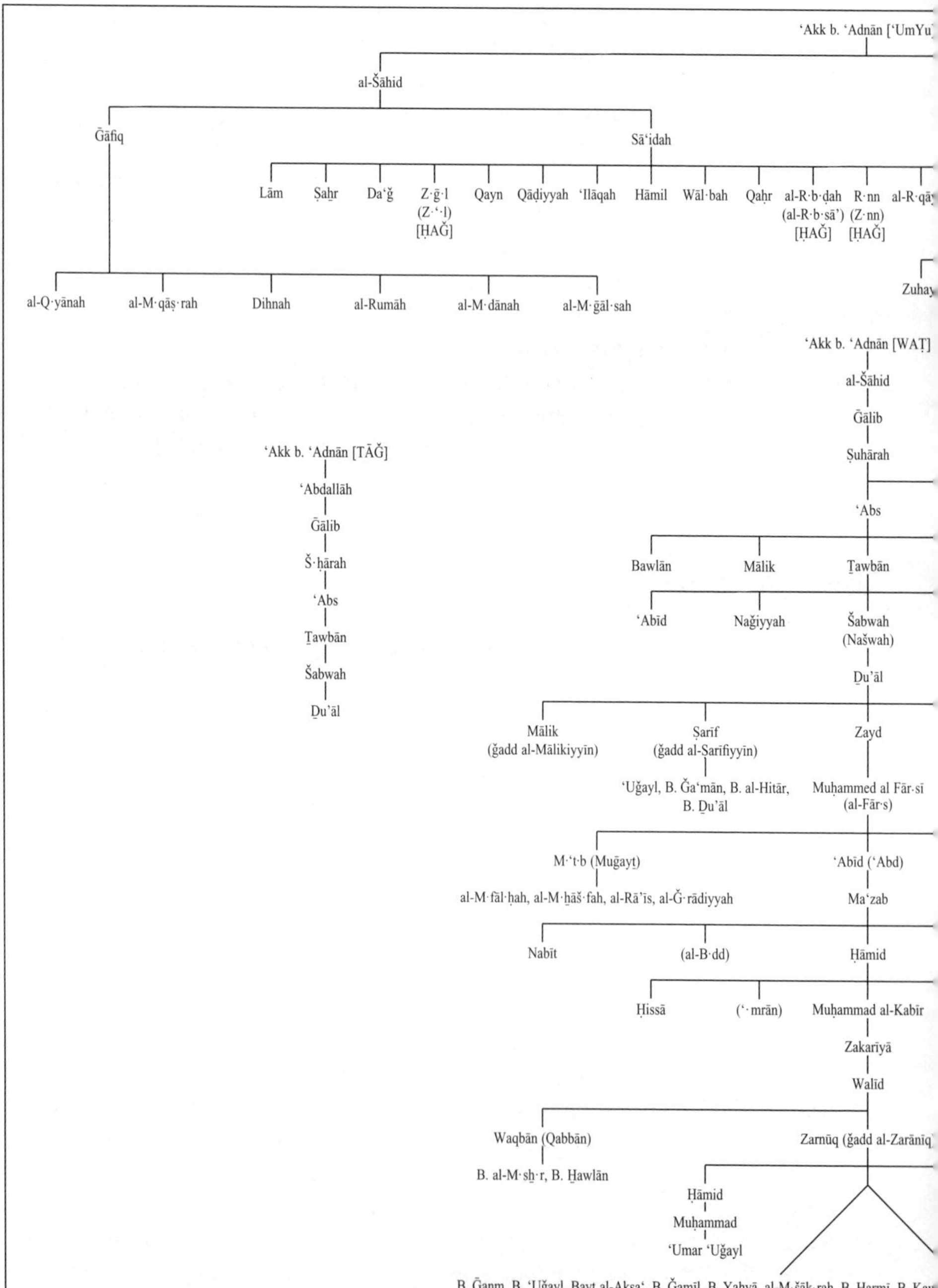

Figure 1. Geneaology of al-Ma'āzibah and Zarānīq.

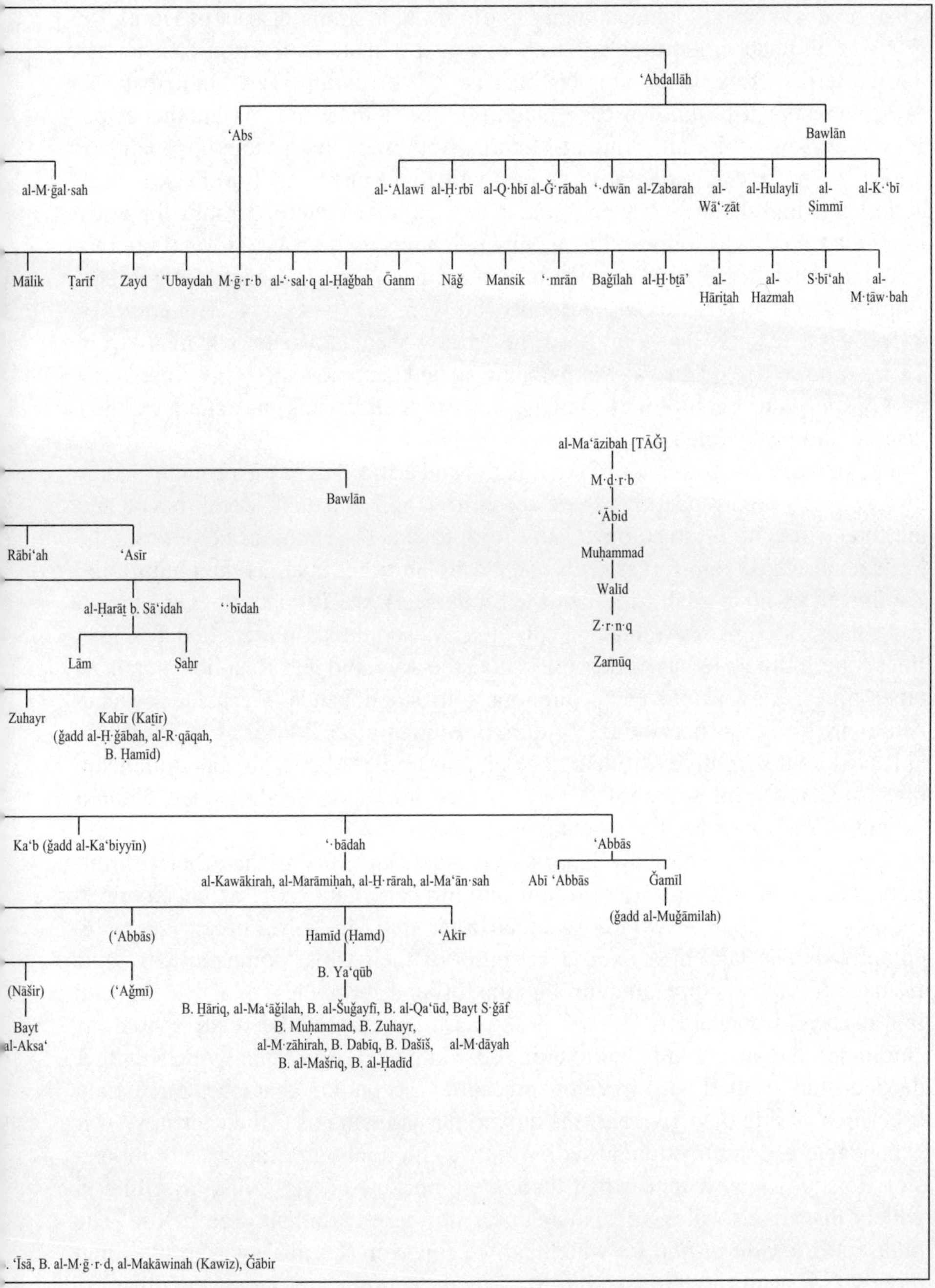
‘Abdallāh
‘Abs
Bawlān
al-M·ğal·sah
al-‘Alawī
al-Ḥ·rbī
al-Q·hbī
al-Ğ·rābah
‘·dwān
al-Zabarah
al-Wā‘·ẓāt
al-Hulaylī
al-Ṣimmī
al-K·‘bī
Mālik
Ṭarif
Zayd
‘Ubaydah
M·ğ·r·b
al-‘·sal·q
al-Ḥağbah
Ğanm
Nāğ
Mansik
‘·mrān
Bağīlah
al-Ḫ·bṯā’
al-Ḥāriṯah
al-Hazmah
S·bī‘ah
al-M·ṭāw·bah
al-Ma‘āzibah [TĀĞ]
M·d·r·b
‘Ābid
Muḥammad
Walīd
Z·r·n·q
Zarnūq
Bawlān
Rābi‘ah
‘Asīr
al-Ḥarāṯ b. Sā‘idah
‘·bīdah
Lām
Ṣaḫr
Zuhayr
Kabīr (Kaṯīr)
(ğadd al-Ḥ·ğābah, al-R·qāqah,
B. Ḥamīd)
Ka‘b (ğadd al-Ka‘biyyīn)
‘·bādah
‘Abbās
al-Kawākirah, al-Marāmiḥah, al-Ḫ·rārah, al-Ma‘ān·sah
Abī ‘Abbās
Ğamīl
(ğadd al-Muğāmilah)
(‘Abbās)
Ḥamīd (Ḥamd)
‘Akīr
B. Ya‘qūb
(Nāšir)
(‘Ağmī)
Bayt
al-Aksa‘
B. Ḫāriq, al-Ma‘āğilah, B. al-Šuğayfī, B. al-Qa‘ūd, Bayt S·ğāf
B. Muḥammad, B. Zuhayr,
al-M·zāhirah, B. Dabīq, B. Dašīš,
B. al-Mašriq, B. al-Ḥadīd
al-M·dāyah
. ‘Īsā, B. al-M·ğ·r·d, al-Makāwinah (Kawīz), Ğābir

when he describes al-Qaḥmah, a city north of Zabīd in the district of D̲u'āl. He refers to an unspecified time when there was a climate of fractiousness across the western sectors of the country because of corruption. The Ma'āzibah, he says, were the tribe known for plundering al-Qaḥmah, as was another tribe, al-Ash'ūb, known for attacking al-Mafālīs. Both were implacable opponents of the two respective administrative centres which, we understand, were extracting levies in a high-handed manner (*'alā ṭāla'*), although there is room for other interpretations of this phrase. Ibn al-Muǧāwir sums it all up as a story of oppressors and rebels, neither one worse than the other.[16] Ibn Ḥātim, a government-employed chronicler, was in no doubt who were the 'bad guys'. His entry for 645/1247–8 records that Our Lord the Martyr went down to Tihāmah (from Ta'izz) and sallied against al-Ma'āzibah who had become restive and were being unruly and causing mischief, and he cut off their means and subdued their discord and he returned.[17]

The subsequent chronicles of the Rasulid and Tahirid dynasties contain scores of accounts which repeat this basic scenario—the Ma'āzibah wreak havoc and the forces of central government sally forth to exact retribution. Sometimes the Ma'āzibah would join forces with other Arabian tribes such as the Quḥrā', the Zaydiyyah (the Tihāmah tribe, not the Shiite sect), the Rumāh, the Qurašiyyah and others. (*'Arab* or Arabian in this context should be understood to mean 'local and indigenous' as opposed to Ǧuzz the Ayyubid and Rasulid rulers.) At other times, they would carry out forays in small bands. Occasionally clan names are given, such as the B. Ya'qūb, B. Muḥammad, B. Masūd, al-Ḥaǧābah, al Kawākirah, B. Yaḥyā, B. Bašīr, al-Maǧāmišah, B. 'Abbās, al-Muǧāmilah and others but more often record is kept of notorious individuals named without benefit of *nisbah* or family affiliation.

The regions where they dwelt are only vaguely specified in the official chronicles. The sultan's troops are sent time and time again into 'Ma'āzibah country' (*Bilād al-Ma'āzibah*). Never do we read what area Ma'āzibah country actually comprised. The lack of a fixed description of their tribal homeland can arise from several factors threading through the 'official chronicles' of al-H̲azraǧī and Ibn al-Dayba' and others.[18] First is the assumption that the readers of these chronicles had a working notion of the Ma'āzibah heartland which neither needed nor wanted any greater precision; secondly, that the marauding tribesmen astride their swift horses moved far and wide as if their territory was expandable and contractible at will. This was no doubt an exaggerated impression. Lastly it would appear that there were pockets of Ma'āzibah dwelling in widely disparate locales, off Tihāmah far up the escarpment. See below. The phrase *Ma'āzibah al-tihā'īm* which can be found in Ibn al-Dayba' proves that there was a need to clarify which Ma'āzibah were meant in a given situation. Unfortunately the distinction was not often observed; therefore one cannot assume that every text is talking about events in the Ma'āzibah heartland of Ḏu'āl.

Reconstructing a map of *Bilād al-Ma'āzibah* from texts which involve events within half a day's distance from Zabīd—the area of Ḏu'āl—one can start with the western boundary. This is not the coast itself but further west still, on the off shore islands and in the coastal waters. Frequently tribesmen and their families made for the sea to flee the sultan's forces, and occasionally they drowned. No accounts have yet come to light in the sources which describe Ma'āzibah seafaring. This is surprising. The only mention of piracy off the coast of Ḥays recorded by al-Ḫazraǧī in 801/1399[19] does not give enough information to identify the pirate's tribe. A further reference by al-Ḫazraǧī to the capture of two Ma'āzibah 'seamen' turns out to be an error in Redhouse's translation.[20] In one instance a Ma'āzibah village on the shore is mentioned, but the reading, al-Q·rayn, is too doubtful to allow identification.[21] Could this be Kurêm on Niebuhr's map on the coast north of Ġulayfiqah?[22] When this village was raided by the Rasulid ruler al-Ašrāf in 798/1395–6, the villagers fled to an off-shore island but were pursued thence and the whole island was torched by the government troops. If Niebuhr's Kurêm is to be identified with al-Q·rayn, the island just off shore is Ǧazīrat al-Muǧāmilah, named for a well-known section of al-Ma'āzibah. See Figure 1. It is clear that Ma'āzibah country included sections of the western seaboard and islets north of Zabīd.

At the centre of the map, one can discern the agricultural zone where the Ma'āzibah had date palm plantations, much as today's Zarānīq farm lucrative tracts of tropical fruit and cotton producing land between Zabīd and al-Ḥusayniyyah. The texts mention palm groves belonging to them at Nakhl al-Madanī[23] and al-Mudabbī,[24] in the northern reaches of Wādī Zabīd,[25] as well as on the road to Bayt al-Faqīh.[26]

The eastern limits of their territory were less well-defined, but they were equally a place of resort when soldiers drove them out of their villages dotted about the centre of the plain. The term *ḥāzzah* means the lowland strip which runs along the base of the foothills. Thus we read of many events in Ḥāzzat al-Ma'āzibah or more often just called al-Ḥāzzah.[27] They were attacked in this sector in 837/1433–4 by soldiers who had encamped at Šuǧaynah a village east of today's al-Suḫnah at the base of Ǧabal Bura'; and again, camels stolen by them from their southern neighbours, al-Qurašīyūn, in Wādī Rima' were spirited away into *al-ḥāzzah*.[28] Also in the eastern sector of the plain lay the dense thorny tangles of acacia woodland known as *al-hayǧah*, ideal places to hide. Further eastward still lay the foothills and canyons of Ǧabal Bura', Ǧibāl Raymah and the foothills of Lower Waṣāb (modern vocalization of Wuṣāb) into which al-Ma'āzibah regularly repaired. As the anonymous Rasulid chronicle reported in 796/1393–4, the Ma'āzibah betook themselves to the feet of the mountains (*aṭrāf al-ğibāl*) and the coasts and the maquis (*al-amākin al-wa'rah*) to hide.[29]

The northern boundary of *Bilād al-Ma'āzibah* is not defined in the sources. There is however one reference in Ibn al-Dayba' to a camel raid staged against a group of people called al-Manāfirah in 803/1400–1.[30] This small clan, a section of al-'Absiyyah, survives today east of al-Ḥudaydah in the scrublands of lower Wādī Sihām. Their main village is al-Mukaymīniyyah which is north east of al-Durayhimī.

The extent of today's Zarānīq territory is described in an article written in 1982 by the Zabīd historian, 'Abd al-Raḥmān al-Ḥaḍramī.[31] Similarly Muḥammad al-Ḥağarī defines the tribe's lands in his 1984 gazetteer edited by Ismā'īl al-Akwa'.[32] Both of these can be compared to the *Bilād al-Ma'āzibah*. There are three divisions (*aqsām*) of today's tribe, and these comprise a southern sector (*ṭarf*), a northern sector and a western one. The northern *ṭarf* begins in the town centre of Bayt al-Faqīh at the *ḥukūmah* building and extends northward through the weekly *sūq* (the colourful tourist attraction) up to al-Manṣūriyyah, al-Lāwiyah on the west and al-Ğanba'iyyah on the east. The shaykh's compound is at Qawqar and another large village is al-Ṣa'īd (Saiid on Niebuhr's map). As for the southern sector, this includes the *ḥukūmah* building at Bayt al-Faqīh and goes through al-Ḥusayniyyah where the shaykh resides. It extends westward to Ġulayfiqah and as far as al-Ğāḥ. The third area includes the coast north of al-Durayhimī and the sandy zone southward through al-Ṭā'īf and al-Ğāḥ where the shaykh has his seat. This can be compared to the *Gazetteer of Arabia* description of the Zarānīq territory: 'Jahbah, a clan of the northern section, occupies the north-west corner from Shurain to Doreihimi, and the Mujamilah are at Jebel Kahmah in the north. The Wādi Reimah, which rises in Jebel Dorān, runs through the Zarāniq country and irrigates a large area of fertile land. The chief town is Beit-el-Faqīh. The principal villages are Ta'if (Sheikh Manāsar Saghīr); Shurain, (Jahbah, 'Abasi Jahbah); Doreihimi (Jahbah and Sa'dah); El-Kahmah (Mujamilah); Mohammed Jābir, Lawīyah (Jahbah); El-Huseinīyah (Mohammed Yahya Fashīk); El-Mahad.'[33]

Figure 2 is therefore a map which collates what we know about *Bilād al-Ma'āzibah* and Zarānīq territory. It includes places from the contemporary sources which can be identified with a fair degree of confidence. It also incorporates modern place names which preserve the names of clans and tribal sections that can be seen in the Ḏu'āl genealogies of Figure 1 and elsewhere. The main towns and villages of today's Zarānīq that have arisen since the medieval period (as far as we know) are plotted. Thus the map reconstructs the *Bilād al-Ma'āzibah* as it was in the medieval period, and it provides a picture of the territory which the Zarānīq inhabit today, highlighting the match between the two tribal territories. Figure 3 provides a key to the place names and the plotted numbers on Figure 2 and it gives a legend that explains how to distinguish between those medieval place names which have disappeared, those which survive from the historical period, and those which have only come to the fore in modern times. On page 155 is an index of the study area place names and their co-ordinates. This should prove useful to anyone researching either modern or historical sources related to this sector of Tihāmah and who is wishing to locate the place names and family names that crop up. Allowances may need to be made for variant forms. Further discussion of the place names in this article can be found in F.L. Stone 1999 'Tihāmah Gazetteer' PhD thesis, and F.L. Stone *Tihāmah Gazeteer* (Curzon Press, London, in preparation).

The genealogy and the map of the Ma'āzibah heartland are powerful proof that these people were not a roving band of recalcitrants with dubious origins. The social organization of al-Ma'āzibah which emerges from contemporary accounts reinforces the fact that here was a group with a 'conventional' tribal structure and fixed abodes. They should not be compared to the non-tribal group, the 'Awārīn, who caused trouble in Zabīd in the Rasulid period. In the annals Ma'āzibah headmen are spoken of, as are certain tribal subsections (*buṭūn*) or clans (*buyūt*), although it is never stated what order of magnitude or importance these terms carry if any. It is related that the tribesmen turned to religious leaders to intercede on their behalf with the authorities. Such interaction between the religious fraternity and the tribes was common on Tihāmah in the medieval period. Holy men (*fuqahā'* or *awliyā'*) at this time assumed a social role normally ascribed to tribal chieftains. Indeed they are termed shaykhs (*mašā'iḫ*). These righteous individuals often commanded the personal respect of the sultan, and they were able to win concessions for the beleaguered Ma'āzibah. The most famous of these intermediaries was Faqīh Aḥmad b. Mūsā b. 'Alī b. 'Umar Ibn 'Uǧayl (d. 690/1291) whose prestige was so great that when he died al-Malik al-Muẓaffar's son helped to wash his body and acted as a pall bearer at his funeral.[34] Nowhere in the official chronicles is it stated that Ibn 'Uǧayl was himself of Ma'āzibah stock. Either the fact was not generally known or, more likely, it was 'politically incorrect' for a man of this religious stature to be identified with the scoundrels whose misdeeds were considered to be their sole stamp on history. A passage from an anonymous Rasulid chronicle encapsulates this relationship between the tribe's religious leaders and its serial outlaws. To paraphrase in English the incident which took place in 832/1428–9:

> Al-Ma'āzibah fell into discord, most of them being B. Ya'qūb and Bayt al-Akīd, and they withdrew to a place they didn't usually assemble ... and al-Malik al-Ẓāhir sent [a commander] to put them to flight and drive them out of al-Madanī and cut down their palms. When al-Ma'āzibah learned of this they sent to the *fuqahā'* and the *ṣūfī* shaykhs to get them to show their kindness toward them to the Sultan in order to obtain his forgiveness as well as to hand

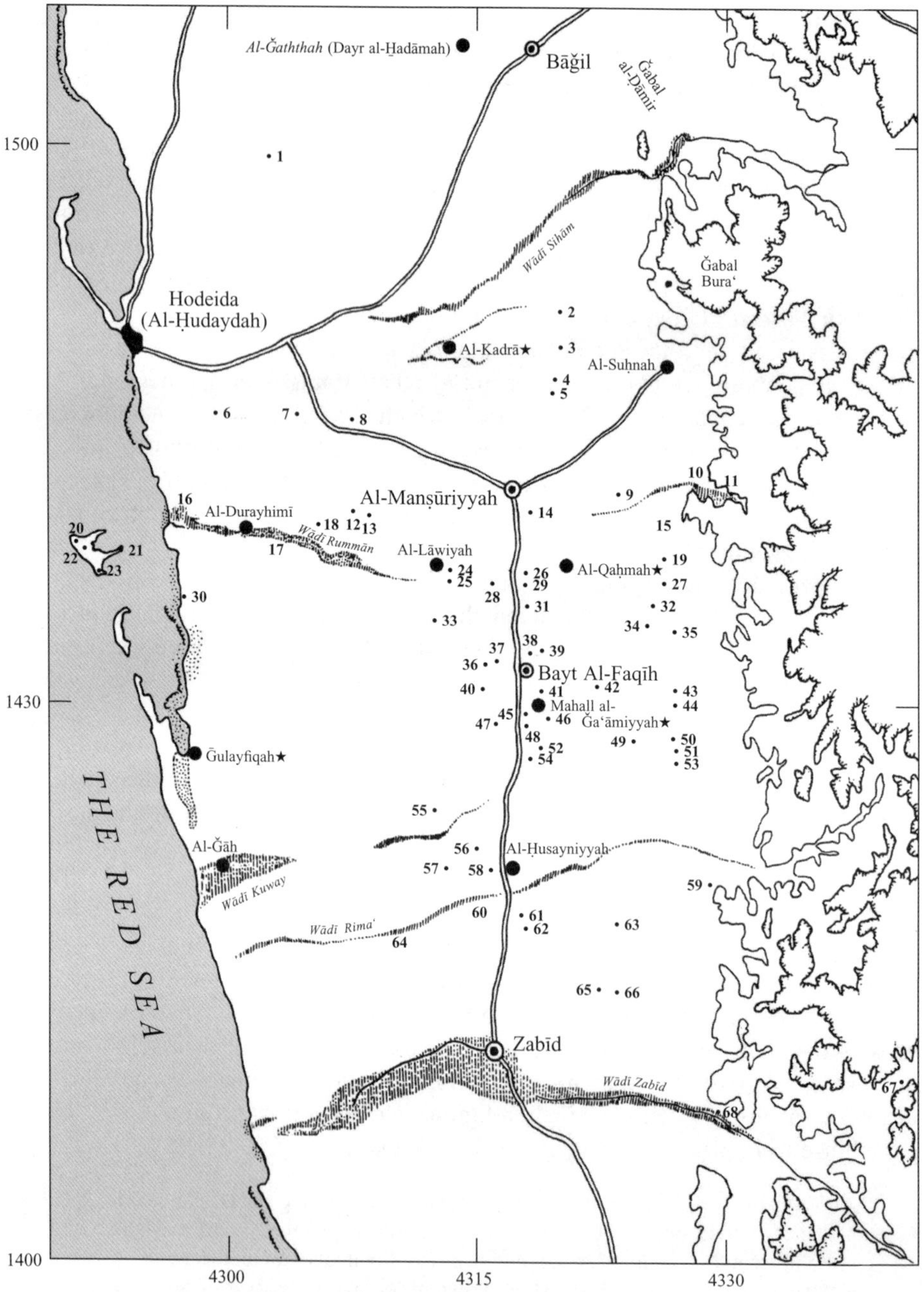

Figure 2. Study area map.
Source: Anderson Bakewell and Keith Brockie (1985) and Francine Stone (2004).

italic = medieval (Ma‘āzibah)
roman = modern (Zarānīq)
bold = medieval and modern
★ = archaeological site
§ = medieval proper name remnant in modern place name

Bāğil
Bayt al-Faqīh
Bura‘, Ğabal
Ḍāmir, Ğabal al-
Ḍurayhimī, Al-§
Ğa‘āmiyyah, Maḥall al-§
Ğāh, Al-
Ğaththah, Al- (Dayr al-Ḫadāmah) ★
Ġulayfiqah (*Ġulāfiqah*) ★
Hodeida (**al-Ḥudaydah**)
Ḥusayniyyah, Al-
Kadrā’, al- ★
Lāwiyah, Al-
Manṣūriyyah, Al-
Qaḥmah, al- ★
Suḫnah, Al-
Wādī Kuway
Wādī Rima‘
Wādī Rummān
Wādī Sihām
Wādī Zabīd
Zabīd

1 Suhayl, Dayr al-
2 Ḥušaybir, Dayr al-§
3 Mağāmilah, Maḥall§
4 **‘Awwāğah, Qaryat**
5 **Šuğaynah**
6 Ğumayš al-Yumná
7 Mukaymīniyyah, Al-
8 ‘Uğayliyyah, Al-§
9 Manāṣirah, Maḥallat al-§
10 Manāṣirah, Sanīf al-§
11 Ma‘zab, Al-§
12 Muğālisah§
13 Muğālisah, Buyūt al-§
14 Kawāziyyah, Qaryat al-§
15 **Wa‘āriyyah, Bilād al-**
16 ‘Abbāsī, Wādī al-§ (W. Rummān)
17 Ğaḥābah, Wādī al-§
18 Ğābir, Bayt Yaḥyā§
19 Ğanba‘iyyah, Al-
20 Muğāmilah, Ra’s§
21 Muğāmilah, Ṭurfat al-§
22 Muğāmilah, Ğazīrat al-§
23 Muğāmilah, Faṣmat al-§
24 *Bayt al-Akīd* (al-Kīdīyah?)
25 ‘Abbāsī, Ṣanīf al-§
26 Ğaḥbah, Buyūt al-§
27 Šaṭṭ, Al-
28 ‘Abbāsī, Al-§
29 Qawqar
30 Ṭā’if, Al-
31 Ma‘ārīf, Quz‘at al-§
32 Ma‘ārīf, Buyūt al-§
33 Muqābil, Maḥall al-§
34 ‘Iğāliyyah, Buyūt al-§
35 **Ṣa‘īd, Al-**
36 *Madālihah,* al- (Ṣaraṭiḥah§)
37 ‘Iğāliyyah, Buyūt al-§
38 *Bayt al-Aksa‘* (Bayt al-Faqīr)
39 **Manāwirah, Dayr al-**
40 Kawākirah, Buyūt al-§
41 ‘Amārah, Ḥillat al-§
42 ‘Amārah, Ṣanīf al-§
43 Rabā‘iyyah, Buyūt al-§
44 ‘Iğāliyyah, Buyūt al-§
45 Sulaykiyyah, Al-
46 Habāliyyah, Buyūt al-
47 Sawlah, Al-
48 Sulaykiyyah, Al-
49 Zunbūliyyah, Al-
50 Nafḥān
51 Ġalābah, Ṣanīf al-§
52 Ḥašābirah§
53 Habāliyyah, Al-
54 Maḥğar, Al-§
55 Habāliyyah, Al-
56 *Fašāl* ★ ca.
57 Ġānimiyyah, Al-§
58 Ma‘ārīf, Buyūt al-§
59 Zunbūliyyah, Al- [sic]
60 **Badwah, Wādī al-**
61 **Badwah, Al-**
62 **Badwah, Al-**
63 Uğaylī, Bayt al-§ [sic]
64 *Madanī, Nakhl al-* (al-Madanīyah) village and area
65 Maḥāğibah, Al-§
66 Ka‘bī, Bayt al-§
67 Maḥrab, Al-
68 Ğa‘arah, Ṣanīf al-§

Figure 3. Key to *Bilād al-Ma‘āzibah* and Zarānīq territory.

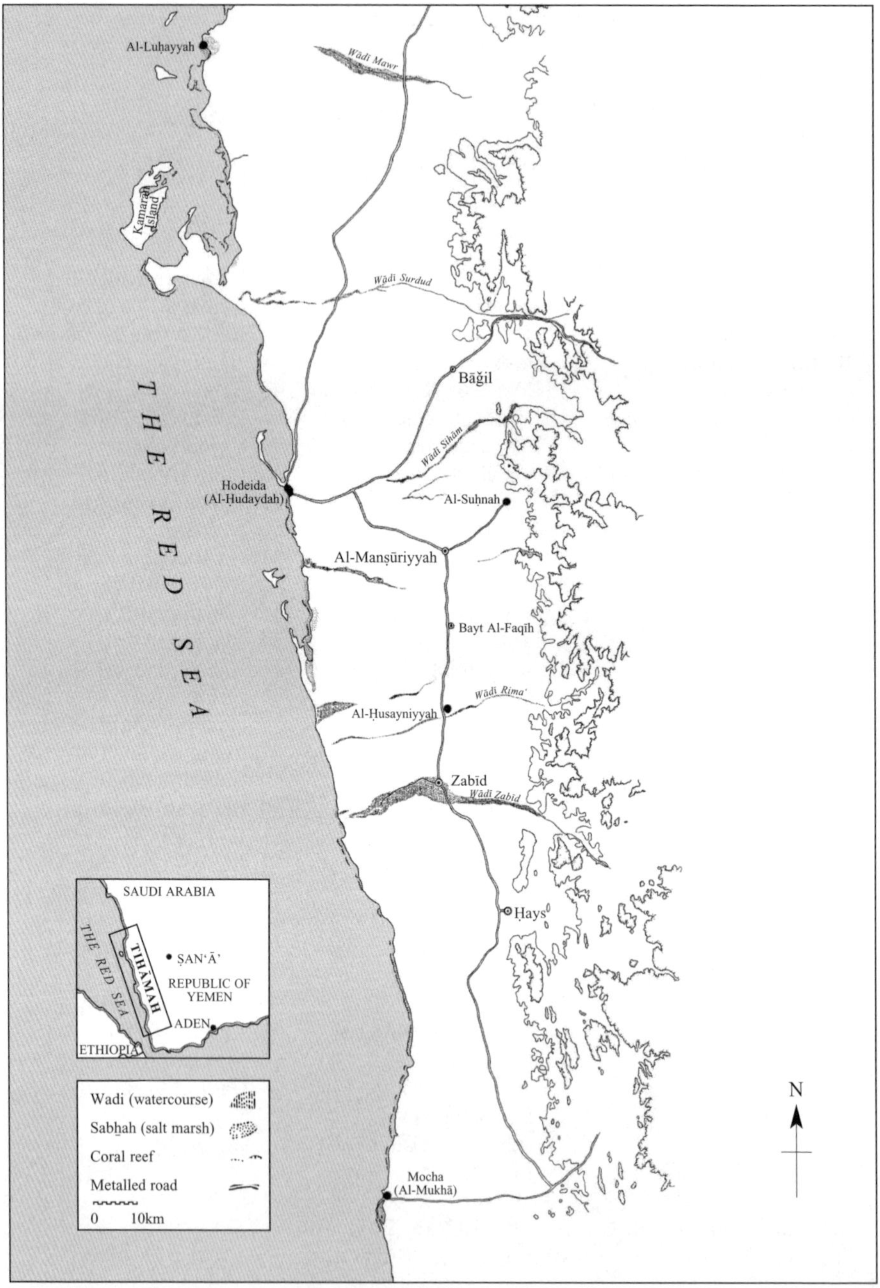

Figure 4. Contextualizing Map.
Source: Anderson Bakewell and Keith Brockie (1985) and Francine Stone (2004).

> over what horses they had with them and to elicit a royal response; and so the *fuqahā'* went, and the Sultan accepted the intercession of the *fuqahā'*. And they wrote to al-Ma'āzibah that their intercession had been accepted and their horses had been handed over and that the Sultan's decree would be published. … And so the cutting down of the palms was halted. …[35]

The religious leaders of today's Zarānīq do not come from their own tribe. Rather they are the *sayyids* of al-Manṣūriyyah. Here is a bifurcated branch of the Ahdal *sādah*, one being al-Qudaymī and the other al-Baḥr. Both claim descent from the Prophet through the Ḥusaynī line. There are also, to this writer's knowledge, Ahdal family members who are *fuqahā'* at al-Ḥusayniyyah, the seat of the southern sector of the Zarānīq.

Despite the identification of the Ma'āzibah and the Zarānīq with the D̲u'āl region of Tihāmah, the fact remains that there were evidently pockets of people called Ma'āzibah elsewhere in Yemen. It is difficult to understand how, if at all, they were related to the Tihāmī tribesmen. Equating them all with the same tribe can cause problems. Translator and annotator, Sir J.W. Redhouse, found at least four instances in al-H̲azraǧī's chronicles where al-Ma'āzibah took part in events in the highlands, namely on the plain of Bawn at Ǧawb, at Kawkabān, Ruḥām and H̲awšān, at al-Mih̲lāfah near Ḥaǧǧah and between D̲amār and Ǧabal Ḥaḍūr. He first met them near Kawkabān in an account from 646/1248–9 where they are named as al-Ma'āzib. He expounded in his annotation:

> The Ma'ázib, more usually called the Ma'ázibah, were a warlike and turbulent tribe or congregation of hill Arabians. They play a very important part in future throughout the history, but are not described in the authorities. The word would appear to mean the Vagrants, men far away from their homes and wives. They infested and ravaged all the hill country near the plains from about lat. 13°30' to 15°30' N., devastating the plains also on occasions. The Imáms were perhaps their secret instigators.[36]

In fact Redhouse may have mistaken al-Ma'āzib المعـــازب for al-Maǧārib المغارب in some of his readings. If so he compounded the problem by attempting to construe al-Ma'āzib as an alternative form for al-Ma'āzibah which it is not. The attested alternative is B. Ma'zab.[37] Editor al-Akwa' in his edition of al-H̲azraǧī prefers al-Maǧārib in many of the passages where Redhouse has read al-Ma'āzib.[38] The Akwa' edition suffers notoriously from typographical errors, however he chose to index separate entries for Maǧāribah and for Ma'āzibah which indicates he was confidant of his readings. Redhouse himself comments on the possibility of confusing Ma'āzibah with Maǧāribah in his note 547 III: 91 (op. cit.). Similarly Abū Mah̲ramah editor, L.O. Schuman cautions that both his author and Ibn al-Dayba' have the names Maǧāribah, 'meaning the Maghribī elements in the Egyptian expedition, and al-Ma'āziba, meaning a

North Tihāma tribe … confused in several places.'[39] Yet other discrepancies crop up in the contemporary sources: 'Umar b. Yūsuf puts M·ḡ·r·b on his 'Akk tree where al-Zabīdī has M·ḍ·r·b and Waṭyūṭ has M·'·z·b. It is difficult to rule out categorically one shape or the other. What editors Redhouse and Schuman overlook is the fact that people and places with names derived from *m·ḡ·r·b* are attested in northern Yemen. Al-Ḥağarī records al-Mağār·b as a territory near Ṣa'fān in the Ḥarāz, as well as a B. al-Maḡrabī who are *ashrāf* and *qudāh* in Ṣan'ā' originating from al-Lā'ah tribe of Ḥağğah and a B. al-Ḡarbī who are people of Ḏamār to the west of 'Ans.[40] Today in northern Yemen there are fifteen places named al-Maḡārib, four named al-Maḡāribah, not to mention over forty-five examples using the toponymic Maḡrabah either alone or in contruct. The impression given by Redhouse that there were Ma'āzibah tribesmen up and down the western central plateau may stem in part from a misreading of Maḡāribah.

Furthermore one needs to consider that there could have been more than one tribe named al-Ma'āzibah in the historical period. It seems certain that there were Ma'āzibah near al-Mihlāfah (west of Ḥağğah) who figure in the historical accounts of al-Ḫazrağī. But were they Ḏu'ālī or not? Waṭyūṭ casually mentions a 'B. Ma'zab man or a Šağādir man', as if there was little difference between the two; the story he tells about him takes place in Ḏu'āl through which this man is travelling on his way home to the mountains.[41] Today there is a tribal area and town named al-Šağādirah 1537 4331, 1543 B3 which lies in the hills southwest of Ḥağğah; nearby one finds the hamlet and village cluster named al-Maḥall al-Ma'āzīb [sic], 1531 4330, 1543 B3.[42] Sifting through other contemporary sources, one reads about relatives of the Ḏu'āl Ma'āzibah both in the Ḥarāz and near 'Ibb.[43] So there may have been contingents of the self-same Tihāmah tribe up the escarpment and on the plateau, or they could have been another people entirely. Various forms—Ma'zab, Mi'zāb, Ma'āzīb, Mi'āzīb and Ma'zabah—exist in northern Yemen today in as many as fifty places, including around Ibb, Ğabal al-Nābī Šu'ayb, al-Maḥābišah, Šaḥārah, Ğabal Milḥān, Ḥaydān, Bāqim and elsewhere. It is fair to say that these may not necessarily all stem from the sons of Ḏu'āl.[44]

Furthermore one should not assume that the Tihāmī Ma'āzibah were agents of the Zaydīs. Nowhere in the historical texts is there hard evidence to suggest that the Ma'āzibah were succoured militarily or economically by highlanders or that the imams were their instigators. It is simply said that they fled 'to the hills'.[45] When the Ma'āzibah of the plains made alliances, these were notably with other Tihāmah tribes, mainly fellow 'Akk descended from Ḏu'āl b. Šabwah. Collusion between Ma'āzibah and highlanders would most likely have been opportunistic, as it is has been between the Zarānīq and the imams at times in the modern period when the Turks held sway. One must reject the belief that the Ma'āzibah were 'hill Arabians'. They were fundamentally Tihāmī, based on the plain and beholden only to themselves, much as the Zarānīq are now.

However one small phrase stowed away unnoticed in the minutiae of Ma'āzibah/Zarānīq history points to a different kind of link with the highland Yemeni world. This phrase concerns religion, not politics or social structure, and it takes us back to an earlier mention of a kind of sufism that was evidently practiced by certain Zarānīq. *Tāǧ al-'arūs* states that the Zarānīq included the *fuqahā'* of the B. 'Uǧayl and a clan which he calls the B. 'Ulays and their immediate kin (*wa-qarābatu-hum*) who were Zaydī sufis of D̲u'āl (*ṣūfiyyah al-zaydiyyah*).[46] The modern historian 'Abd al-Raḥmān al-Ḥaḍramī repeats this information almost verbatim in his article on Tihāmah history.[47] But in Waṭyūṭ there are three more versions. One has it that among the Zarānīq were the B. 'Isā and their immediate kin who were '*ṣūfiyyah al-zaydiyyah* in D̲u'āl'.[48] A second version, attributed to al-'Allāmah Muḥammad 'Uǧayl (see above), names a Zarānīq clan, the B. Ḡānim, as *ahl al-zaydiyya*h.[49] The third relates that Faqīh Aḥmad b. Abī Bakr b. Muḥammad b. Mūsā 'Uǧayl's father knew of a people said to be *ahl al-zaydiyyah al-ṣūfiyyah*, who were the closest of the Ma'āzibah clans (*buyūt*) to the 'Uǧayl clan. Although he does not name them he says they were among the Zarānīq.[50] Al-Šarǧī, the 9th/15th century hagiographer, includes in his *Ṭabaqāt al-ḫawāṣṣ* an entry on a group which could explain who these so-called B. 'Ulays of the *Tāǧ al-'arūs* were. Al-Šarǧī describes the B. Ḡulays (which he spells out definitively) saying they are a small tribe (*qawm*) on the borders of Bilād al-Ma'āzibah who are known for their goodness and righteousness.[51] The modern author, Muḥammad al-Ḥaǧarī, explains that al-Muǧālisah, a tiny tribe of 'Akk tribe, are still known today on Tihāmah in the area of al-Manṣūriyyah.[52] He adds an unattributed anecdote which suggests that they possessed superior credentials:

> Some Tihāmah people came upon a man of the Muǧālisah and they asked him, 'Are you one of the Zarānīq?' He answered, 'Higher (*fawq*)'. 'One of the Rumāh?' And he said, 'Higher.' 'One like that?' And he said, 'Higher.' And they kept on naming tribes until there only remained the Muǧālisah. And they said, 'Muǧlasī?' And he replied, 'Yes, I am *sayyidī*.' And he told them, 'I revolve above you in the heavens while you are way down there below, you might say [as lowly as] the sandal (*al-na'l*).'[53]

It seems that the Muǧālisah believed themselves to be a cut above other tribespeople, but it is contradictory that a man carrying a tribal name would be claiming descent from the Prophet. What is inferred is that his family were in some way elite, possibly of a superior religious standing.[54] This could definitely be said for the B. ʻUǧayl, B. Aksaʻ and others in the Zarānīq constellation. If the B. ʻUlays should be read Ġulays it would appear that their religious devotees adhered to the Zaydī sect, as did the B. ʻĪsā and the B. Ġānim. This is manifestly unusual on Tihāmah. It is occasionally recorded that renowned individuals in the medieval period went up to the mountains to acquire advanced learning (*fann min al-ʻilm*) before returning to Tihāmah,[55] but there is no suggestion that they adopted the Zaydī sect. To the contrary, Zaydī tenets were refuted by Aḥmad b. Mūsā Ibn ʻUǧayl himself.[56] It is so unusual that one might wonder if *al-zaydiyyah* is meant to refer to al-Zaydiyyah the village and people in lower Wādī Surdud rather than the sect of the same name. But the context requires a religious interpretation, not a geographical one.[57] Whatever was going on, it is evident that the Zarānīq harboured certain religious affinities with the highlands in the medieval period. The modern tribe is Shāfiʻī as are most Tihāmīs. If there are any residual Zaydī leanings amongst the Zarānīq today they are not common knowledge.[58]

Just as Redhouse's belief that the Maʻāzibah were 'hill Arabians' must be reassessed in the light of their Tihāmah origins, any suggestion that the Zarānīq are somehow not of Arabian stock can now also be set aside. Such a misnomer surfaces in tourism literature presumably having percolated through European travellers' accounts. Peter Wald in his *Pallas Yemen* Guide wonders whether the Zarānīq were of African origin.[59] It is not surprising that such a notion would take hold, given the seafaring exploits of the Zarānīq back and forth across the lower Red Sea. They were notorious pirates, not to mention traders, smugglers and gun runners, whose reputation for able seamanship was undoubtedly deserved. Caesar Farah has researched an Ottoman report in the Naval Museum library in Istanbul dated around 1906 which targets the contraband activities of the Zarānīq. The report 'stresses the urgent need to patrol off the ports of Ḫawḫah, al-Qāḥ [sic] and Ġulayfiqah … where many of the tribal chiefs have the fire arms to keep would-be interceptors at bay with their fast-moving sail boats (*falūkahs*).'[60] The *Gazetteer of Arabia* in 1917 noted that al-Ṭā'if on Ḫawr Ġulayfiqah was the chief port of the Zarānīq adding 'they own many sea-going *dhows*, and have much of the trade between Aden and the important towns of Zebīd and Beit al-Faqīh in their hands.'[61] With ready access to the African coast it is plausible that some of them intermarried. Evidence of this can be found not on the Arabian but the African side where members of an ʻAfar tribe, the Dammohoytá on Wādī Dammáhu behind ʻAsab, claim descent from the Zarānīq, according to Didier Morin.[62]

Coastal Zarānīq on Tihāmah do display distinctive physical features and these give rise to speculation about their origins. This writer recorded the Tihāmah Expedition team's first impressions upon encountering them on 11 January 1982 between al-Ṭā'if and Ġulayfiqah on the coast:

> The fisher people here are a pure type, perhaps aboriginal to this place or from a pure stock of immigrants whose facial type we don't recognize at all. They are dark, have semitic noses, low brows, pointed chins, dark flat-lying hair, large hands and shortish legs. They all look alike. … They differ markedly from the Tihamis around them inland.

However physiognomy is not a valid indicator of place of origin. It cannot be used to propose that the coastal Zarānīq came from 'African' stock, nor that the inland ones who have refined features are 'Arabian.' All that can be said is the way these Zarānīq look stimulates the imagination and adds to their mystic. Josef Kessel's romantic rendition of the swashbuckling Zarānīq in his novel *Fortune Carrée* makes a fitting end to this paper which began with accounts of the Ma'āzibah. Novelists, travellers, tourists and historians alike have been fascinated by the Zarānīq:

> —Boss, said Hussein, the Tihama is a no-good place. Everywhere you look there's misery. And most of all you've got the Zaranigs.
> —The Zaranigs? said Igricheff, you're so afraid of them?
> —To serve you, Chief, there's nothing that scares me. But they are really terrible devils.
> —Tell me.
> Ilusscin squatted on his heels by his employer stretched out on the sand. His spoke in a distant, chant-like recitation, his voice muffled in the darkness.
> —Their skin's almost totally black, thanks to the Tihama sun, hard as leather from the salt sea air. They have the fastest boats around, they know how to trim them for speed, they can sail like nobody's business. From time immemorial they've been attacking the sambouks and the villages of this coastline, always getting away with it. They're afraid of nothing. They submit to no one. Past imams couldn't subdue them. The Turks tried a dozen times and got no where. The Zaranigs take no prisoners. They don't know the meaning of flight. If one of them tries to run the women will knife him. On land they're as bold as at sea. No one's better armed. With all their plunder they can afford it. They've got rifles with silver bands all over them. They grow good Qat, but they don't chew much, less than us. They choose the bravest for their shaykhs, the most cruel, and they obey them to the death. They've got low foreheads, flat noses, shocks of straight hair on their heads. They like to call themselves the Prophet's pirates, 'cause other than him, they will have no other master.

and again:

> They didn't look like mountain men, nor yet like Tihama folk. They were short, stocky, muscular of arms and thigh. Their hair was black as jet, thick and coarse, hanging in straight shanks on their round heads and half way down their foreheads. Their noses were sort of crushed and they had muzzle-like mouths. They wore loin-cloths and tunics of indigo so starched the cloth hung in stiff folds.

> They were carrying musket length rifles, decorated with silver bands, and wearing daggers that were longer and sharper than those of the Yemenis. In every sinew of the face and body was evinced something violent, unfeeling. One would have said a pack of hounds, disciplined and mute.

and again:

> This population in arms had all the force and all the cohesion of a clan. Taken singly these men and these women might not have uniform qualities but taken as a whole—on a swift boat, in a shock force or at the siege of a town—one could sense the vigour, the courage and the tenacity of each individual amplified ten times by profound mutual understanding and the mystery of the blood tie.[63]

If al-Ḫazraǧī had been an adventure writer instead of a chronicler, his rendition of al-Ma'āzibah in the 8th/14th century would have echoed Kessel's lurid but well-observed account of the Zarānīq fighting for their independence in 1928.[64]

To conclude, there can be no doubt that the Ḏu'āl region of Tihāmah was the homeland of the medieval Ma'āzibah and the Zarānīq. Their genealogy shows that they believed themselves to occupy the same branch of the tree descending from 'Akk b. 'Adnān. What is more they coexisted in the 8th/14th century if not earlier. At some point after the arrival of the Ottomans in the mid 10th/16th century, the Ma'āzibah and the Zarānīq swapped roles as the dominant tribal faction on central Tihāmah, and the Ma'āzibah name faded into obscurity. Study of their shared family tree gives one the confidence to refute suggestions that either the Ma'āzibah or the Zarānīq hails from some place other than Tihāmah, or that they are of mixed ethnic or racial backgrounds. Furthermore this genealogy provides a key to clan names preserved in the place names between Wādī Sihām and Wādī Rima'/Wādī Zabīd from the mountains to the sea. With Waṭyūṭ's genealogies one can read the map of central Tihāmah afresh. The picture Waṭyūṭ paints of his local tribes and their interconnections is complex and deserving of close attention. It invites many questions about how tribal genealogy informs geography. The subject of this paper has been the identity of the Ma'āzibah with the Zarānīq, but one hopes that this case study will point the way to a wider understanding of Yemeni tribes in their landscape.

Bibliography

Abū Maḫramah. 1991 reprint. *Tārīḫ ṯaġr 'Adan*. In *Arabische Texte zur Kenntnis der Stadt Aden im Mittelalter*. Löfgren, O. (ed.), Cairo. 1960. *Qilādat al-naḥr fī wafayāt a'yān al-dahr*. See Schuman, L.O.

Al-'Aršī, Ḥusayn b. Aḥmad. 1939. *Bulūġ al-marām fī šarḥ misk al-ḫitām fī man tawallā mulk al-Yaman min malik wa-'imām*. A-M al-Karmilī (ed.), Cairo.

Bury, G.W. 1915 reprt 1998. *Arabia Infelix*. Reading.

Dresch, P. 2000. *A History of Modern Yemen*, Cambridge.

Farah, C. 2000. Smuggling and International Politics in the Red Sea in the Late Ottoman Period. In G. Rex Smith, J.R. Smart & B.R. Pridham (eds), *New Arabian Studies 5*. Exeter.

Al-Ǧanadī, Bahā' al-Dīn Muḥammad b. Yūsuf. 1983–89. *Al-Sulūk fī ṭabaqāt al-'ulamā' wa-al-mulūk*. Ismā'īl al-Akwa' (ed.), Ṣan'ā'. 2 vols.

Gazetteer of Arabia. 1917. Simla. 3 vols.

Al-Ḥaḍramī, 'Abd al-Raḥmān. 1980. Tihāmah fī al-tārīh. *Al-Iklīl* 2: 41–82.

Al-Ḥağarī. Muḥammad. 1984. *Mağmū' buldān al-Yaman wa-qabā'ilihā*. Ismā'īl al-Akwa' (ed.), Ṣan'ā'. 3 parts.

Al-H̱azrağī. 1981. *Al-'Uqūd al-lu'lu'iyyah*. Muḥammad al-Akwa' (ed.), Ṣan'ā'. 2 vols. 1906–18. See Redhouse, J.W.

Ibn Baṭṭūṭah. 1954–2000. *The Travels of Ibn Baṭṭūṭa A.D. 1325–1345*. H.A.R. Gibb & C.F. Beckingham (eds & trans), London. 5 vols.

Ibn al-Dayba'. 1977. *Qurrat al-'uyūn bi-aẖbar al-Yaman al-maymūn*. Muḥammad al-Akwa' (ed.), Cairo. 2 vols.

——1979. *Buğyat al-mustafīd fī tārīẖ madīnat Zabīd*. 'Abdallāh al-Ḥibšī (ed.), Ṣan'ā'.

——1982. *Al-Fadl al-mazīd 'alā Buğyat al-mustafīd fī tārīẖ madīnat Zabīd*. Muḥammad 'Isā Ṣāliḥiyyah (ed.), Kuwait.

——1983. *Al-Faḍl al-mazīd 'alā Buğyat al-mustafīd fī tārīẖ madīnat Zabīd*. J Chelhod (ed.), Ṣan'ā'.

Ibn al-Muğāwir. 1954. *Tārīẖ al-mustabṣir* in Löfgren, O. *Description Arabiae meridionalis*. Leiden.

Ibn Ḥātim. See Smith 1974–8.

Kessel, J. 1955 paperback 1968. *Fortune Carrée*. Paris.

Morin, D. 1997. The Kingdom of Dankali, Ethiopia and Yaman (Baylûl Revisited). *Orbis Aethiopicus*: 53–57.

Našwān ibn Sa'īd al-Ḥimyarī. 1999. *Šams al-'ulūm*. Beirut & Damascus. 12 vols.

Redhouse, J.W. (ed. & trans.). 1906–18. *The Pearl strings; a history of the Resúliyy Dynasty of Yemen*. London. 5 vols.

Al-Šarğī. 1986. *Ṭabaqāt al-ẖawāṣṣ*. 'Abdallāh al-Hibšī (ed.), Ṣan'ā'.

Schuman, L.O. 1960. *The Political History of the Yemen at the Beginning of the 16th Century*. Groningen.

Smith, G.R. 1974–8. *The Ayyubids and early Rasulids in the Yemen*. London. 2 vols.

Stone, F.L. 1999. Tihāmah Gazetteer. PhD thesis. University of Manchester.

In preparation. *Tihāmah Gazetteer, the Southern Red Sea Coast of Arabia to 923/1517*. Curzon Press, London.

'Umar b. Yūsuf b. Rasūl, al-Malik al-Ašraf. 1949. *Ṭurfat al-aṣḥāb fī ma'rifat al-ansāb*. K.V. Zetterstéen (ed.), Damascus.

Wald, P. 1996. *Pallas Yemen*, London.

Waṭyūṭ, al-Ḥusayn b. Ismā'īl al-Bağalī. MS. *Tārīẖ al-mu'allim Waṭyūṭ*. Ṣan'ā', Great Mosque, Ǧarbiyyah, MS 2208.

Wenner, M.W. 1967. *Modern Yemen 1918–1966*. Baltimore.

Wüstenfeld, F. 1883. *Die Çüften in Süd-Arabien im XI. (XVII.) Jahrhundert*. Gottingen.

Yajima, Hikoichi. 1976. *A Chronicle of the Rasūlid Dynasty of Yemen*. Tokyo.

Al-Zabīdī, al-Murtaḍā. 1888. *Tāğ al-'arūs min ğawāhir al-Qāmūs*. Cairo 10 vols.

Notes

1. Redhouse 1906–18: II 88–89, 96.
2. Bury 1915 reprt 1998: 23–4.
3. *Gazetteer of Arabia* 1917: III 1937, 1943 & 1977.
4. See Wenner 1967: 73–5.
5. See al-Zabīdī 1888: VI 370; al-Ḥağarī 1984: III 636–8; al-Ḥaḍramī 1980: 52.
6. MS 2208. There is a copy made in 1333/1915 of the original which is said to be dated 810/1407–8. Such is the information given by Dr Daniel Varisco, to whom this writer is indebted for having brought the manuscript to her attention and to 'Abd al-Raḥīm Ğāzm for having provided her with a photocopy of it. It should be noted however that a date of 815/1412–13 appears in the text (page 138). Therefore the original manuscript should not be dated before that year.
7. The writer was al-'Allāmah Muḥammad b. Mūsā b. Aḥmad 'Uğayl and the intermediary was Muḥammad b. 'Umar al-Nahārī who died in 747/1346–7 (Waṭyūṭ: 122).
8. 'Umar b. Yūsuf b. Rasūl 1949: 17. Al-Zabīdī 1888: VI 370, VII 328–9.
9. Idem. See also Ḏu'āl in F.L. Stone 1999: 191–2.
10. Al-Zabīdī 1888: VI: 370. The full passage from the *Tāğ* is problematic because it does not occur in the *Qāmūs* entry for *z·r·n·q* and it contains what look like corruptions. These might be explained if al-Zabīdī, who was a modern author in terms of this paper, was adding his own information from the 12th/18th century to the earlier 9th/15th *Qāmūs*. Another indication that he might have incorporated 12th/18th century information is his comment that 'Zarnūq was a large territory.' Medieval authors only refer to the territory as belonging to the Ma'āzibah.
11. Waṭyūṭ: 154.
12. Waṭyūṭ: 122.
13. Waṭyūṭ: 154–5.
14. Similarly in *Ṭabaqāt al-ẖawāṣṣ* al-Šarğī says that the B. al-Aksa' are of an educated and righteous family (*bayt*) and they are relatives of the B. 'Uğayl all of them numbering among the Ma'āzibah, well-known Arabs from the children of Ḏu'āl (1986: 237).
15. Muḥammad al-Ḥağarī alludes to information in al-Hamdānī's *Ṣifat* that al-Ma'āzibah originated from al-Ašā'ir الاشاعر (1984: II 636). Neither the Müller nor the Akwa' edition of the *Ṣifat* contains such a comment.
16. Ibn al-Muğāwir 1954: 62.
17. Smith 1974–8: I 224, also II 166.
18. Redhouse 1906–18. Also Ibn al-Dayba' 1977 *Qurrat*; 1979 *Buğyat*; 1982 *al-Faḍl*; 1983 *al-Faḍl*. Also Abū Maẖramah 1991 reprint *Tārīẖ ṯağr 'Adan*; 1960 *Qilādat*. Also Hikoichi Yajima 1976.
19. Redhouse 1906–18: II 275.
20. Ibid.: II 229, III n. 1538. Rather than 'seamen', the term *baḥrī* means a small, fleet camel. It is common usage amongst modern Zarānīq who still race them.
21. Yajima 1976: 64 and n. 3.
22. In Niebuhr's transliteration system *qāf* = k, and the dipthong *-ay* = ê. The final *mīm* may instead be *nūn*, as is the case with the neighbouring village to the north which Niebuhr marks as Shurêm. This village is given as Shurain in the *Gazetteer of*

Arabia (1917: III 1943), but note Shuraim in the *Red Sea and Gulf of Aden Pilot*. 1932. London: 324.

23. Al-Ḫazraǧī 1906–18: II 39; Waṭyūṭ: 121; Ibn al-Dayba' 1977: II 84–5; Yajima 1976: 123.
24. Al-Ḫazraǧī 1906–18: II 56, 117, 229, 280; al-Ǧanadī 1983–89: I 478; Ibn al-Dayba' 1983: 75/2, 88/1.
25. Ibid.: 78/2.
26. Ibid.: 87/2.
27. Waṭyūṭ: 158. Many editors mistake this for a village name, or mistakenly point it al-Ḥārrah. See Stone 1999: 272–3.
28. Ibn al-Dayba' 1983: 84/2 and Yajima 1976: 180.
29. Ibid.: 61. See *al-hayǧah* in Stone 1999: 264–5.
30. Ibn al-Dayba' 1983: 59/2. See also *Gazetteer of Arabia*. 1917: III 1942.
31. Al-Ḥaḍramī 1980: 52.
32. Al-Ḥaǧarī 1984: III 636–8.
33. 1917: III 1943. Shaykh Muḥammad Šu'ayb al-Fāšiq of al-Ḥusayniyyah in March 1987 gave this writer yet other names of sections in his tribal confederation. Those noted down were: Ma'āzibah (!), Madd, Zarnūq, Zahrah, and Ǧumaylah.
34. Redhouse 1906–18: I 221–3. See Figure 1 for the genealogy of 'Umar 'Uǧayl according to Waṭyūṭ and his source, al-'Allāmah Muḥammad b. Mūsā (the brother of Aḥmad). F. Wüstenfeld produced another genealogy based on other sources, thus: 'Omar el-'Ógeil b. Muḥammed b. Ḥâmid b. Zureik [sic] b. Walîd b. Zakarîjâ b. Muḥammed b. Ḥâmid b. Mugrib [sic] b. 'Îsá b. Muḥammed el-Fârisí b. Zeid b. Dsuwâl b. Schabwa b. Thaubân b. 'Îsá b. Suḥâra b. Gâlib b. Abdallah b. 'Akk b. 'Adnân (1883: 100 and 'Die Çufiten in Beit el-Fakîh Ibn 'Ógeil' Tab. VI Nr. 155–173: 99). As Wūstenfeld points out, this traces the 'Uǧayl family back through 'Akk's son 'Abdallāh rather than al-Šāhid. In this respect Wūstenfeld's version replicates that of the *Tāǧ al-'arūs* given in Figure 1.
35. Yakima 1976: 123.
36. Redhouse 1906–18: III 62 n. 358; see also III 91 n. 547 where he surmises that 'the Ma'áziba were an indigenous though possibly a mixed race.'
37. Waṭyūṭ: 9.
38. See al-Ḫazraǧī 1981: I 76 *et passim*.
39. Schuman 1960: 78 n. 137.
40. Al-Ḥaǧarī 1984: III 715.
41. Waṭyūṭ: 9.
42. Furthermore on the *Yemen Arab Republic* 1:50,000, 1-DOS edition maps there are several al-Ma'zab and one instance of al-Ma'zabah on the 1543 C2 sheet (Ǧabal Milḥān); also, al-Ma'āzibah, hamlet 1520 4316, 1543 C2 (Al-Ṭūr); al-Ma'āzīb, hamlet 1529 4323, 1543 C2; al-Ma'āzīb, village 1530 4322, 1543 A4 (Ǧabal Milḥān). The long *ī* was added by the Survey Authority in Ṣan'ā' in March 1986 although the Permanent Committee on Geographical Placenames heard al-Ma'āzib on the field tape recording at this place.
43. See for instance al-Ǧanadī 1983–9: II 302, 376. This writer in 1993 met a man from a village in the Ibb region who was named Amīn al-'Uǧaylī.
44. Al-Ḥaǧarī lists two Ma'āzibah tribes without making any connection between them.

One is a tribe of Milḥān, and the other of Bayt al-Faqīh Ibn 'Uǧayl (1984: III 711).

45. L.O. Schuman feels that there was probably Zaydī influence but he confirms this writer's analysis of the documents, saying 'As far as I can see, Abū Makhrama and the other sources at my disposal do not mention such connections, or even hint at them' (1960: 57).
46. Al-Zabīdī 1888: VI 370.
47. Al-Ḥaḍramī 1980: 51.
48. Waṭyūṭ: 154.
49. Waṭyūṭ: 122.
50. Waṭyūṭ: 154–5.
51. Al-Šarǧī 1986: 421.
52. In al-Malik al-Ašraf 'Umar b. Yūsuf's genealogy shown on Figure 1 one can see this tribe named twice as off-spring of both sons of al-Šāhid b. 'Akk b. 'Adnān. If the B. Ḡulays were from the Muḡālisah as the name would indicate, it appears they had been absorbed in the Zarānīq branch of the Ma'āzibah.
53. 1984: III 715, also III 608.
54. R Dozy offers 'dominical' for *sayyidī* (1927. *Supplément aux dictionnaires arabs.* Leiden & Paris. 2 vols: I 699.)
55. As did the uncle of the great Aḥmad b. Mūsā Ibn 'Uǧayl, Faqīh Ibrahīm b. 'Alī b. 'Umar b. Muḥammad 'Uǧayl (d. ca. 640/1242–3) who studied for two long periods in the highlands (*ǧibāl al-Yaman*) before returning to Tihāmah. See al-Šarǧī 1986: 45–6; Waṭyūṭ: 155.
56. See Ibn Baṭṭūṭah: III 368. The Zaydī sect on Tihāmah is mentioned explicitly by al-Ǧanadī in connection with the B. Sawd of al-Qanāwīṣ who were said to be highly respected in spiritual matters except that they got mixed up with some Zaydī imāms to the point that they were drawn to entering their sect and even writing panegyrics to them. This led to at least one of their numbers being incarcerated along with his associates by the Rasulids in a Zabīd prison. They had become followers of Imām al-Muṭahhar b. Yaḥyā of Ḏarwān Ḥaǧǧah who died in 697/1297. The B. Sūd were not from the same branch of 'Akk as the Zarānīq. They were descended from Qahb b. Rāšid b. 'Akk b. 'Adnān (al-Ǧanadī 1983–9: II 315; al-Šarǧī 1986: 150–1). The tomb of Abū Muḥammad Sūd b. al-Kumayt (d. 436/1044–5) is tucked in the hills east of al-Qanāwīṣ in a wadi named Wādī Ḡulaysī, as it so happens. See al-Fāshiq in Stone 1999: 210.
57. Furthermore, Schuman rightly points out that the people in Wādī Surdud are known as *al-Zaydiyyūn* 'in obvious distinction of the politico-religious appellation *al-Zaydīya'* (1960: 57 n. 44).
58. For the Shafiite character of the Zarānīq, see for instance M. Piamenta's *Dictionary of Post Classical Yemeni Arabic* (1999. Leiden. 2 vols: I 199). Discussing the lack of doctrinaire distinctions between the two sects in Yemeni society, Dr Paul Dresch nevertheless finds it curious that the Zarānīq (i.e. Shafiite) were the personal body guards of Imām Aḥmad (i.e. Zaydī) in Ta'izz (who came to power in 1948). Perhaps in light of the evidence for their historical Zaydī tendencies, it is not so surprising (see Dresch 2000: 69).
59. 'In the early millennia whole tribes certainly crossed the Red Sea between Africa and Arabia. It has therefore been assumed that the dark-skinned people of the

Saranik [sic] tribes, the largest tribal federation of the Tihamah, were the earliest inhabitants of the region, but in fact it is not clear whether they first lived on the Arabian or African side of the Red Sea' (Wald 1996: 125).

60. Farah 2000: 58–9.
61. 1917: III 1943. There is reference in the same passage to a 'highland section' of Zarānīq under a Sheikh 'Ali Ibn Hamūd with no further information. The suggestion that there are non-Tihāmī Zarānīq fits with the existence of Ḏu'ālī Ma'āzibah near Ibb and in the Ḥarāz in the medieval period. However there is no place today in northern Yemen where the name Zarānīq survives in any form according to the *Yemen Arab Republic* 1:50,000, edition 1-DOS map series. This is despite the fact that *zurnūq/zurnūqān* has carried a common utilitarian meaning—the upright posts supporting crossbar and pulley at a well head. See al-Zabīdī 1888: VI 370; also Našwān 1999: V 2784.
62. Morin 1997: 54 n. 5. In communication with this writer, Dr Morin has added that his informants 'refer to a so called 'Umar "Darnûgi" (az-Zarnûgi)' and that 'other tribes claim this mythic hero as their common ancestor.' However an Ad'ali tradition preserves a genealogy where 'the very first ancestor who came from Arabia is called 'Abbâs' (Pers. comm. 10 April 2001).
63. Kessel 1955 paperback 1968: 61, 71–2. Excerpts were translated from the French by this writer.
64. Manfred Wenner gives a useful summary of the Zarānīq uprising with references (1967: 73–5).

Index to *Bilād al-Ma'āzibah*/Zarānīq territory

Co-ordinates correspond to the *YAR* 1:50,000 series, edition 1-DOS (1979–90). Superscript = key number on Figures 2 and 3.

'Abbāsī, Al-[28] 1435 4315
'Abbāsī, Wādī al-[16] 1438 4310 (W. Rummān)
'Abbāsī, Ṣanīf al-[25] 1436 4314
'Amārah, Ḥillat al-[41] 1430 4321
'Amārah, Ṣanīf al-[42] 1430 4323
'Awwāğah, Qaryat[4] 1447 4320
Badwah, Al-[62] 1416 4320
Badwah, Al-[61] 1417 4320
Badwah, Wādī al-[60] 1418 4319–1416 4315
Bayt al-Akīd (al-Kīdīyah?)[24] 1436 4314
Bayt al-Aksa' (Bayt al-Faqīr)[38] 1432 4319
Bayt al-Faqīh 1431 4319
Durayhimī, Al- 1438 4303
Fašāl*[56] *ca.* 1422 4315
Ğa'arah, Ṣanīf al-[68] 1409 4330
Ğa'āmiyyah, Maḥall al- 1429 4321
Ğaḥābah, Wādī al-[17] 1437 4314–1437 4259
Ğaḥbah, Buyūt al-[26] 1435 4320
Ğanba'iyyah, Al-[19] 1437 4327
Ğābir, Bayt Yaḥyā[18] 1438 4310
Ğāh, Al- 1420 4303
Ğumayš al-Yumná[6] 1445 4304
Ḡalābah, Ṣanīf al-[51] 1427 4329
Ḡānimiyyah, Al-[57] 1421 4313
Ḡulayfiqah (Ḡulāfiqah*) *ca.* 1425 4301
Habāliyyah, Al-[55] 1422 4311
Habāliyyah, Al-[53] 1425 4329
Habāliyyah, Buyūt al-[46] 1429 4323
Ḥašābirah[52] 1426 4320
Ḥusayniyyah, Al- 1421 4319
Ḥušaybir, Dayr al-[2] 1453 4322
'Iğāliyyah, Buyūt al-[44] 1430 4329
'Iğāliyyah, Buyūt al-[37] 1432 4318
'Iğāliyyah, Buyūt al-[34] 1432 4324
Ka'bī, Bayt al-[66] 1414 4327
Kadrā', Al-* *ca.* 1447 4314
Kawākirah, Buyūt al-[40] 1430 4317
Kawāziyyah, Qaryat al-[14] 1440 4321
Lāwiyah, Al- 1437 4312
Ma'ārīf, Buyūt al-[58] 1422 4318
Ma'ārīf, Buyūt al-[32] 1434 4325
Ma'ārīf, Quz'at al-[31] 1434 4319
Ma'zab, Al-[11] 1442 4329
Madanī, Nakhl al- (al-Madanīyah)[64] 1416 4311 (vil) and 1417 4312 (area)
Madālihah, Al- (Ṣaraṭiḥah)[36] 1432 4317
Mağāmilah, Maḥall[3] 1449 4321
Maḥāğibah, Al-[65] 1414 4324
Maḥğar, Al-[54] 1424 4319
Maḥrab, Al-[67] 1410 4343
Manāṣirah, Maḥallat al-[9] 1442 4325
Manāṣirah, Ṣanīf al-[10] 1442 4327
Manāwirah, Dayr al-[39] 1432 4320
Manṣūriyyah, Al- 1441 4318
Muğālisah, Buyūt al-[13] 1440 4313
Muğālisah[12] 1441 4311
Muğāmilah, Faṣmat al-[23] 1435 4255
Muğāmilah, Ğazīrat al-[22] 1435 4256–1437 4254
Muğāmilah, Ra's[20] 1437 4253
Muğāmilah, Ṭurfat al-[21] 1436 4256
Mukaymīniyyah, Al-[7] 1444 4305
Muqābil, Maḥall al-[33] 1433 4314
Nafḥān[50] 1428 4329
Qaḥmah, Al-* *ca.* 1438 4321
Qawqar[29] 1435 4318
Rabā'iyyah, Buyūt al-[43] 1430 4328
Sawlah, Al-[47] 1428 4316
Suhayl, Dayr al-[1] 1459 4309
Suḫnah, Al- 1447 4326
Sulaykiyyah, Al-[48] 1428 4319
Sulaykiyyah, Al-[45] 1429 4319
Ṣa'īd, Al-[35] 1432 4328
Šaṭṭ, Al-[27] 1436 4327
Šuğaynah[5] 1446 4319
Ṭā'if, Al-[30] 1434 4300
Uğaylī, Bayt al-[63] [sic] 1416 4326
'Uğayliyyah, Al-[8] 1444 4309
Wa'āriyyah, Bilād al-[15] 1439 4326
Zabīd 1411 4319
Zambūliyyah, Al-[59] 1419 4328
Zunbūliyyah, Al-[49] 1428 4327

The Muslim Qāḍī and the Peasant Bedouin of the Emirates*

Abdullah A. Yateem
Bahrain National Museum

Introduction

Reading about the late 19th and early 20th century history of the area which is now the United Arab Emirates, one notices that its social structures in that period did not exhibit the features inherent to those of the neighbouring countries: Oman, Yemen and Saudi Arabia. In those countries, respectively Ibadhi, Zaydi and Wahhabi theocratic regimes, religious and social practice constituted part of everyday life and power structures. The history of the social structures of the Emirates shows that it has escaped the experiences which the others went through. The early chiefdom-form of political system in the Emirates, on the contrary, gave a larger role and greater power to its secular ruling shaikhs and emirs. Men of religious knowledge in the Emirates gained, as a result, a less important political role.

It is assumed that the reasons for the less significant role of religious men in the modern history of the Emirates are several: amongst them, for instance, the lack of one single, centralized political system in the whole country. The civil war of the 18th century, in which the entire country of Oman (of which the Emirates was only part, and during which its main tribal factions, the Hinawi and Ghafiri, participated) led to the rise of several chiefdoms (*imārāt*).

* Acknowledgment: Data for this essay are based on my residence in the coastal region of the Emirates (1976–1983) and, later, on field research in its Western Hajar (1987–1995). My research has been carried out largely among the semi-nomadic tribal groups who reside in the mountain zone of the Emirates, al-Hajar. I gratefully acknowledge support from the University of Bahrain for the research period between 1987 and 1988.

While the Ibadhis, Zaydis and Wahhabis united their countries by overriding their tribal factions and rivalries, thus leading the polities towards a form of centralized system, the Emirates engaged in a sequence of segmentation which generated several chiefdoms scattered around the country.

These features may be considered as one of the general trends in the socio-cultural structures of the Emirates, especially when these structures are compared with those of other Arabian societies. The question remains, if Ibadhi, Zaydi and Wahhabi men of religious knowledge formed such a historically important role in their societies, why have their counterparts in the Emirates lacked such a role. Given that this is so, then what role have they played in the absence of a single, centralized political system?

Some interesting recent studies on the history of the social and political transformations in the Emirates have noted, for example, the remarkable role of a religious elite in such transformations, including that of Muslim *qāḍī*s in the coastal towns.[1] These studies have hinted, as a result, that this type of role is to be considered as one of the endogenous sources in those transformations. This current study, as a result of its ethnographic findings, suggests also that further ethnographic and historical investigations in the various cultures and societies of the Emirates, including those of the mountains, the desert and the coast, can reveal more heuristic aspects of Islamic religious authority practices.

Based on ethnographic research in one of the Emirates' communities, in the Hajar mountain range, this study aims to throw some light on the role of the Islamic religious authority (based in the town) in the social and cultural life of the Hajari Bedouin in the mountain region. Since this question has generated considerable attention in anthropological theory and ethnographic studies, it is worth elaborating on the theoretical dimension before looking at the case.

What is Anthropologically Important here?

I found social control and authority the most suitable contexts for the examination of the Islamic *qāḍī* role in the Hajar but this very statement itself creates a problem for the author. The question which this study is intended to deal with is not totally new; several aspects of it have been dealt with by anthropologists working in Middle Eastern societies. These anthropologists' works have shaped the theory of the very phenomena which have been studied. Therefore, it will be interesting to see how the question of the Emirates can be related to those problems studied by the anthropologists of the Middle East.[2]

Some Islamic tribal societies studied by anthropologists like Evans-Pritchard (1949) and Gellner (1969) in North Africa, Barth (1959) and Ahmed (1980) in North Pakistan, Lewis (1961) in Somalia, and Bujra (1971) in South Yemen, present us with important characteristics of authority and social control in

Islamic societies. In these societies, certain aspects of leadership and authority have always been embedded or vested in lineages which claim to be descendants of the Prophet Muhammad. Such lineages are treated in Islamic tribal societies as holy and have thus acquired higher social status. As a result, the leaders of these lineages become very influential and powerful in their societies. It is also clear that such leaders have built up an authority which is accepted by all tribal factions in the society. As a consequence of this authority, the leaders of these lineages are strongly effective in establishing social control and maintaining social order. Clearly, what makes the role of these leaders legitimate is their position in the social organization as members of holy lineages, and the society's belief system which grants a special status to holy religious men.

It is worth looking at Geertz's notion of religion, since his approach has been influential in the field of Islam. Unlike previous approaches—which were mainly preoccupied with the theory of segmentation, ecological constraints, dynamic relationships and religion as authority in making social control, Geertz derives his notion of Islam from his view of religion as: 'sociologically interesting not because … it describes the social order … but because, like environment, political power, wealth, jural obligation, personal affection, and a sense of beauty, it shapes it' (Geertz 1975: 119). So religion not only describes how the system of social order functions, but also affects the latter, as do other factors such as environment, political power, and so on.

Most importantly, Geertz deals with religion as a cultural system and also as a system of meaning (1975: 123–25). Thus, according to him an anthropologist when studying religion must analyse 'the system of meaning embodied in the symbols which make up the religion proper, and, second, the relating of these systems to social structural and psychological process' (1975: 125).

Furthermore, he believes that the cultural dimension of religion can reveal for us a system of life, a way of communication and attitude toward life (1975: 89). He stresses the significance of viewing religion as a 'religious perspective, mode of seeing, … a particular way of looking at life, [and] a particular manner of construing the world' (1975: 110). Geertz, therefore, argues that only a 'thick' description of the cultural system of a religion can allow us to understand religion in its proper context. In his *Islam Observed* (1968), he suggests that certain steps should be taken in order to create a better understanding of religion in local contexts, including 'the description of the wide variety of forms in which it appears; the uncovering of the forces which bring these forms into existence, alter them, or destroy them; and the assessment of their influences, also various, upon the behaviour of men in everyday life' (Geertz 1968: 97).

Geertz's approach has in recent years been much appreciated by his students who have carried out fieldwork in different Islamic societies. Unlike Evans-Pritchard and his students who saw the problem in the context of the relationship between Islam and tribalism, Geertz's students are not only concerned with the individuals as social actors; they are also deeply interested in the symbolic meanings of social actions, and how an ordinary tribal man views Islam. For these students, if this symbolic meaning is revealed, then the cultural system of Islam will be fully understood. This was, for instance, the approach of Dale Eickelman in his *Moroccan Islam* (1976), when he studied the role of Islamic authority in a traditional pilgrimage centre in Boujad in Morocco.

Within the same theoretical framework, Lawrence Rosen (1984) has applied these concepts in his study of an Islamic community of Sefrou in Morocco in order to see how social reality has been attained by the ordinary Muslim. The most relevant study of the concept of social control among Geertz's students is by Brinkley Messick on Yemen (1986, 1993). Messick sees the *muftī*'s job in solving Muslim problems as an indigenous cultural interpretation of Islamic legal texts. Messick also sees the Yemeni *muftī* as a mediator between the ordinary Muslim in the community and the Muslim judge in the Islamic Court. Therefore, the *muftī* derives his authority from his interpretation of legal texts and through solving people's disputes before they reach the court.

Finally, along this line, Richard Antoun has studied the importance of religious authority by examining the role of an Islamic judge in a tribal village community in Jordan. He viewed the judge's role as a culture broker who introduces changes to the village's values through his role in the Islamic court. The judge, through settling disputes, is required to interpret the law, to accommodate it, or to reconcile it with the people's day-to-day problems. Thus he introduces changes to the community as well as to the law (Antoun 1980).

Comparing these above-mentioned ethnographies to my own, there arise several interesting observations. For instance, the problem we encounter here, especially among the British social anthropology school, is that most of its anthropological studies have drawn their examples from ethnographic regions where holy lineages or saints play a significant part as leaders or authorities in the segmentary lineage system. The question which could be raised here is, what would be the case in other Islamic tribal societies where holy lineages or sainthood systems do not exist? How does authority then legitimate itself in such societies? Does a religious authority without a holy descent or sainthood possess a lesser or greater role in these societies?

The area in which I have carried out my fieldwork, the Hajar region of the Emirates, as well as other regions in the Middle East, such as those which have been studied by Talal Asad (1970), Richard Antoun (1971, 1979), Donald Cole (1975) and William Lancaster (1981), do not possess holy lineages or saints to function as leaders or authorities. Yet religious and tribal leaders still play a powerful role. In the tribal societies in the Emirates there are no holy lineages. On the contrary, the societies are ruled by a shaikhly authority, whose members act as leaders and rulers of the country. These shaikhs have local representatives, who are mostly leaders of the native tribes or clans. In some communities the shaikh has appointed village headmen (*wālīs*) to act as representatives for him. The shaikhs here do not derive their power from saintly or holy descent, instead their source of power is based on bravery and generosity, and on their reputation as wise leaders in time of wars and conflicts. Thus, the tribes to which these shaikhs belong are considered and treated as noble.

The shaikhs are very powerful and popular men in their societies. As a sign of their popularity, for instance, the ordinary tribesmen call the shaikhs in their conversations by their name alone, such as Salim, Nassir or Abdullah. They never say Shaikh Salim or Nassir, as other citizens of the Arab Gulf call their shaikhs.

An interesting characteristic of the authority of the shaikhs in the Emirates is that while they have an effective role in the political life in the tribal villages, they do not reside in these villages. Instead, they live in the coastal towns like Abu Dhabi, Dubai, Sharjah and Fujairah. The fact that these shaikhs live in the towns, while their followers live in the deserts and mountains, has been established since the shaikhly families came to power in the mid-18th century.

A further important characteristic of authority in the tribal societies of the Emirates is that, while there are no holy men or saints to practise as a religious authority, the religious authority consists mainly of pious men who have gained their religious status not through heredity, as is the case with the saints of the holy lineages, but through religious learning, or by being pious and devoted Muslims. According to their personal traits and skills, a religious practitioner can either stand at a higher level on the ladder and thus become a *šar'* (Islamic judge and jurist: see later for more detail), or at a lower level and thus become the village priest (*muṭawwa'*). In the history of the Emirates (Heard-Bey 1982; Abdullah 1978) the most learned religious men, such as the judges and jurists, have always come from the towns. Hence, until recently the Islamic courts were largely run by these judges from their centre in the towns.[3] Consequently, the tribal villages on the periphery are left with their village priests who carry out the prayers, the sermons, and other formal and informal religious services.

Islamic tribal society in the Emirates presents the problem of the relationship between the political and religious authorities which practise their domination from their centre in the towns on the one hand, and the peripheral tribal societies which consist of tribal followers, on the other. The question here is how these two authorities, the political and religious, have continued to maintain their authoritative role in these societies despite the belief which sees peripheral tribal societies as being in continuous conflict with the state or central authority. One anthropologist stated the problem: 'The commonest view is that which sees the two in simple dichotomous terms, as representing radically different principles of social and political organization. In this paradigm tribe and state are in a relationship of systematic opposition, each threatening (generally through rebellions) and the attempts of centralized states to control recalcitrant tribesmen form one of the great themes of the history of the region' (Christensen 1986: 286). In this case, therefore, I want to restrict the study to one of these authorities, that is the religious one. By doing so, I hope to show how the Islamic judge in the towns has gained authority and power over the peripheral tribal villages, and how the Islamic institutions have provided the judge with power to mediate and arbitrate in local village disputes.

The Hajar and the Hajari Bedouin

In order to locate the Hajaris within their proper social and cultural context, and to demonstrate the distinctiveness of the Hajari sub-culture as compared to those in the rest of the Emirates, I will provide a description of the Hajari environment, with the aim of showing its influence on the Hajari social and cultural systems.

The Hajar region in the Emirates is part of a larger region known as the Hajar Mountains (*Jibāl al-Ḥajar*), a mountain range covering an area of about 35,000 square kilometers of south-eastern Arabia. The Hajar plateau stretches from the steep cliffs in the Strait of Hormuz, in the north-east, to Ras al-Hadd in the south-east of Oman. The range is divided by the plateau of the Jabal al-Akhdar, whose altitude reaches over 3,000 metres, into two sections known as the Eastern Hajar and the Western Hajar. Most of the Eastern and Western Hajar ranges are situated in Oman, and only a small part of the Western Hajar stretches into the Emirates. The part which lies in the Emirates constitutes one tenth of the whole country. Territorially, the Hajar is divided between the Sultanate of Oman and the Emirates. The section of the Western Hajar which occupies the south-eastern region of the Emirates is also sub-divided territorially between the seven emirates which constitute the federation of the United Arab Emirates. Thus each of the Emirates has a portion of its country and people stretching into the Hajar region.

Due to its ecological characteristics, the Hajar region has had a powerful influence on the society and culture of the Emirates. The Hajar, thus, formed a society that is different from the desert one, the Dhahirah (*ḏāhirah*), and from the maritime one, the Batinah (*bāṭinah*). Traditionally, the coastal villages and towns formed a society that was dependent on trade and fishing, and was exposed to direct contacts with foreign cultures, such as those of Persia, India and Africa. This geographical positioning offered the coastal region the power to dominate and hence to operate as the centre. The desert, on the other hand, was also a region with its own character. With its large tract of sandy land, the desert region acted as a homeland for the camel-herding tribes, whose people and tribes formed the backbone for the ruling shaikhs of the centres.

In contrast to the desert and coastal regions, the Hajar formed a society and culture that was, and still is, remarkably different from those of the other two regions. The Hajar society is composed of tribes which are neither town-dwellers nor desert nomads. The Hajaris of the Emirates, as well as those of Oman, form sections of tribes, some of whom are totally dependent on mountainous pastoralism, while others depend on agriculture or both.

Of the various Hajari tribes who occupy the Hajar range, the Sharqiyin (*šarqiyīn*) are considered the largest. The Sharqiyin who reside in the mountain zone of the Hajar region are part of the Sharqiyin confederacy of the Fujairah emirate. The Sharqiyin, in general, can be divided into two distinct groups. Those who live in the small towns and villages in the coastal area of Fujairah are the town-dwellers and villagers (*ahl al-bāṭinah*). The rest of the Sharqiyin, which constitutes two-thirds of the emirate, reside in the mountains of the al-Hajar region. The people of this region are known as *ahl al-ḥayar*; they are the tribal people of the mountain zone. The Sharqiyin are scattered among several valleys in the part of the Hajar range which lies under the sovereignty of the Fujairah emirate. Of these valleys, Wādī Hām is the most strategically and regionally important.

Geographically, the Hajar region belongs to the arid zone environment. The terrain is extremely barren and the mountains are dominated by bald, dark rocks. The fertile soil in the small pockets of terraces is mostly deposited by infrequent floods. The soil is of silt and red clay, and very grainy in texture. The scarcity of loamy soil, combined with its loss through winds and floods, makes it precious to the villagers. With the exception of light rainfall over a very few months, the Hajar remains dry for most of the year. The valleys of the Hajar region are surrounded by steep and high mountains. The altitude of these mountains varies from north to south: the highest mountains are in the north where their altitude is 2,000 metres above sea level; in the south, it ranges between 1,000 and 1,500 metres. The overall average annual rainfall in the Hajar region is 140 mm (Ministry of Agriculture and Fisheries, 1986) but the Hajaris do not rely directly on it: the village's winter crops are not irrigated by rain. Instead, the village depends on water storage beneath the wadi-basin. The villagers irrigate their farms and gardens by using an underground canal system known as falajes (*falağ*/*aflāğ*). Agricultural products vary according to the season: a single agricultural year-cycle would take a Hajari peasant from growing tobacco, sorghum, wheat, barley, millet, fodder and alfalfa, in winter, to dates, mangos and limes in summer. The Hajar, furthermore, is famous for its livestock, which includes mountain goats, sheep, camels and a few local cattle.

Beliefs and Ritual

Moving now to the belief system of the Hajari, it is here, in this sacred zone, where the judge, in the town, and the Hajari, in the mountain, can find a common ground for dialogue. It is here also where a remote person, like the *qāḍī*, can find the legitimacy and the source of power for his authority. In the following description of the Islamic Hajari belief system, and in order to show the type of environment in which he has to operate, I will try to strike a balance between official and practical Islam.

The Hajaris are known to be amongst the first tribal groups in Arabia to have adopted Islam as their religion and way of life during the 1st/7th century. Today, the Hajaris do not differ very much in their Islamic ritual practice from any other Islamic tribal society that consists of mixed groups of peasants and mountain nomads. By this, I mean that Islam has a great influence on the values and belief system of the Hajari. The personality of the Prophet Muhammad and his practice constitute an important element in the Hajari ideal-type. For instance, one aspect of the Hajaris' admiration of the Prophet Muhammad is their tradition of growing a full beard to show they follow the Prophet's practice of manhood and religiosity. It is also the case that the Prophet's name is the name with which every Hajari poet ends his poem.

In principle, all the Hajari tribes are *sunnī* Muslim, but within them there are a few tribes or sections of tribes who adhere to the Shafi (*šāfi'ī*) doctrine (*maḏhab*), while others to the Hanbali (*ḥanbalī*). Tribes such as the Kunūd, Jalājilah, Banū Ka'b, Sufadnih and 'Abādilah are Shafi; others like the Zuyūd, Yamāmanah, Dahāminah, Zuḥaym, Ḥafaytāt and Surīdāt are Hanbali. In general, there are few differences in the ritual practices of these two doctrinal groups.

In the Hajar, the tribesmen who follow the Shafi and Hanbali doctrines attend the same mosques and are buried in the same cemetery. All of their other rituals which are carried out throughout the life-cycle (birth, circumcision, marriage and death) and their practices of observance and avoidance are the same. Thus the Hajaris of the Shafi and Hanbali doctrines are led by the same prayer leader and have their disputes regarding marriage, divorce or inheritance settled by the same Islamic judge. The Shafis and Hanbalis also both observe the Prophet Muhammad's birthday celebration (*mawlid*), which is a ritual practice in which blessings are brought to the dead, the sick, and to those recovering from illness; and also to share the happiness of the birth of a child after long years of waiting. But there are quite large numbers of Hanbalis in the urban towns of the Emirates who do not celebrate *mawlid*, and who consider it instead as a heretical practice (*bid'a*).

The Hajaris celebrate the birth of the first child with great happiness, especially if it is a boy. Every new-born child is celebrated after one week by slaughtering a sheep or goat. This ritual is known among the Hajaris as the *'uqūqah*. The meat of the sacrificed animal is usually distributed to the relatives and neighbours and small portions are cooked for a feast, or another feast takes place for the men, a few days later. Until forty days after the birth of the child, no sexual contact can take place between the spouses, and then the mother of the child has to purify her body with a powder made from the lotus tree's (*Zizyphus spina Christi*) leaves (*sidr* in Arabic). The *sidr* is taken to a *muṭawwa'* to read some verses of the Quran over it, as a matter of blessing, and then the new mother will use the *sidr* to clean her hair and body before putting on new clothes. On the next day, she will declare her purification and the accomplishment of her forty days by offering a feast for the women in the neighbourhood. This feast is called the Forty (*al-arba'īn*). On the same day the child will have his or her hair completely shaven. This hair shaving is also treated as part of the purification ritual.

Circumcision (*taḥlīl*) is the second ritual in the life cycle. Both boys and girls are circumcised. At the age of one year the girl will be taken to a specialist woman who will make only a small cut which allows a little blood to come out. Girls' circumcisions are carried out quietly with no sign of celebration. A boy's circumcision, however, sometime between the ages of four to ten, is celebrated with a large feast offered to the entire village. Since the late 1970s all boys' circumcisions have been carried out in the town's hospital. Girls' and boys' circumcision is considered a purification ritual which every new-born child must undergo.

Puberty does not have any public ritual celebration, except that girls reaching puberty are instructed by their mothers to purify their body, and in particular their head-hair, at the end of every monthly menstruation (*ḥayḍ*). When the girl has her first menstruation, the mother informs the father that their daughter has ended her childhood (*kisrayt*). There is not a long period for a girl between puberty and marriage, for once she is known to be '*kisrayt*', the girl will be prepared for a suitable husband. At the age of fifteen most girls will have been married.

The puberty of the boy is celebrated a little later, usually when he is fifteen. This celebration will involve the finding of a suitable wife for him, for between the age of fifteen and eighteen years most boys will be married. The marriage in the life-cycle also serves as a social announcement of the fact that the boy has reached puberty and manhood. At this stage, the boy gives much care to his beard and the girl will start wearing her mask, *burqa'*. Once a girl has reached puberty she must strictly avoid all her non-incest kin both before and after her marriage.

When a man or a woman dies then they are again washed and purified with *sidr* (women and men must be purified only by their own sex), before being covered in a white shroud and taken first to the mosque to carry out a special prayer for the dead (*ṣalāt al-mayt*). Then the dead person, whether man or woman, is carried to the cemetery (*madīnah*) and buried by the men. The burial (*dafn*) must be during the day. Later at night a feast (*waḥšah*) will be offered to the villagers. The mourning (*'azā'*) goes on for one week. A wife who has lost a husband has to undergo a period of complete seclusion (*dīn*) in which she locks herself in her house for 90 days. During this period the only people she is permitted to see are her sons and daughters and a few of her incest kin. Those women who happen to be seen outside their houses during this time will be regarded as disgraced. After passing the *dīn* period the widow has the right to marry another man if she wishes to do so and to continue her normal life.

Apart from those rituals relating to the life-cycle, the Hajaris, as part of their religious beliefs, strongly believe in envy (*ḥasad*), called locally *'ayn* (evil eye). They also believe in witchcraft and sorcery (*siḥr*). Though *siḥr* is condemned and prohibited as a practice in the Quran and equally so by the Hajaris, they believe that some of the crises that occur amongst them can be attributed to *siḥr*. Belief in *siḥr* is related to other beliefs in demons (*ğinn*). According to the Quran and the Hajari belief, there are two types of *ğinn*, those which are useful and those which are harmful. Those who practise witchcraft and sorcery make contact with *ğinn* and direct them to do either bad or good work. Those who consider themselves victims of *siḥr* or *ḥasad* seek either a *muṭawwa'* or a diviner (*bāṣir*) who uses different methods, such as the reading of Quranic verses on a sick person who is a victim of the evil eye, or the use of divination to counteract the harm caused by a bad *ğinn* directed by a sorcerer (*sāḥir*). The Hajaris also believe that a number of areas and places in the valleys are occupied (*maskūnah*) by harmful *ğinn*. Some of these *ğinn* also inhabit the villages at night; therefore young children are always told to be home before sunset and are advised not to play or remain in the village's alleys. Children who become sick suddenly with no obvious reason are always considered to be the victims of these *ğinn*, or victims of *ḥasad*. To keep those *ğinn* and evil-eye people away from family members, mothers usually burn large amounts of incense in the house at sunset.

One common type of *ğinn* influence or effect on Hajari health is spirit possession (*zār*), which is mostly experienced by adult men and women. The *zār* can be the result of being inhabited by either a bad or a good *ğinn*. Most people involved in *zār*, as healers, are the *ḫuddām* (black people, descendants of slaves), but victims of *zār* can be of both sexes and of any social category. Special sessions are prepared by the healers (*ubwah*) for their patients (*'iyyāl*), but those who are possessed by *zār* can easily be exorcised during the playing of music and dancing (*razfah*) at wedding parties, and also during the recitations at the *mawlid* celebrations.

Amongst the Hajaris, ritual and knowledge related to religious practice are not as sophisticated as among the urban learned pious men in the coastal towns. The harsh environment and the absence of literacy have made Hajari society lack sophisticated religious figures, and so their religious practice is a simplified and practical version of Islamic ideals. This does not mean, as is frequently said in the ethnographic literature about Arab Bedouin or Muslim tribesmen, that the Hajaris are lax in their religious duty or observance. My own observation of the Hajaris is quite different. Until very recently, the Hajaris did not have any rock or mud buildings for their mosques, and they still do not have any decorated cemeteries. Their mosques have always been simply a clean piece of land circled with small stones located near the *amīr*'s house, or in the village's outskirts (such as the Friday and *'īd* prayers mosques). During my stay in one of the valleys, the *wālī* of one of the villages ordered his servants to clean up the *'īd* mosques twice, once a few days before the Ramadhan feast (*'īd al-fiṭr*) and again before the *ḥağğ* feast (*'īd al-ḥağğ*).

Each village in a valley today has a main mosque with a tall minaret, used normally as the Friday grand mosque, and a place for the daily prayers plus a few others without minarets. These smaller mosques consist mainly of a single small prayer room built by the leaders or prominent families of the quarter. These and the old mosques possess no features of elaborate decoration. There are no lineages of saints or learned families dominating these mosques as religious centres, as is the case elsewhere in Islamic tribal societies, but even so the religious life in the villages is very active. Most mosques are full of men and young boys during the daily prayers. Prayers such as the mid-day (*ẓuhr*) or afternoon (*'aṣr*) may be less well attended than others, for those are the times when men are busy in their farms or gardens or in the towns, but during other prayers the mosques are fully occupied.

The Hajaris are very strict in observing their prayer duty; young sons are encouraged by their fathers to join them in the prayer times at the mosque. Going to Friday and *'īd* mosques is not only considered as a religious duty but also as a social obligation. The Hajaris expect to meet and greet each other and their guests, first at the mosque's doorsteps, and then to meet each other for a feast or social gathering at their homes. For instance, it is a tradition after Friday prayers, and after the prayers for the Ramadhan and *ḥağğ* feasts, for the *amīr*s and *wālī*s to wait near to the mosque entrance to receive the greetings of their fellow villagers.

Of the five pillars of Islam which the Hajaris observe, besides believing in the oneness of God and praying, the Hajari observe the fasting days of the month of Ramadhan. Except for young children, and women who are menstruating, all other people abstain from eating, drinking and sex. People also refrain from social gatherings, visits and excessive work in the farm during the daytime.

After sunset, the villagers, particularly the men, spend their time at the mosques for the elaborate night prayer (*tarāwīḥ*). During the month, notable Hajaris such as the *amīr*s, *wālī*s and heads of each quarter offer daily feasts for the villagers. These important men are also invited by various members of the village to be their guests. Those landlords and landowners who endowed some date-palms in their gardens as a type of *zakāt* (*fuṭra*), will distribute the produce of these palms, or the equivalent in wheat, to their neighbours and relatives in the village.

Regarding the fourth pillar, *zakāt*, the Hajaris practice *zakāt* and see it as a way of purifying and making their income and the food they eat permissible (*ḥalāl*). The Hajaris believe that if they do not make the land they own, along with its produce and their livestock, permissible by the payment of the required *zakāt*, then the income from the land and livestock will be *ḥarām* (forbidden). A further result of not giving *zakāt* is that God will not give the rest of his land and livestock any blessing (*baraka*). The *zakāt* of livestock used to be collected by the *wālī*s as recently as the late 1960s. The *zakāt* on dates is still levied on land in some cases (*bidārah* tenure), whereas the tobacco *zakāt* is no longer collected but is left for their owners or holders to execute. Today, *zakāt* is becoming more and more the individual's religious responsibility to fulfil. While a few years ago *zakāt* was collected and sent to the state, today it is collected by the *wālī* and individuals' offerings are distributed among the needy families of the village. In the Hajar, there is in every traditional date garden between one and four date-palms that are endowed by their owner for religious purposes: they are either for the passer-by (*sabīl*) or *fuṭra* of the Ramadhan month. Whole gardens or farms are also endowed as *waqf*. Landlords and landowners seek, by making such endowments, to bring blessing on themselves and their families, and to purify their property.

The last aspect of the formal practice of Islam is the fifth pillar, the pilgrimage, or the *ḥaǧǧ*. Until very recently, this was a practice which was carried out only by the wealthy Hajaris. Since the Hajar was connected by a recently-constructed highway, many Hajari tribesmen have been able to go once or twice to Mecca. Buses organized by a pilgrimage agent collect the pilgrims from the villages in the valleys and take them to the towns, whence they are flown to Jeddah and thence by bus to Mecca and Madina. Some pilgrims, seeking more rewards from God for their *ḥaǧǧ*, prefer to travel by coach across the Arabian desert.

The Hajaris in their valleys and their pilgrim relatives in Mecca celebrate the *ḥaǧǧ* feast (*'īd al-ḥaǧǧ*) on the 10th of the month of *ḏū al-ḥiǧǧah* (the *ḥaǧǧ* month) as a mark of the sacredness of this month. Among the Hajaris coming back from *ḥaǧǧ* are villagers who, by fulfilling the pilgrimage, enter into the elder category. The pilgrim will acquire the *ḥāǧǧ* title, which will place him amongst the wise elders of the village. Becoming a *ḥāǧǧ* forms part of the

Islamic rituals of the Hajari, but the title itself bestows upon those men seeking social prestige and status power which allows them to achieve high ranking in the village. Today, for instance, it is very rare to find a leader in any of the Hajar's valleys who has not become a *ḥāǧǧ*.

Besides the *ḥaǧǧ* feast as a form of ritual to celebrate the holiness of the month, the Hajaris also celebrate the return of their relatives from *ḥaǧǧ* by paying a visit to the pilgrims' homes to congratulate them for carrying out the *ḥaǧǧ* duty. The pilgrims' houses are usually decorated with the state flag to celebrate their return, and a few days after their arrival pilgrims offer a feast for the villagers and give their visitors gifts from *ḥaǧǧ* such as rosaries and men's head-cloths and skull-caps. Pilgrims also bring some posters of Mecca and Medina, and inscriptions of Quranic verses to hang in the men's guestroom.

Advanced religious knowledge amongst the Hajaris is quite poor; those who were able to read the Quran in the past were counted on fingers. Well-to-do men in the Hajar would normally bring a private Quranic teacher to teach their sons the skill of literacy through studying the Quran. The rest of the men and women of the area were illiterate until the 1970s, when the new generation of boys and girls started going to school. The boys of this generation are very much encouraged by their parents to study the Quran in order to be able to lead the men of their quarters at prayer times. It is in such an environment of illiteracy that the learned men or men of religious knowledge (*muṭawwa'*), or men of divination (*bāṣir*) and men of advanced learning in Islamic theology (*šar'*) gained much influence and power and thus had more authority. The Islamic rituals and beliefs of the Hajaris thus tend to produce specialists and practitioners who, either because of their advanced knowledge, such as the *šar'* and *muṭawwa'*, or because of their personal characteristics and qualities, put forward certain claims of divinatory power, such as the *bāṣir* and the *zār* healer.

Village Priest vs. Town Qāḍī

The *šar'* is a category of religious functionary and is the term used by the Hajaris for their Islamic judges. In comparison with other religious practitioners, the *šar'* is considered the highest both in terms of power and authority. The Hajaris use the word shaikh when addressing the judge or talking to him personally, but in daily conversations they use the term *šar'* to mean both the judge and the Islamic court. Thus the word *šar'* is a reference to a type of authority, as well as being the usual word for the canonical law of Islam.

The *šar'* derives his power and legitimacy from his status as a man of the Book (Quran) and the *sunna* (the Prophet Muhammad's actions and sayings). He is the man who is capable, because of his formal religious training, of distinguishing between what is permissible (*ḥalāl*) and what is prohibited (*ḥarām*), and guiding people on which course to follow. Because of his prolonged religious learning which lasts many years, this puts the *šar'* in a more powerful position than the *muṭawwa'*.

Unlike the *muṭawwa'*, the *šar'* behaves in a very reserved manner and keeps a distance in his social interactions with people. His status as the highest religious authority means that people treat him with respect and dignity. He is not like the *muṭawwa'* who is a fellow villager and mixes with the villagers in everyday life and exchanges jokes with them. The *šar'* is usually an old man who has spent most of his life in religious learning and devotion to Islam. For a Hajari, the *šar'* is the person who can give him the final word on what is religiously considered as *ḥalāl* or *ḥarām*, and as such there is no advice that is more respected and followed than that of the *šar'*.

The involvement of the *šar'* in the daily life of the Hajari is very important and is quite different from that of the *muṭawwa'*. At the level of local village politics, the *muṭawwa'* may find himself involved in playing the role of mediator in solving local disputes, but none of the disputants is obliged to accept his settlement. The *šar'*, however, is more powerful, and is also vested with the authority to act as a formalized legal institution. Thus, once a case is taken to the *šar'*, it is solved either by means of reconciliation, or a formal verdict is reached with the *šar'* having enough power to enforce it. Thus while the *šar'* acts as an authoritative consultant (*muftī*) by providing a formal religious opinion (*fatwā*), he also acts as a formal legal religious judge (*qāḍī*). The *šar'* influence over village life is therefore quite considerable. An example of the range of his powerful authority and influence is the *fatwā* given to some of the villagers regarding the excavation done by a foreign archaeological team who were excavating, during the month of January 1988, some graves dating from 1,000 BC, in one of the Hajar villages' outskirts. The *šar'* in this particular case issued a *fatwā* in which he stated that as long as the graves were not of Muslim people and the graveyard was not part of the Muslim *waqf*, then such an excavation was *ḥalāl*. The *šar'*'s *fatwā* ended an argument among the men who used to attend daily the *wālī*'s majlis.

The *šar'* meets the villagers at his court in the town and plays an effective role as the most powerful religious authority. The Hajaris visit his court to seek his advice or consultation on private or public matters. They either go to his court voluntarily, or are referred to him by the shaikh to examine their dispute. The case can be as simple as the issuing of a marriage deed, as complicated as dividing a family's patrimony, or forcing a divorce upon a reluctant and oppressive husband. Thus there is no limit on the type of case examined by the *šar'*, nor is there a limit on his authority over the disputing parties.

At the other end of his range of authority and influence are the many land and marital disputes in the various villages. All such issues are brought before the *šar'* for his legal verdict and for settlement according to Islamic rules (*ḥukm al-islām*). In their disputes, the Hajaris usually end their arguments by one party challenging the other to take the case to the *šar'* if he thinks that he is in the right. A common phrase used is 'between you and me is the *šar'*', or 'you say whatever you like but the *šar'* will judge whether what you have done is *ḥalāl* or *ḥarām*'. If fellow villagers are not sure about the religious legality of a certain attitude or behaviour one will often hear them say: 'Distance yourself (*ḥallīk ba'īd*) from the *ḥarām* by knowing the *ḥalāl* one from the *šar'*.'

The Hajari may consult any *qāḍī* he likes, but when he needs a sharia (*šarī'ah*) verdict in a disagreement, then he is expected to take it to the judge who operates within the jurisdiction and the sovereignty of the emirates to which both he and the *qāḍī* belong. In most cases, however, the Hajaris go for a *šar'* in the nearest coastal town to them, such as Fujairah, Kalba, Khor Fakkan and Dibba; or will go as far as towns such as Sharjah, Dubai, Ajman, or Ras al-Khaimah. Whereas in the years before the 1970s, the *qāḍī*s operated their courts in their own houses or in the ruling shaikh's majlis, today all *qāḍī*s have to carry out their duties in a new building in the town which is designated as a place for the Sharia Court. Today, most *qāḍī*s still use their own houses, especially between and after the prayers, to either issue a *fatwā* or answer a question, but serious cases are always referred to the court.

Before going any further, it is necessary to turn to individual judges and their history. Throughout the remembered history of the Hām valley and the other main valleys in the Hajar, the *šar'* have always settled in the towns, where the ruling shaikhs live. There has never been a *šar'* who married or resided in any of the villages in the Hām valley. A *šar'* might come to a valley for a visit or with the shaikh, but his job requires him to remain in the town.

Most men who served as a *šar'* gained their early knowledge and training in the remote towns of the emirates, such as Sharjah or Ras al-Khaimah. The knowledge of Islamic jurisprudence was mostly taught to them by religious scholars (*ahl al-'ilm*) from Saudi Arabia and southern Persia (Faris). The Saudis taught according to the Hanbali Islamic doctrine, whereas the Farisi scholars taught according to the Shafi. In the early part of the 20th century, most of the native Emirates *šar'* scholars travelled to different religious centres in Saudi Arabia and Faris to gain advanced religious knowledge and training.

Major towns on the eastern coast, especially those which are regularly visited by the Hajaris, have had a non-Emirates *šar'* at some time. In the Shamailiyah region, especially in its coastal towns of Khor Fakkan, Dibba and Fujairah, some of the Farisi and Saudi religious scholars have served as *šar'* for decades. For instance, the *šar'* of the Sharqiyin in Fujairah town, from the late 1930s until the late 1950s, was 'Īsā bin Mūsā, a learned theologian from Faris. He was fluent in Arabic and a man who had great knowledge of the *šar'*.

When 'Īsā bin Mūsā retired, no one replaced him in Fujairah. The Sharqiyin, as well as the Hajaris, consulted the *šar'* in other towns of Shamailiyah such as Kalba, Khor Fakkan and Dibba. In Kalba, a native local judge, Ḥumayd bin Fallaw, served for a while as *šar'*. Ḥumayd received his training in Sharjah and later in Qatar, under the instruction of Wahhabi scholars from Saudi Arabia and their Emirates students. In Khor Fakkan, the *šar'* were Aḥmad bin Ḥasan and Aḥmad bin 'Abdullah, sons of Farisi migrants, who both trained earlier in Faris and were subsequently taught by Saudi scholars in Sharjah. Later, when the *šar'* of Kalba, Ḥumayd bin Fallaw, retired and went to Ras al-Khaimah, one of the Khor Fakkan *šar'*, Aḥmad bin Ḥasan, replaced him, running the Kalba Sharia Court twice a week. Aḥmad used to travel from Khor Fakkan to Kalba on those days for this purpose. Another judge also served in Murbah, one of the coastal towns of Fujairah. He was Shaikh Rāshid bin Ḥusayn, a man who came originally from Faris and acted as the *šar'* until he died in 1967.

In the late 1960s, however, the Shaikh of the Sharqiyin appointed Saudi *šar'*, amongst them Shaikh 'Abd al-Karīm al-Šiha, who acted as the senior *šar'*. Shaikh 'Abd al-Karīm was assisted by various junior judges. The junior judge during my first period of fieldwork (1987–1988) was Shaikh Muḥammad al-Dakhīl. Both *šar'* had been trained and gained their religious education in Saudi Arabia.

The most obvious reason for the existence of Saudi and Farisi *šar'* in the northern emirates, in general, and in the Shamailiyah region in particular, is the fact that both Saudi Arabia and southern Persia have been the main centres for religious training for many centuries. In addition, we must exclude Oman and Yemen: the former being Ibadhi and the latter Zaydi. In the early part of the 20th century, the Emirates religious scholar, as a Muslim *sunnī*, would be left with the choice of the two nearest countries from which to gain his religious training: Saudi Arabia and southern Persia. Nowadays, however, the existence and influence of Farisi *šar'* has declined considerably in the northern emirates, thus leaving the highest religious authority, the *šar'*, under a majority of Saudi jurists. Most of the recent Saudi jurists have received their religious education from the Islamic University in the holy city of Madina in Saudi Arabia.

Having described the *šar'*, let me now illustrate their role by providing an ethnographic description of the Islamic court. The judge's role and the type of disputes that are examined and settled by the judge will be illustrated with a case study. This will show how the judge mediates between the local Hajari traditions, customs and the formal legal traditions of greater Islam, and how, by doing so, he introduces changes to the native Hajari traditions and culture.

My personal and fieldwork experiences were connected largely with the *qāḍī* and courts of Dibba, Kalba, Fujairah and Khor Fakkan: hence I have chosen one of them as an illustration.

The Court and the Judge in Kalba

The Islamic court in Kalba town is the central one in this region of the emirate.[4] There are other Islamic courts in the northern region of the Emirates which operate either daily or once a week. The Kalba court works every day. It is located on 10,000 sq. metres of land beside the Amiri Court and municipality building. Over the main gate of the court there is a white sign-board with black Arabic writing carrying the name of the court: the Sharia Court of Kalba (*al-maḥkama al-šar'īyah bi-Kalbā*).

The court building, the main hall and the judges' offices, are built on only one-third of the court area. The rest of the area is used for the court's mosque and a car park. The court building consists of two floors. The ground floor constitutes the office of the senior judge, a main hearing hall or court-room measuring 30 × 20 metres, a 40 × 40 metre waiting area, the record office and a rest-room. In addition, there is a waiting hall for men, within which there is a small secluded hall for women; and then there is the record room and, finally, the toilets. On the second floor there are only two offices. One large office is used as a courtroom for the junior judge and beside it is a private office for the judge to interview women in the case of very private hearings.

Before 1970, the judge used to hold the court in the majlis of his own house, or otherwise the session would be in the Shaikh's majlis. No records were kept by the previous judges, and any deeds issued by them were usually kept by the parties to the dispute. Since 1970, however, the court has kept a register of the cases and a record of each case examined by the judge. Today the judges are assisted by two clerks, two policemen and a messenger.

The working hours of the court are between 7.30 a.m. and 1.30 p.m. Men and women who have business with the court wait in separate halls. The judge usually arrives about 8 a.m., and all men in the court greet him at the entrance door and, leaving his footwear behind, he enters the courtroom. It is as a matter of respect to the court that the judge and all those who are in his courtroom should attend with bare feet.

There are two desks in the courtroom, a large one for the judge and a small one for his clerk. Round the other three sides of the room there are rows of chairs. In front of the judge's desk there are also four chairs set beside each other for the disputants or petitioners to sit and present their cases. Behind the judge, there is a large bookcase which is full of various religious books on Islam and some old and new Islamic calendars, the new ones being hung on the shelves.

Once the judge has entered the courtroom, all the court attendees will enter after him. Before the judge starts to hear the first case, he spends a few minutes signing newly issued deeds. As he signs the deeds and looks into his papers he keeps repeating loudly praises of God (*tasbīḥ*). Then he calls for the first claimant (*mudda'ī*), a case's protagonist (*ṣāḥib qaḍiyah*), or a petitioner to come forward and sit in front of him.

Cases in the court are heard and examined publicly. All the other attendants can sit and listen to the proceedings. In many cases, the judge invites the other attendants to help bring reconciliation or to settle the dispute before considering it himself and issuing his verdict (*ḥukm*). However, cases which involve women and deal with very private matters, such as the sexual relationship between a wife and her husband, are usually heard in the judge's private office. During the court's sessions, the judge eases the seriousness by making some jokes, telling entertaining stories, or by making some witty comments about the cases being presented. He sometimes brings in stories from Islamic history. He also repeatedly asks the messenger to serve tea. Meanwhile, he gives the litigants (*mudda'īn*) a chance to learn a lesson from his jokes and stories and he encourages the other attendants to persuade the litigants to forgive each other and be reconciled. The language of the judge is very distinguished. He speaks a local dialect but formal Arabic terms are quite dominant in his conversation. At about 12 noon the judge ends the session temporarily and goes with the court's staff and the people attending to the court's mosque (*masǧid al-maḥkamah*) in order to perform the midday prayer. Once the prayer is over the sessions start again and will continue until 1.30 p.m.

There are no written rules for the court's legal procedures. The judge listens to the claimant, and then gives the defendant (*mudda'a 'alayhi*) the chance to reply. There is no lawyer for the disputing parties; the sharia expects the *šar'* to act both as the judge and the lawyer. In the sessions that I attended with the senior and junior judges, I found that both judges may, after hearing both sides of the case, ask for a testimony (*šahādah*) if they think the matter is serious enough. If the witnesses (*šuhūd*) are in the courtroom they are immediately asked to give their accounts of the matter in hand. If they are not available, the judge requests the parties to the dispute to bring them to the court. When the witnesses arrive, the case is examined again.

The judge will examine cases of litigants who personally bring their problems to him. Cases can also be transferred to him by the ruling shaikh, or from the police and the land department in the municipality.

There are some cases that are not disputed, and are straightforward, such as the issuing of birth certificates, ownership deeds, marriage or divorce deeds and court registration of commercial transactions; in addition to the issuing of deeds of authorization, guardianship and custodianship. Because such cases involve no litigants, the judge examines them immediately by taking testimony and then issues a court deed to prove the legality of the matter. There are cases, however, which clearly violate Islamic law, such as by-passing Islamic law in contracting a marriage or divorce, committing adultery or the incorrect or unjust division of a patrimony. The judge examines these by listening to the litigants and the witnesses, and if they are all available in the same session he then announces and issues his verdict.

The judge's verdict in these instances aims at settling things correctly, and at preventing a *ḥarām* practice continuing in an Islamic society. The judge also has the aim of teaching a lesson to those who, because of their ignorance or direct intention, want to violate the rules.

Cases of litigation presented to the judge by disputing parties are resolved in a similar way to the above. The judge offers enough time for the disputants to present their arguments, but a testimony also has to be provided. The *šahādah* for the *šar'* is the main pillar of the verdict, for Islam gives the Muslim's testimony (*šahādat al-muslim*) an invaluable weight. A Muslim's *šahādah* is a representation of his faith. Thus, when the litigants put forward their claims and counter-claims, the judge considers the testimonies provided by the witnesses as a determining factor in reaching his judgement on the issue at hand. The judge, in any disputed case, is in no hurry to give his verdict. He offers several opportunities for a reconciliation (*ṣulḥ*) to be reached. On many occasions he asks the witnesses of both parties to sit with him and to draw up a plan for reconciliation, or he may invite notable men to his court from the disputants' village or town and ask them to mediate between the disputants in order to reach a reconciliation. In most of the cases that have been taken to the Islamic court in the town, and also those that I witnessed myself in the court, the judge tried to achieve a reconciliation through the efforts of the village. Many of the Hajar's land and marital cases were settled this way. If such an attempt fails, the judge usually blames the litigants for allowing hate and enmity to grow between them.

The judge, in his effort to mediate, brings a reconciliation and a reasonable settlement, or when he announces his sharia judgement (*ḥukm šar'ī*), appeals to the Hajaris by imploring them as 'proper Muslims, as followers of the Prophet Muhammad and worshippers of God who himself is the most merciful'. He also invokes the tribesmen's own values, customs and traditions. Thus, if the tribal customs do not contradict Islamic law, the judge settles the dispute by making use of such customs. I once asked the judge if the use of local customs is permissible in Islamic jurisprudence. The judge said: 'Islam was born in Arabia and those customs contradicting Islam died a long time ago. I don't see any reason why we should not use customs which do not oppose the sharia. The sharia permits such use of local customs if it will bring benefit to the Muslim community.' Thus, for example, the *šar'* will in many cases of dispute or conviction appeal to the great value the Hajaris place on their tribal loyalty as members of the same tribal alliance (*šaff*), that is the various *šaff*s the Hajaris belong to. If the litigants are of the same tribe, he will blame them for not allowing their dispute to be kept in the village and for letting it be brought to his court. In many instances, the way the judge challenges the Hajaris by appealing to their values and traditions persuades the Hajari litigants to accept his mediation and so avoid any sharia verdict.

There are also numerous Hajari customary institutions for resolving or avoiding disputes. For instance, those which protect the right of pre-emption (*šafī'*), another for land which is made sanctuary by the Shaikh or tribal council (*marfūqah*), another for minor compensation (*raḍwā*), and also one for fine (*ğarāmah*) and compensation (*murāḍāh*). These institutions, and several others, are not seen as contradictory in their nature with the sharia law. The judge, therefore, will permit any good use of these institutions, but he will also prevent any bad use which could give rise to deviant practice. For instance, he will forbid and abolish any marriage contract where force has been used to make the bride accept her father's brother's son (*ibn 'amm*). Even if *šafī'* is given as a justifiable reason, the judge will abolish the marriage contract and will give the right to the bride to reject a groom that she does not want.

Consequently, the judge, while relying on many local Hajari customs to settle the dispute in his court, also has to make a choice between those customary institutions which coincide with or accommodate to the sharia law, and those which contradict or deviate from it. The following brief cases are examples of the judge's use of customary institutions. They are examples that were seen by the judge on one particular day. The type and number of cases seen by a judge in the space of one year are presented in Table 1.

Table 1. Type and Number of Cases Heard by a Junior Qāḍī, 1986.

Type of Case	*No.*
Marriage Contracts	9
Reinforcing deeds of contracted marriage	75
Divorce	30
Deeds for women becoming widows	19
Birth certificate deeds	39
Dividing patrimony	63
Ownership deeds	26
Authorization	37
Filiation	9
Acknowledgment	19
Correcting personal and family name	12
Total	338

Everyday Life in the Court

Today is Monday, the middle of the week, the month January 1988. The judge arrived at 8.30 a.m. and at about 9 a.m. he started examining the first case. The court's session ended at 1.45 p.m. after an interruption around 12 noon, of about half an hour, for midday prayer.[5]

Case No. I

The first case started with a man who came forward and sat on the chair. After he was asked by the *šar'* about his case, the man said: 'Shaikh, I came to tell you that my sister's husband died recently and my sister is now in the seclusion period (*dīn*). She authorized me to be her representative (*wakīl*) in all matters regarding her husband's patrimony, particularly the portion of her husband's land.' The judge asked him: 'Do you have witnesses?' Two men sitting far back in the courtroom said: 'We are the witnesses, Shaikh.' The two men told the judge that they heard the sister telling the brother that she gave him her authorization (*tawkīl*). The judge, after taking the names of the sister, her brother, the deceased husband and the two witnesses, asked the clerk to write out an authorization deed and told the man to come and collect it the next day.

Case No. II

The judge asked for the next people to come forward and present their problems. A woman in her fifties, with her young son, moved forward and sat on the chair. The son told the judge that his father died a long time ago and now his father's brother wanted to divide their patrimony. His mother now wanted him to be her *wakīl* in matters regarding the gaining of her share. The judge asked the mother if what he son said was true. She said, 'Yes, Shaikh' (*na'am šayẖ*). The judge asked two of the attendants in the courtroom if they could be witnesses for this authorization. They said yes. He asked the mother, the son and the two witnesses for their names. He wrote them down, and then asked the son to come the next day for the deed.

Case No. III

This third case is of people who are related to the Kunūd tribe of Wādī May. A father and his son asked the judge to divide the patrimony of one of his sons who used to work in the army as a soldier and who had died recently. They also informed the judge that the deceased's widow wanted the deceased's brother to be a custodian (*wālī*) over her children until they reached the age of maturity.

The deceased was in his thirties. He left behind him a family which consisted of a wife, two sons and two daughters. His patrimony consisted of 45,000 dirhams cash from the army which comprised his service reward. Three men came with the deceased's father and offered their testimony. The judge, before starting to divide the patrimony, since he knew the family, asked how the death had occurred and offered his condolences to the father and his son. He said, 'This is God's wish. We are not better. Every one of us will have to face his death sooner or later.' Then he began calculating the deceased's total inheritance. After a few minutes the judge left his pen and paper and told the father that he would receive one-sixth, his wife one-sixth, the deceased's wife one-eighth and the rest was to be divided amongst the deceased's children. The female children must receive a share which was equivalent to half of the male children's share. This division of the deceased's inheritance was based on the Islamic law of inheritance.

The judge informed the deceased's father that two deeds would be issued the next day. One was for the division of the patrimony and the other was about the custodianship (*wilāyah*) of the brother over his deceased's brother's children.

Case No. IV

The last case was a dispute over a divorce. The litigants were two parties in the courtroom. The first party consisted of a husband, who was a young man in his early twenties and his father. The second party consisted only of the wife's father, the wife herself being absent from the court.

The judge asked the disputants, 'What is your problem?' The husband's father said, 'My son married one year ago to this man's daughter. She was good in the first few months, but later she began to visit her father's house very frequently and finally she refused to do any work in our house. My son advised her many times. Two weeks ago she answered him very badly, thus he has beaten her and sent her home. Please, Shaikh, my son wants to divorce her, we have had enough of these people.'

The judge then asked the wife's father if this was true. The father said that his daughter was very young and her health was too poor to do a whole day's work for such a large family as her husband's. The father added that he did not mind if they wanted a divorce. As the wife's father finished his story the judge said in a very angry voice that he blamed the two fathers for encouraging their siblings to sue for divorce. The judge added, 'If you are unwise fathers, I am sure there are wiser men than you where you live. I shall not permit a divorce to take place. Come to me tomorrow with your *wālī*, and think a hundred times before talking about divorce. Divorce is the most hated thing for God.'

Next day the litigants came with their *wālī*. The *wālī* suggested to the judge that they reach a compromise between the two families. The wife's family agreed that their daughter would not be allowed by them to come every week and that they would try their best to make sure that their daughter carried out her duties in her husband's house. For his mistake, the husband should pay his wife 500 dirhams and her father 500 dirhams as *raḍwā*.

The judge agreed and congratulated the two families on their reconciliation. He also warned the two fathers not to let their children lead them into choosing the wrong path. The *wālī* promised to follow up their case and assured the judge that he would hear only good news about it in future.

The four cases above show the type of routine job carried out by the judge. They also show the weight given to a Hajari's *šahādah* as a representation of a Muslim's faith and as the base on which the judge reaches for a reliable sharia judgement. Moreover, the cases, particularly the fourth one, illustrate the importance of the ideology of reconciliation amongst the Hajaris and its significance for the judge and the court.

Now follows the case of a dispute over inherited land between members of 'Iyāl Muḥammad bin Ḥasan. The case aims at showing the role of the *šar'* at the village level. In addition, it will illustrate how the shaikhly and *šar'* authority and the Wadi's notable leaders co-operate to reduce conflicts by mediating between the people of the Wadi and reconciling the disputing parties. The *šar'* here tries his best to act successfully as a mediator and arbitrator, and he uses his role as adjudicator only when it is absolutely necessary. The result of the *šar'*'s attitude towards his role is reflected in that he reduces the conflicts amongst the Hajaris and so allows the ideology of consent to be the dominant one. The reason why the *qāḍī* has such an attitude is that if he insists on acting only as an adjudicator, then there will just be more discord and rivalry amongst the Hajaris rather than solidarity and consent. For although the Islamic judge must be firm, he must not lead the Muslim community to division. Thus a compromise must always be reached between the great ideal tradition of Islam in the centre and the local practice of the Muslims on the periphery.

The Qāḍī and the Disputant Hajari

'Iyāl Muḥammad bin Ḥasan was a sub-lineage of the bin Sa'īd clan of the Zuyūd tribe. It consisted of four families: a widowed mother (Dabiah), three married sons (Salim, Ali and Hassan), and two married daughters (Fatima and Ruda). Muḥammad, the father, died at the age of seventy-five after a long illness and left behind him a date garden and a tobacco farm, called al-Hanya. When the father died in 1975, the three sons were working together on the land while also serving in the army as soldiers. They employed farm labourers and continued cultivating tobacco on a share basis. The two sisters were married to men who were not members of the same tribe and valley (*ğurbityah*). They did not get a share of the crops, but they were quite happy that their share of the land was collectively cultivated and the land was being taken care of by their brothers.

In 1985, the two sisters, Fatima and Ruda, found that their elder brother, Salim, was in a dominant position over the land, since the other two brothers, Ali and Hassan, were absent for weeks due to the nature of their army work. Salim made use of their absence and invested more money in the land. He carried out many repairs to fencing and rebuilt the terrace walls. Moreover, he had started to use part of the *ḥarām* land (no-man's land) surrounding their cultivated land: he reclaimed, and then cultivated it the following season. In addition, he grew new date-palms and dug a new well and some canals. Salim also raised a large protective wall on the main side of the land facing the wadi-bed in order to protect the land from damaging floods.

As a result of Salim's investment in and expansion of the land, the villagers began to talk and exchange gossip on the hidden motivations of Salim. They said that he was intending to use the investment he had made as an excuse to control the land and then later to ask for a larger share if the land was to be divided. These rumours had been heard daily by Fatima and Ruda at women's meetings. As a result, Fatima and Ruda sent their husbands to check on what Salim had been doing on the land.

Fatima and Ruda met many times and they told their mother of Salim's purpose, accusing their younger brothers of being careless and naive. They saw Salim's purpose as a plan by him to use his brothers' frequent absence and their reluctance to invest in the land to make the present situation a *de facto* one of his dominance. The mother rejected Ruda's and Fatima's claims and asked them to keep out of land business. She said that they should praise Salim for the attention he gave to the land. The two sisters were not satisfied with their mother's attitude or her reply and so resolved to speak to their brothers, Ali and Hassan.

A few weeks later, Fatima and Ruda each met separately with Hassan and Ali. Hassan and Ali did not agree with Fatima's and Ruda's claims and accusations, since they saw Salim's efforts to improve the land as a sacrifice on his part, while the rest of them were taking no care of it. The two sisters, however, did not listen to their younger brothers and instead they went to see Salim and demanded that if he wanted to continue cultivating the land alone then he must give them their share of the crops in cash. They argued that if Salim did not agree to this then the land must be divided amongst them since they were equal, legitimate heirs.

Salim's reaction was very angry. He abused them soundly and then accused them of greed, saying that while he had been keeping the land alive they just sat and waited for the ready money to come to them. Salim surprised his sisters by going to the Shaikh's majlis next morning to seek a partition of the land as a patrimony inherited from his father.

The Shaikh was not surprised to see Salim in his majlis, nor to hear what he was asking, since the dispute among the 'Iyāl Muḥammad members had become known in the village. However, no one had expected that the families would ask for partition. The Shaikh asked a notable man of the Zuyūd present in the majlis to ask his colleagues, the members of the land-dispute committee of the valley, to look into the case and report back to him.

The committee consisted of the wālīs and amīrs in the valley, and four other notable men of the Zuyūd. A leading man of the committee, Hajj Saif, was deputized by the committee to see Salim, and his brothers and sisters. The Shaikh and the committee recommended that his mission was to reconcile the lineage's members by advising Salim to give a certain amount of money as an annual income from the land to his sisters. When Hajj Saif met Fatima and Ruda they agreed to his suggestion; the brothers also agreed but Salim refused, and told Hajj Saif that the committee would have to divide the land if they did not want more conflict in the future. Hajj Saif used a number of means to try to persuade Salim, but failed. Hajj Saif had to return to the committee members and tell them of Salim's insistence on division.

With the failure of Hajj Saif's mediatory efforts, another notable member of the committee, Hajj Abdullah, asked permission from the other members to try to convince Salim to accept the committee's suggestions. This time Hajj Abdullah found that it was not only Salim who wanted the partition but Ali, Hassan, Ruda and Fatima as well. Hajj Abdullah returned to the committee and informed them of the 'Iyāl Muḥammad members' decision about the division of their land.

Hajj Saif and Hajj Abdullah, who were deputized by the committee's members, met the Shaikh and informed him of the result of their efforts, and of the fact that the Muḥammad sons and daughters had requested the division of their land. Hajj Abdullah and Hajj Ali informed me, 'that in order to avoid more disputes amongst 'Iyāl Muḥammad lineage we agreed to divide their land. We also put this decision before the Shaikh for approval.' The Shaikh agreed, after a discussion about the committee's efforts, but insisted that there should be no walls or fence (*ḥiḍār*) between the divided land. This meant that none of Muḥammad's heirs would have the right to erect or build fences or walls to show the borders of his or her land. Only stones, known as *yawāmīd*, were to be placed in the corners of each piece of land. The wells were also to be collectively owned by all the parties. The use and access to the wells were to be free for all. This method of land division proved to be useful in the long run, for it reduced the tension and kept the members dependent on each other.

The Shaikh finally ordered the committee to take the case to the Islamic court before any division took place. Six months after the start of the dispute, the judge held a session which was attended by the three brothers and two sisters.

Hajj Abdullah and Hajj Saif also attended the court. The litigants sat on the chairs facing the judge. Hajj Abdullah and Hajj Saif sat on the chairs which were on the right side of the judge's desk. Since they were known to the judge, Hajj Abdullah and Hajj Saif informed the judge that they were referred to him by the Shaikh. They also briefed the judge on the case and the decision which they had reached.

The judge started the session after calling every one of 'Iyāl Muḥammad to say loudly his or her name. He also wrote down Hajj Saif's and Hajj Abdullah's names as witnesses in the case. He told the Muḥammad men that there was no harm in what they wanted to do with their land, but there would be harm if they kept any hate for each other and then increased this hate by erecting walls and fences over a 'land that was inherited from one father.'

The judge praised the efforts of the committee and announced his authorization in the way the land should be divided according to the laws of Islamic juridical division of patrimony (*al-qismah al-šar'īyah*). Hajj Abdullah reminded the judge of the existence of Muḥammad's widow (Dabiah) who did not want to attend the court, but had authorized the committee to represent her there. The judge wrote her name down as dictated by Hajj Abdullah and then began calculating the number of shares for each of the legitimate heirs. After fifteen minutes he announced the shares of each member. These shares were as shown in Table 2.

The judge explained to me later that the share of each member was according to his or her kinship closeness to the deceased and their sex. The judge said: 'I should always take out first the wife's share, which is one-eighth, and then study the relation of the heir to the deceased and their sex. It is easier for me to divide the shares (*naṣīb*) of the heirs (*wirāṯah*) in this way.'

Table 2. The partition of 'Iyāl Muḥammad land according to Islamic Law.

Name of the Heir	*Relation to the Deceased*	*No. of Shares in the Patrimony*	*%*
Dabia	Wife	8(1/8)	12.0
Salim	Son	14	22.0
Hassan	Son	14	22.0
Ali	Son	14	22.0
Fatima	Daughter	7	11.0
Ruda	Daughter	7	11.0
Total	6	64	100

At the end of the session, the *qāḍī* repeated his wish that the heirs should 'avoid a quarrel (*ḍirābah*) over a land that all of you will die on, like your father, and then you will leave everything behind you and go to your graves with pieces of cloth as your shroud (*šiffan*). So why should one run greedily after material life.' Later the judge shook hands with Muḥammad's sons and Hajj Saif and Hajj Abdullah and promised to give them the deeds in three days. Three days later deeds were issued for each of the heirs.

The committee members assembled on the 'Iyāl Muḥammad land a day after the court session. They started by touring the garden and farm, calculating the type and numbers of date-palms, and the number of beds in the farm. They met again beside the well, while Salim and his two brothers sat together, and began to suggest which parts of the land each of the heirs would take, bearing in mind the equal division of the type and number of the date-palms and the closeness of each bed to the well.

With a few modifications, the brothers agreed to the committee's proposals, and at about 1 p.m. the committee members were invited to one of the *amīr*'s guest-rooms where a feast for Muḥammad's sons and the committee members was held to celebrate the reconciliation. The reconciliation culminated with an agreement by Muḥammad's lineage members to keep only pieces of stone as markers at the corners of their land to show their borders, and not to build any fences or walls. They also agreed that Salim should use the whole land and cultivate it. His use of the land was considered a means of keeping the land alive and fertile.

Next day Hajj Abdullah and Hajj Saif met the Shaikh and reported to him the result of the reconciliation. They also met Muḥammad's widow and daughters to inform them about their parts and location of their land.

Conclusion

In a society that lacks any place for what Gellner called a 'religious aristocracy' (Gellner 1983), I intended in this paper to demonstrate how the non-saintly, religious men, lacking any status of holiness, still retain a place of authority in an Islamic tribal society like that of the Hajar. Religious men of the Hajar such as the community's *muṭawwa'*, and the *šar'* of the Islamic court in the town, were seen as individual actors who use personal and community resources in order to execute their role successfully.

Recently, there have been two interesting studies on the role of the Muslim community preacher, or the *muṭawwa'* as he is known among the Hajaris, the first by Gaffney on authority and the mosque in Upper Egypt (Gaffney 1994), and the second by Antoun on a Jordanian Muslim preacher (Antoun 1989). Both Gaffney and Antoun focused on the role of these individual preachers at the community level and showed how significant are the Islamic ritual, sermons and, ultimately, the role of the mosque in shaping the face of social reality in Muslim societies.

The preacher or *muṭawwa'* in the Hajar will similarly perform the prayers and deliver the Friday sermons for the congregation in the mosque, and at the same time perform the role of a religious authority which plays its part in maintaining control and order in the community. What is different here is that the *muṭawwa'* does not have the same power and authority as the *šar'*, or those saints of the Swat or Atlas valleys. However, his status as a preacher and prayer-leader continues to offer him the power and influence to control the community's rituals, and also enables him to enforce the ideology of equality and solidarity among the Hajaris, as brothers in Islam and members of the Hajari *šaff*.

The *muṭawwa'* maintains control in the valley through his status as the community preacher and prayer-leader. The role of religious authority in the field of the community's social control does not cease there but extends further and more profoundly through the influential role of the Islamic judge, and his court in the town. The importance of the *šar'*'s place in Hajari life not only signifies the role of the religious authority in the town over the peripheral community of the valley, but also demonstrates how significant it is for a Hajari to be consistent with his Islamic belief in his practice. While the existence of religious authority shows how relevant it is for Hajaris to make a clearly demarcated distinction between *ḥalāl* and *ḥarām* practices by using the judgement of the Islamic authority, it also shows that the maintenance of Hajari identity requires them to maintain both a tribal and an Islamic identity.

The involvement of the *šar'* in community life shows not only the type of chiefdom form of centralized political system which seems to have existed as a dominant type at the level of each emirate, but also reveals the interdependence between the centre and the periphery. By being in the centre, the *šar'*, with his sophisticated religious knowledge and experience, is capable of using this power to bring control and order either by reconciling the litigants, observing the legality of the Hajari Islamic practices, or offering his legal opinion which the Hajaris require in order to be consistent with their own religious belief. As such, the areas of the judge's involvement are varied, and are not confined to legal affairs alone. His role is to be looked on as a part of a cultural system in which he becomes a cultural broker, as a mediator between the peasant and tribal culture of the Hajar and the sophisticated culture of the town. Thus he introduces new values and norms and above all new interpretations (*iğtihād*) in Islamic practices. An Islamic judge is therefore not to be seen as a type of judge who bridges the gap between the sharia, as an ideal law, and the social reality by non-methodical and tyrannical procedures as Weber viewed it (1956: 821). Neither is such a judge to be viewed as one belonging to a religion, Islam, 'that lacked the requirement of comprehensive knowledge of the law and lacked the intellectual training in casuistry' (1956: 262). An Islamic judge, rather, is to be understood within the cultural concepts and social relations in which he operates (Rosen 1989: 18).

The status of the *šar'* amongst the Hajaris and the source of power upon which he builds his authority appear to show that he is a cultural broker in both his role as a judge and in his court as a form of legal institution. Through his position in the town court, the *šar'* represents the great tradition of Islam: of Islamic literacy; of the formal theology and jurisprudence that are gained through years of education and only in those remote centres of learning; of the absolute jurisdiction and the observation of the implementation of Islamic law. Seen as a *šar'*, and as a man of knowledge (*'ilm*), the Islamic judge is not only responsible for maintaining social control in the village community of the Hām valley, but is also a culture broker who mediates between the great tradition of Islam and the local tradition of the Hajaris. Richard Antoun (1980) asserted that the roles of the Islamic judge and court are to accommodate the Islamic law to the traditions and customs of the peasant community. One could add that the judge also has a political position in establishing order and control through the settlement of disputes. In addition, he is the man who gains his authority through his mediatory role between the ordinary Muslim Hajari and the Islamic text (Quran and *sunna*). Understanding the text needs his knowledge and the courageous responsibility to interpret the text and to make it accessible (Messick 1993; Lambek 1990).

A further point has to be added here, that is to say that I desired, like most anthropologists who wish to study a particular group of people, to be practical about my mission. I wanted a small group of people living within a bounded community. That condition, as I thought, would give me much opportunity to use the limited time and resources that were at my disposal. Having moved to the Hajar, however, that personal desire was altered very much by the reality of the Hajari life.

I found that the Hajaris, who were described to me by my urban, Emirates friends of the coastal towns as isolated and wild, are not in fact like that. The Hajaris that I came to know have had a constant economic, political, social and cultural relationship, not only with coastal and desert regions of the Emirates, but also with other more remote regions, ones that are further than those of southern Arabia itself.

I have found, as the case in hand shows, that the Hajaris in their remote communities have both individuals and groups who were and still are entering into relationships with individuals and institutions operating at the central emirate level, in the past, or national federal state level, in the present. Should we, the anthropologists, take this relationship between community and national, or little and great traditions or centre and periphery into consideration, and to what degree? Several anthropologists have argued the benefit of such an approach (Redfield 1956; Wolf 1956; Geertz 1959).

With a different emphasis on the way peripheral communities communicate and interact with centres, these pioneering studies all have one thing in common: they are interested in seeing how changes are brought about in the remote cultures by the centre. They want to see what role an individual or an institution has in such changes. This study, in its turn, would like to add that further ethnographies and historical investigations into the nature of the individuals' and institution's roles in the cultures of complex societies of the Middle East are required in order to throw more light on the way these societies have been historically transformed.

Bibliography

Abdullah, M.M. 1978. *The United Arab Emirates: a Modern History*. London.

Abdulrahman, A. 1989–90. *Al-Imārāt fī Ḏākirat Abnā'ihā*, 2 vols. Sharjah/Dubai.

Ahmed, A.S. 1980. *Pukhtun Economy and Society: Traditional Structure and Economic Development in a Tribal Society*. London.

Al-Tabur, A.A. 1993. *Riğāl fī Tārīḫ al-Imārāt*. (Vol. I). Dubai.

Antoun, R. 1971. *Arab Village: a Social-Structural Study of a Transjordanian Peasant Community*. Bloomington.

—— 1979. *Low-Key Politics: Local-Level Leadership and Change in the Middle East*. Albany.

—— 1980. The Islamic Court, the Islamic Judge, and the Accommodation of Tradition: A Jordanian Case Study. *IJMES*. 12: 455–67.

—— 1989. *Muslim Preacher in the Modern World: a Jordanian Case Study in Comparative Perspective*. Princeton.

Asad, T. 1970. *The Kababish Arabs: Power, Authority and Consent in a Nomadic Tribe*. London.

Barth, F. 1959. *Political Leadership among Swat Pathans*. London.

Bujra, A.S. 1971. *The Politics of Stratification: a Study of Political Change in a South Arabian Town*. Oxford.

Christensen, R.O. 1986. Tribes, States and Anthropologists. *MES*. 22: 286–92.

Cole, D.P. 1975. *Nomads of the Nomads: the Al Murrah Bedouin of the Empty Quarter*. Chicago.

Eickelman, D.F. 1976. *Moroccan Islam: Tradition and Society in a Pilgrimage Centre*. Austin.

Evans-Pritchard, E.E. 1949. *The Sanusi of Cyrenaica*. Oxford.

Gaffney, P. 1994. *The Prophet's Pulpit: Islamic Preaching in Contemporary Egypt*. Berkeley.

Gellner, E. 1969. *Saints of the Atlas*. London

—— 1983. The Tribal Society and its Enemies. In Tapper, R. (ed.), *The Conflict of Tribe and State in Iran and Afghanistan*. London.

Geertz, C. 1959. The Changing Role of the Cultural Broker. *Comparative Studies in Society and History*. 2: 228–49.
—— 1968. *Islam Observed: Religious Development in Morocco and Indonesia*. New Haven.
—— 1975. *The Interpretation of Cultures*. London.
Heard-Bey, F. 1982. *From Trucial States to United Arab Emirates: a Society in Transition*. London.
Lambek, M. 1990. Certain Knowledge, Contestable Authority: Power and Practice on the Islamic Periphery. *Am Eth*. 17: 23–40.
Lancaster, W. 1981. *The Rwala Bedouin Today*. Cambridge.
Lewis, I.M. 1961. *A Pastoral Democracy: a Study of Pastoralism and Politics Among the Northern Somali of the Horn of Africa*. Oxford.
Messick, B. 1986. The Mufti, the Text and the World: Legal Interpretation in Yemen. *Man* (N.S) 21: 102–19.
—— 1993. *The Calligraphic State: Textual Domination and History in a Muslim Society*. Berkeley.
Ministry of Agriculture and Fisheries. 1986. *Meteorological Reports on Rainfall of the Eastern Region and Mountain Zone*. Dubai.
Redfield, R. 1956. *Peasant Society and Culture*. Chicago.
Rosen, L. 1984. *Bargaining for Reality: the Construction of Social Relations in a Muslim Community*. Chicago.
—— 1989. *The Anthropology of Justice: Law as Culture in Islamic Society*. Cambridge.
Weber, M. 1956. *The Sociology of Religion*. London.
Wolf, E. 1956. Aspects of Group Relations in a Complex Society: Mexico. *American Anthropologist* 59
Yateem, A.A. 1993. Review of 'The Emirates in the Memory of its People', by Abdullah Abdulrahman. *Journal of Social Affairs* 39: 233–8 (in Arabic).
—— 1993–4. Anthropological Approaches to Social Control in Islamic Tribal Societies: A Critical Review. *Dilmun* 16: 65–86.

Notes

1. See Abdullah (1978); Heard-Bey (1982); Abdulrahman (1989, 1990).
2. For a clearer and more elaborated view of the relevance of these works to my ethnographic experience in the Emirates, see my review of these works in Yateem (1993–94).
3. I mention here the recent and interesting contributions made by two local historians (Abdullah Abdulrahman, 1989–90; Al-Tabur, 1993, who have written about the biographies of some of the Emirates' *qāḍīs*. See, for instance, my review (in Arabic) of the two volumes of Abdulrahman (Yateem 1993).
4. For ethical reasons, I have changed the name of the original court to Kalba. So this is not a description of the Kalba court; it is one of the four courts mentioned.
5. All the names of individuals and tribes mentioned in this and the following cases have been changed to preserve anonymity.

Notes on Contributors

Hussein A. al-Amri has recently returned to Yemen after serving as Ambassador to the Court of St James in London. He is author of numerous publications on the 19th–20th century political and intellectual history of the Yemen.

Elizabeth Lambourn was awarded her PhD in Islamic Art and Archaeology in 1999 from the School of Oriental and African Studies, University of London. She is currently an Honorary Research Associate of the Centre of South East Asian and Chinese Studies at S.O.A.S. and specialises in Islamic material culture in South and South East Asia.

James Onley is an Assistant Professor of History at the American University of Sharjah and an Honorary Fellow of the Institute of Arab and International Studies at the University of Exeter.

Clive Smith was the first British Council Director in the then Yemen Arab Republic from 1973 to 1978, and Director in Saudi Arabia from 1988 to 1992. He has written a number of articles about Yemen, and now is Honorary Secretary of the British Archaeological Mission in Yemen.

G. Rex Smith has recently retired, having been Professor of Arabic at the University of Manchester. His major research interests continue to be in the early and medieval political economic history of the Yemen.

Francine Stone has edited *Studies on the Tihāmah* (1985) and a monograph issue of *Arabian archaeology and epigraphy* (1995) on pre-Islamic Tihāmah, as well as authoring articles on ethnography and co-authoring natural history studies of the Yemen Red Sea littoral and the Gulf of Aden. Her *Tihāmah Gazetteer* (in preparation) provides a tool for the study of historical geography of the Red Sea coastal plain up to 923/1517. She is currently convening a set of Red Sea Studies symposia for the Society for Arabian Studies at the British Museum.

Abdullah A. Yateem is Director of the Bahrain National Museum, and serves on the Academic Advisory Committee of the Bahrain-British foundation.